ALLIANCE
COMPETENCE

ALLIANCE
COMPETENCE

MAXIMIZING
THE VALUE OF
YOUR PARTNERSHIPS

Robert E. Spekman
Lynn A. Isabella
with Thomas C. MacAvoy

John Wiley & Sons, Inc.

New York ■ Chichester ■ Weinheim ■ Brisbane ■ Singapore ■ Toronto

Published by John Wiley & Sons, Inc.

Published simultaneously in Canada.

This publication is designed to provide accurate and authoritative information in regard to the subject matter covered. It is sold with the understanding that the publisher is not engaged in rendering professional services. If legal, accounting, medical, psychological or any other expert assistance is required, the services of a competent professional person should be sought.

Designations used by companies to distinguish their products are often claimed by trademarks. In all instances where the author or publisher is aware of a claim, the product names appear in Initial Capital letters. Readers, however, should contact the appropriate companies for more complete information regarding trademarks and registration.

Library of Congress Cataloging-in-Publication Data:

Spekman, Robert E.
    Alliance competence : maximizing the value of your partnerships /
Robert E. Spekman, Lynn A. Isabella, Thomas C. MacAvoy.
       p.   cm.
    Includes index.
    ISBN 0-471-33063-9 (cloth : alk. paper)
    1. Strategic alliances (Business)—Case studies.   I. Isabella,
Lynn A., 1948–   . II. MacAvoy, Thomas C., 1928–   . III. Title.
HD69.S8S67 2000
658'.044—dc21   99-41223

Printed in the United States of America.

10   9   8   7   6   5   4   3   2   1

*To Nancy, your support and love through the years
have been a source of both strength and peace.*
Robert

*To Katherine and Matthew Booth,
daughter and son extraordinaire.
I love you both very much.*
Lynn

To Peggy, my lifelong partner and best friend.
Tom

Preface

To say that alliances are pervasive throughout the corporate landscape almost seems to trivialize their true impact on the conduct of business across the globe. The sweeping reach of alliance strategies is stretching from traditional, old-line businesses where vertical integration was a source of great pride to new digital companies whose entire business is through partnerships. The days of the old Ford River Rouge plant in Michigan where coal, iron ore, and sand entered one end of the factory and an automobile exited the opposite end are gone. Now Chrysler's cost of goods sold exceeds 65 percent and it has become more an assembler than producer of cars. Compare vertically integrated heavy industrial plants to the myriad start-ups in the world of the Internet and e-commerce where alliances are the rule and not the exception. Dell Computers revolutionized the PC market through its partnerships with Intel and Federal Express, mass customizing and delivering computers faster than most of its key competitors. In fact, FedEx talks about having dedicated warehouses for Dell that are airborne at 500 miles per hour.

Alliances make it possible for firms to move nimbly across a convergence of technologies that, almost by definition, mean that no one firm has all the technical tools and/or expertise needed to compete successfully in these burgeoning markets. But each of the firms captures and provides value through these networks of alliances. This value is realized across every sector of the economy, evidenced by accessing markets and/or technologies, developing new skills, building new businesses, improving costs through new processes, or leveraging size and scope. Simply stated, alliances permit companies to gain advantages that are too slow or costly to achieve alone.

The harnessing of such value, however, comes at a cost. Companies must sacrifice some autonomy and engage in joint decision making and control. Alliance partners cannot use a hierarchical command and control mentality—it just won't work. Partners no longer can focus solely on their self-interests but now must pursue policies that are mutually beneficial to all alliance members. Control as a concept is no longer relevant; verbs like influence, educate, persuade, and collaborate enter the alliance conversation to describe how work gets done.

We see this book as a "second generation" alliance book that raises the alliance discussion to the next level—the concept of alliance competence. Our interest in alliance competence grew from the observation that many alliances fail to live up to their potential. These alliances realize only a small fraction of the value possible. We've seen alliances whose strategic intent makes perfect sense. Partners are chosen with considerable care. Yet, the anticipated value-added capability never materializes and partners become increasingly frustrated. Dysfunctional effects of conflict begin to surface, eventually eroding not building value.

When we observed such difficulties, a critical but unrecognized variable seemed to be the alliance management process. Errors occurred because the firm was not alliance competent. That is, it lacked the skills to find, nurture, and manage partners who were aligned with its objectives and goals, shared a similar sense of what it meant to partner, or had the capability to maximize the skills/capabilities that each partner brought to the table. Yet, problems were far greater than partner selection or an ability to engage in meaningful due diligence.

Of equal importance, many individual managers are extremely frustrated although they appreciate and attempt to engage in alliance-supportive and relevant behaviors. Their frustration is linked directly to structural, process, and system barriers in their firm, which in the end inhibit the growth of alliance-like skills. The misalignment between the managers and their understanding of the need to develop these skills and the firm's inability to facilitate and support these efforts does not bode well for building an alliance-ready culture.

Alliance competence is partly a function of individual skills and capabilities and firm-level attributes that enhance, encourage, and support alliance-like thinking and behavior throughout the firm. These competencies become part of the fabric of the firm and are embedded in its culture. Our premise is that alliance-competent firms will outperform others and will have a sustainable competitive advantage in global markets.

In the following chapters, we outline and discuss the foundations of alliance competence. The book begins with a question: "What does it mean to partner?" We invite our readers to actively consider their answer to this question as they proceed. Chapters 1 and 2 are introductory chapters and set the stage for the rest of the book. These chapters define strategic alliances, the range of alliances, and the importance of strategic intent to alliance development.

Chapter 3 focuses on the building blocks of business and relationships. Developing an understanding of the power of relationship management to alliance development and alliance competence ground this chapter. Concrete steps are offered to achieve the delicate balance between business and relationship. We suggest steps managers can take to shore up the relationship side of the alliance equation. The role of alliance management is another primary focus of this chapter.

Chapter 4 addresses the concept of alliance spirit, the implicit psychological contract about what it means to partner. The power of the alliance spirit and ways to build a strong spirit are documented. Spirit, to a large extent, sets the rules of engagement. It sets the norms that govern how partners will interact and work with one another.

Chapter 5 describes the forces of static, the ever-present background noise that has the potential to undermine an alliance's stability. The sources of static are discussed, as are ways to counteract its potentially deleterious effects. Certain kinds of static can be managed, other forms are much larger than the alliance and become part of the contextual space in which the alliance attempts to conduct its business. In either case, knowing what "noise" affects the alliance helps managers better adjust their actions and align their expectations.

Chapter 6 focuses on the issues and challenges that an alliance experiences over its lifetime. This chapter documents the problems and challenges that alliances tend to face at certain points and offers concrete suggestions for managing through the evolutionary cycle. An alliance grows and develops through a series of defined phases and each phase must contend with unique challenges and managerial issues.

Chapter 7 focuses on alliance conflict. We discuss the root causes of conflict and present general approaches to resolving conflict. At the heart of this chapter is a process we call *The No Blame Review*©. This process, original to our research, helps alliances constructively confront times when the alliance seems off track. This chapter also discusses the pros and cons of exit contracts, as future sources of conflict in an alliance.

Chapter 8 emphasizes the role of the alliance manager. We explore the skills and competencies needed by alliance managers throughout the life cycle of an alliance. At the core of this chapter is a straightforward premise: Develop alliance managers and your company takes a huge step toward becoming alliance competent and acquiring the essential skills for management in the future. Yet, a cadre of strong alliance managers are not sufficient for the firm to be considered alliance competent.

Chapter 9 pulls all the ideas together by focusing on alliance competence—what it is and how to achieve it. Alignment is needed among structure, processes, and systems if the firm is to develop and foster a culture that supports alliance-like behavior. In addition, the notion of alliance competence is incorporated into a brief discussion of the balanced score card, which demonstrates how being alliance-capable impacts company performance.

Chapter 10 includes three special alliance cases: alliances as research probes, fast-paced alliances, and supply-chain related alliances. We highlight these alliance types and show how each accomplishes specific goals within the book's general framework. Each alliance type has grown in importance as more and more managers are finding that R&D and innovation can be better accomplished, that alliances in fast-paced industries have certain special characteristics, and that an ability to link firms along a supply chain is likely to result in competitive advantage.

Finally, Chapter 11 emphasizes that to develop an alliance competence is not business as usual. For many firms, substantial changes are necessary, and managers should be prepared for a massive change effort. This chapter discusses the steps needed to accomplish those changes.

One of the alliance managers with whom we have spoken said: "Alliances are for today and for tomorrow." We agree. Alliances help companies do business better today *and* alliances can help position companies for future opportunities. Being alliance competent is not just another detail for management's attention. Being alliance competent is central to business of the future.

ROBERT E. SPEKMAN
LYNN A. ISABELLA
THOMAS C. MACAVOY

Acknowledgments

This book is itself the result of an alliance and an alliance journey. Each of us approaches the study of alliances from different perspectives. Through these different lenses come the richness of thought and complementarity of experiences and ideas from which the book benefits. There is no question that each of us has benefited from our colleagues' contribution and all of us have raised our collective and individual "level of play." There is also no question that as we lived the alliance journey ourselves, we have gained greater appreciation for the difficulties and challenges of integrating unique perspectives.

Our journey began in late 1993 with the formation of the Darden Alliance Research Team. From those beginnings, the support of both the Darden School Foundation and the International Consortium for Executive Development Research (ICEDR) has been essential. Darden Business School Deans Lee Higdon, now president of Babson College, and Ted Snyder have been very supportive of our work; we thank them both for their encouragement and efforts on our behalf. ICEDR funded our initial field studies and facilitated access to member companies as study participants. Both were essential to the success of this research. Equally essential has been the continuing and enthusiastic support of Doug Ready and Joanne Hering of ICEDR. For their comments and suggestions as the studies were unfolding and for their unwavering assistance throughout our journey, we owe our sincerest thanks.

Applause is in order for several members of Darden's executive education staff. Ray Smith and Brandt Allen, former and current deans for Executive Education, respectively, have each encouraged and supported us in taking our academic research into the classroom through original case studies, through innovative pedagogy, and a series of unique educational experiences. Most importantly, Darden's executive development program managers, who contribute every day to creating the kind of atmosphere in which learning is encouraged and facilitated, deserve special recognition. Without their hard work and dedication, many of the practical foundations of this book would have been impossible.

This book has also benefited from the managers and companies with which we have worked or had the opportunity to learn about. As a result of our executive program at the Darden School, we have spoken with and heard the stories of hundreds of executives from all corners of the globe. To all our former CSA (Creating Strategic Alliances and Partnerships) participants, we offer another round of applause. In addition, we want to thank the many managers with whom we have interacted and worked over the years. We have shared ideas and have struggled with them through the many problems and challenges created by their attempts to build their own alliance competencies. Our thinking has been shaped by these interactions and many of the learnings (both positive and negative) have been incorporated in this book. We thank these managers for their candor, their receptivity to our work and thinking, and the opportunity to work with a broad range of companies from all over the world. In many instances, we have chosen not to mention companies or individuals by name; nonetheless, thank you for your support.

This book would not have been possible without the efforts of many people who labored behind the scenes over the years. Debbie Quarles, Robert's administrative assistant, is responsible for the final production of this manuscript. She has also assisted in many ways over the years in the production of many articles and has been instrumental in helping with survey development and data input. Joseph Spear, doctoral candidate in sociology, has been our "data guy" over the life of the alliance project. Joe has analyzed all the data shown in the book and has consistently met tight deadlines with a smile. Jay Lambe, former doctoral student and now assistant professor at Texas Tech, contributed to the intellectual development of our chapter on interimistic alliances and helped shape our early thinking on the notion of alliance competence. Niklas Myhr, currently a doctoral candidate, contributed to the thinking on the supply chain management chapter. Jean Gibbons, research associate, assisted in the development of numerous tables and figures and did background searches on many topics and issues, with good humor under stress and attention to detail.

We owe a special debt of gratitude to Ted Forbes, currently an Instructor at the Darden School. It was Ted who initially suggested "an alliance" between Robert and Lynn. As a Darden MBA, class of 1993, Ted saw a complementarity in topical interests and suggested that we talk. Ted became the project's first research associate and case writer extraordinaire. Currently rounding out the Darden Alliance Team as our fourth member, Ted has unselfishly contributed to our work, provided key insights over the years, augmented communication to the practitioner worlds, been a good friend and a joy to work with.

In addition to our Darden colleagues, each of us wishes to acknowledge and thank others. Lynn wishes to thank her colleagues and friends, June West, Jeanne Liedtka, Pat Werhane, Jeff Dreyfus, and Suzyn Ornstein for their friendship, encouragement, support and counsel before and during the writing process.

Robert is indebted to a number of people for their counsel, advice, and willingness to listen to half-baked ideas. Dave Wilson (at Penn State University), Bob Bruner, Ed Davis, and Paul Farris (all at Darden) have helped shape his thinking over the years. Tom MacAvoy, one of the coauthors, has been a valuable alliance resource, a wonderful friend, and a source of wisdom.

Tom wants to thank his colleagues from Corning Incorporated and Corning's many joint ventures and alliances for their examples and counsel, especially Amo and Jamie Houghton, Dick Dulude, Forrest Behm, Bob Turissini, Al Dawson, and Lee Wilson. He is also indebted to Ben Gomez-Casseres (of Brandeis University) who has enriched his understanding of strategic alliances in all its forms.

Despite the input, advice, and counsel of many colleagues at the Darden Business School and at other universities, and the insights derived from our conversations with practicing managers, any errors or omissions are our sole responsibility. We have labored to share our thoughts and convey them in a cogent and managerially useful fashion. Our separate alliance journeys converged five years ago when the Darden project on alliances began. Our journey continues and this book documents our thinking to date.

R.E.S.
L.A.I.
T.C.M.

Contents

1

Alliance

A Set of
Complex Interactions

We work with companies on a global basis often conducting seminars and workshops to assist managers in their understanding of the complexities associated with alliance formation. Those engagements involve spending a great deal of time on problems associated with alliance management. Yet, there exists a gap between practice and theory. Much alliance research neglects dealing with the problems of alliance management. Most books on alliances start with a discussion of alliance imperatives. The typical opening chapter begins with the observation that alliances are driven by a series of economic factors such as global competitive pressures, costs associated with both market entry and new product development, and the rate and speed of technological change. We take these imperatives as a given and spend time in this introductory chapter exploring the meaning of partnering. We focus on the complex interactions and expectations that are established once firms commit to engage in an alliance.

The rate of alliance formation has exploded. Access to developing nations, continued deregulation and privatization, the opportunities created by the Internet and the rise of electronic commerce, rise of businesses based on the convergence of technologies (e.g., voice and data, biotechnology, and pharmacology) have all contributed to the rising tide of alliance formation. The number of alliances formed each year is estimated to run into the tens of thousands. Despite this growth, there is much confusion. The term alliance is overused. Many managers do not know what an alliance really is!

1

It makes little sense to debate how many alliances are formed on a worldwide basis; whether the actual number is 10,000 or 12,000 is not important. What is important is to develop an understanding of both the alliance phenomenon and the alliance process. We often start our inter-actions with managers by asking: "When we say alliances, what do you say?" The responses from a recent workshop conducted for a foreign na-tional petroleum company were:

Complementary	Common goals
Long-term	Win-win
Synergy	Create value
Empathy	Competition
Survival	Trust
Market/technology access	Cultural mix
Need cash	Shared objectives

Several key points emerge from the responses of the senior managers. First, there is the notion of alliances as a means of survival and value creation. Managers convey a sense of urgency associated with the alliance phenom-enon. Survival might appear to be an extreme response, but there are many industries (e.g., petroleum and airlines industries) where alliances are the rule and not the exception. For this energy company, alliances provide opportunities to leverage the market presence and prowess, technological capability, and financial resources of other major oil companies so it can most effectively utilize its precious national resources.

Yet, alliance formation can be essential to the viability of some busi-nesses. In the airline industry, US Airways "strategic rationale for its al-liance with British Air (BA) was partly a matter of survival. In 1992, USAir was losing about one million dollars per month! Labor costs were out of control and competitive pressures were mounting in several of its hubs, its image was not the most positive in the industry, and it could not decide the extent to which it could play in the international arena. Join-ing forces with BA gave USAir several benefits. Through its alliance, USAir could be a global player. First, USAir gained access to BA passen-gers who would travel from the United Kingdom to USAir hub locations for destinations within the United States. The ability to feed passengers into each partner's network would increase the revenue stream for both airlines. Second, USAir could learn from BA those capabilities that give BA such consistently high marks for outstanding customer service. Third, the alliance incorporated the joint purchasing of services, fuel, aircraft, and the like. Negotiating with suppliers as a single airline would enable both partners to save millions of dollars in annual costs.

Beyond these advantages, both CEOs shared a vision of creating a truly global airline. For BA, the United States was the single largest piece of its global puzzle given the large percentage of all international traffic that either begins or terminates in North America. For USAir, the ability to link with BA to Europe and beyond and with Quantas to Australia and Asia gave it a truly seamless global presence. In addition, BA's equity stake provided a much needed infusion of cash. BA paid over $400 million for 20 percent ownership and several seats on the board.

From the responses on page 2, one can infer also a notion of complementary resources and synergistic effects. Managers felt that potential alliance partners should look for skills, expertise, and competencies that do not overlap. Together, partners add value that each alone would be hard pressed to contribute within a meaningful period of time. This oil company has formed many technology alliances in which it relies on the skills of its partner to bring much needed capabilities and competencies. Other alliances focus on the production of petrochemicals and other specialty chemicals. In almost all instances, production projects require very large investments. Risk sharing lies at the heart of many alliances.

Parallel behavior exists in the development of new drugs. The cost of drug development and then the mechanics of navigating the FDA approval process can run into the hundreds of millions of dollars. In recent years, many large pharmaceutical firms have sought alliances with smaller biotech companies to avail themselves of the smaller firm's innovative technology. The smaller firm, in turn, looks to the larger firm to manage the FDA approval process and to commercialize the venture. For example, Schering–Plough and Immune Response formed a research alliance to develop gene therapy products for hepatitis B and C. As part of the agreement, Schering–Plough will receive rights to the gene therapy technology developed by Immune Response using Schering–Plough's proprietary genes.

The majority of these alliances focus on new forms of technology and often involve the convergence of branches of biological sciences. In most instances, the basic scientific knowledge was contributed by the

Table 1.1   Biotech Alliances by Technology, 1995 to 1997

Type of Technology	Number of Alliances
Carbohydrates/cell adhesion	10
Gene/cell therapy	48
Genomics	44
Molecular diversity	56
Monoclonal antibodies	27
Antisense	12
Photodynamic therapy	5
RDNA	48
Signal transduction	29
Transgenics	8

Source of data: Biotech '97 Alignment-An Industry Annual Report, Ernst & Young (LLP).

smaller technology company. Table 1.1 summarizes the range of biotech alliances formed between 1995 and 1997.[1] Smaller companies appear to drive the exploratory phase of the innovation engine in this industry.

Alliance Spirit: An Introduction

The term alliance conveys a set of expectations regarding how partners should engage each other. Managers talk about relationships based on trust, win–win, and empathy. They further imply a sense of long-term shared goals and objectives. These descriptors suggest that managers associate certain norms with alliance-like behavior. Chapter 4 expands on these rules of engagement, and introduces and explores the concept of *alliance spirit*. The importance of the alliance spirit cannot be emphasized enough. It is essential that partners share a similar perspective of what it means to partner. If partners do not share the same view, an alliance is likely to face hard times and probably will fail. In alliances based on technology sharing, if one partner uses the alliance to further its own agenda at the expense of its partner and expropriates the other's technology, the relationship will suffer. Although partners should learn from each other, it is also prudent to protect information that is core to the firm's competitive advantage. Related to this problem is the belief that partners must set expectations early in the relationship regarding what information and/or capabilities they will share. Such expectation setting helps partners understand the scope of the alliance and what is "in bounds" and "out of bounds."

Changing Expectations

When Shell Oil attempted to reenter the Italian retail gas market during the early 1990s, it formed a joint venture with MontEdison. MontEdison purchased retail stations from TOTAL, a French oil company, and then sold half of the business to Shell to form the joint venture MonteShell. Both partners brought complementary skills and resources to the joint venture. MontEdison had refining capability and distribution resources, while Shell had retail experience and brand recognition. The gas stations were adorned with the well-recognized yellow shell. At the time the joint venture was established, MontEdison's parent company experienced severe financial problems. After a series of events (including political scandals, defaults on loans), several U.S. banks entered the picture and pressured MontEdison to begin to shed assets to reduce its indebtedness.

These external pressures had a profound effect on how MontEdison viewed its relationship with Shell. While Shell viewed its reentry into Italy as part of a long-term investment strategy, MontEdison now saw the joint venture as an opportunity to generate cash to retire its debt. Expectations changed, partners no longer viewed the joint venture with similar goals, nor did they approach problems with a consistent management philosophy. Jointly managing the venture became very frustrating as the partners drifted apart. To protect its investment, Shell purchased MontEdison's share in the retail business. Events external to the joint venture affected one partner's definition of and goals for the alliance and, as a consequence, the alliance fell apart. This inability to agree on the alliance's direction affected Shell's long-term retail strategy and jeopardized its market position. Both partners saw the alliance through a different lens and these differences affected their purpose and expectations.

Fundamental Lessons Learned

Three key points are worth repeating:

1. *Alliance formation is driven by competitive pressures.* These reasons can run the gamut from corporate survival to attempts to set standards within a burgeoning industry. Many of the alliances in the software industry as they relate to the Internet, electronic commerce, and security are based on the desire of one coalition to become the dominant design. Remember that alliances are intended to create value so that one set of alliance partners can achieve a competitive advantage.

2. *Alliance partners should possess complementary skills and/or expertise.* When partners have overlapping capabilities, conflicts are likely to emerge. These problems typically converge on issues related to role definition as well as on the calculus used to value each partner's contributions to the alliance. When role definition is unclear and partners possess duplicate skills, conflict is likely to emerge. The duplication-of-skills problem is particularly acute in alliances where equity interests exist (either in joint ventures or in alliances where one partner takes an ownership stake in the other). It becomes difficult to assess value to skills/expertise that both partners possess. Not only does the negotiation process become difficult, but management problems surface during the life of the alliance. A determination of contribution is hard to assess and partners begin to question the costs and benefits associated with the alliance.

3. *Alliances are not only about business; alliances are also about people and relationships.* There are expectations surrounding the rules of engagement and how partners are expected to behave with each other. Acceptable alliance behavior is based on norms that typically emerge as partners interact. When partners share a basic understanding of what it means to partner, governance becomes easier. Successful alliances are built on the premise that partners share similar views of acceptable alliance behavior. Norms encourage collaborative actions in pursuit of a shared vision.

Alliances as a Source of Competitive Advantage

Based on the level of global alliance activity and the resources committed to alliance development and management, many corporate managers appear to view alliances as a key element in their growth strategies. Alliance activity can stimulate growth by:

- Focusing corporate attention on activities that are core to the business and away from nonessential efforts where the firm lacks expertise, cost advantage, or scale.
- Leveraging the skills of partners to develop and introduce new products and services, enter new market segments, new geographic markets.
- Accelerating its revenue opportunities by getting greater returns from its existing customers, channels, and products through the addition of complementary skills and expertise.

Alliances enable firms to develop competitive advantage by leveraging the skills and capabilities of its partners to improve the performance of its value chain. Firms no longer compete as individual companies, they compete as constellations of companies that cooperate to bring value to the ultimate consumer. Across virtually all sectors of the economy, alliances have reshaped the interactions of companies. Not long ago, one could observe adversarial relationships between manufacturers and suppliers or witness high levels of conflict between manufacturers and their distributors. Each party attempted to maximize its gain to the detriment of the other. Not only were potential synergies lost, competitive positions often suffered.

Witness the U.S. automobile industry: Both Chrysler and Ford enjoy closer ties with their suppliers than does General Motor (GM). Chrysler has become an assembler of cars relying on its suppliers to provide, in addition to parts and services, innovation and state-of-the-art engineering know-how in their area of expertise. Both Chrysler's costs are lower and its return on investment (ROI) is greater than GM's as a direct consequence of its willingness to forge and manage close ties with its first-tier suppliers. While GM's Saturn division understands the contribution world-class suppliers can make to the design and production of its cars, the rest of GM struggles with the management of its supplier relation-ships. Honda, on the other hand, has a more enlightened view of its sup-plier alliances and proactively invests time and resources to ensure that its key suppliers can meet its strict requirements. Ironically, all the au-tomakers realize that their long-term viability is partly a function of their ability to manage their far-reaching alliances. However, not all of them manage their supplier alliances well enough to achieve a demon-strable competitive advantage.

Alliances in the auto industry extend beyond buyer-supplier rela-tionships. Globally, U.S. automakers have taken equity stakes in the local manufacturer in numerous countries. Figure 1.1 presents an overview of some of the alliances that exist. Reasons for these alliances vary from wanting to extend one's global reach, to improving economies of scope and scale, to gaining access to new technology and other complementary skills. The message is that if you want to succeed, you have to be global. PriceWaterhouse Coopers estimated that in 1997 alone there were 750 auto-industry deals valued at $28 billion.

Alliance formation has been tied to a desire to achieve a competitive advantage. Researchers in the strategy area suggest that competitive ad-vantage evolves from skills and assets that are unique to the firm.[2] These skills and assets are viewed as resources that not only ensure a firm's abil-ity to compete effectively but also can contribute to its differential ad-vantage. These resources can lead to cost advantage through scale of economy, unique manufacturing processes, and access to raw materials. Similarly, these resources can lead to differentiation through specialized knowledge, reputation, market position, and innovative capabilities.

Partner Selection Is Key to the Process

FedEx has assembled a range of alliances that spans their concerns for meeting their customer needs and building on their core skills. This range of partnerships includes, but is not limited to, technology alliances, distribution and logistics alliances, and electronic commerce alliances.[3] FedEx first attempts to define what it needs from a partner and then tries to answer questions related to strategic fit. Driving its selection process is the search for partner resources that contribute to its quest for competitive advantage. If one traces the competitive interplay between FedEx and United Parcel Service (UPS), it becomes clear that a sustain-able advantage is difficult to achieve in this business.[4] Technology can be

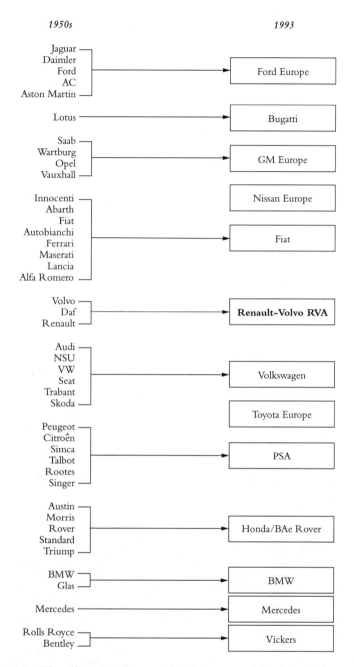

1950s	*1993*
Jaguar, Daimler, Ford, AC, Aston Martin	Ford Europe
Lotus	Bugatti
Saab, Wartburg, Opel, Vauxhall	GM Europe
	Nissan Europe
Innocenti, Abarth, Fiat, Autobianchi, Ferrari, Maserati, Lancia, Alfa Romero	Fiat
Volvo, Daf, Renault	**Renault-Volvo RVA**
Audi, NSU, VW, Seat, Trabant, Skoda	Volkswagen
	Toyota Europe
Peugeot, Citroên, Simca, Talbot, Rootes, Singer	PSA
Austin, Morris, Rover, Standard, Triump	Honda/BAe Rover
BMW, Glas	BMW
Mercedes	Mercedes
Rolls Royce, Bentley	Vickers

Figure 1.1 The Changing Competitive Structure of the Auto Industry in the Early 1990s. (*Source:* AB Volvo, *Information Prior to Extraordinary General Meeting of Shareholders in AB Volvo, November 9, 1993*, 39.)

imitated, service offerings can be copied, and pricing schedules are easily matched. Close ties with partners who bring world-class resources to the alliance offer an opportunity for FedEx to sustain its competitive position. Since UPS is several times larger than FedEx, FedEx must utilize its resources carefully. Partner selection becomes an important consideration for FedEx since the wrong choice can have a profound effect on its ability to execute according to plan. To formalize its partner selection process, management at FedEx developed a series of key questions aimed at determining a potential partner's value-adding capabilities. Among the questions are:

1. What skills capabilities does the partner have? To what extent do their resources complement ours?
2. How does the partner add value?
3. How similar are our management styles, philosophies, and approach to business? Are our corporate cultures compatible?
4. How is the partner perceived in the marketplace? What is their reputation?

Each alliance is predicated on achieving a competitive advantage and looks to the partner's skills and capabilities as an essential ingredient. At the same time, FedEx recognizes that fit cannot be limited to complementary resources. There must also exist a high level of compatibility in management philosophy, culture, and other factors that affect how well the partners are aligned and the manner in which they will engage each other.

Sustaining a Competitive Advantage

Beyond consideration of the nature of an alliance's competitive advantage, one must consider also the degree to which it can be sustained over time. That is, competitive landscapes change, new firms enter the market, and technological change is often the norm. A primary concern is the degree to which a firm's resource can be replicated or imitated. Skills that now convey advantage might become obsolete as technology changes, markets mature, or consumer tastes change. Moreover, a resource base can be copied. There are few guarantees that skills cannot be learned or replicated. People can be hired away, processes can be reverse engineered, patents can be designed around, and so on. A firm's resources become more difficult to imitate if:

- There is a tacitness that makes it hard to codify a process or skill.
- The asset is specific to the firm and cannot easily be transferred or traded.
- The resource consists of a complex interaction among skills and assets.
- The time required to replicate either the asset or the skill is prohibitively long.[5]

Corning is noted for its ability to innovate and commercialize glass and ceramic products that have unique properties. Table 1.2 lists some Corning joint ventures (JV) that illustrate their scope and global reach. Over the years, Corning's technical expertise has contributed to the glass for the light bulb invented by Edison, to the TV picture tube in partnership with RCA, to the windshield for the space shuttle, to innovations and market leadership in the development of fiber-optic cable. Although Corning has licensed to others the technology to manufacture fiber-optic cable, and glass for both light bulbs and TV picture tubes, their skills and capabilities in basic ceramic/glass chemistry cannot easily be replicated. The depth and breadth of Corning's R&D experience provides a sustainable competitive advantage based on a long-developed tradition of research that would be difficult to replicate. Because these resources cannot be easily imitated, Corning brings technical value to its alliance partners. From the list of Corning's joint ventures, the importance of their basic R&D capabilities becomes obvious.

Reputation as a Source of Competitive Advantage

Valuable resources need not only be based on technology and manufacturing expertise. Many companies have resources that are market facing and bring value because of their reputational effects. For example, the court decision that "broke up" the Bell System occurred in 1984, and for several years many consumers believed that AT&T still provided their local telephone service. The brand equity that is attributed to the AT&T name and its logo had taken years to build. Their advertising expenditure is among the highest in the United States. From 1985 to 1988, AT&T spent in excess of $280 million in advertising in newspapers, radio, and TV. In 1984, they were the number two business-to-business advertiser. For a new company to establish a brand identity in competition with AT&T would take both time and considerable financial

Table 1.2 Corning, Inc. Joint Ventures

Joint Venture	Partner(s)	Business	What Corning Brings
Dow Corning Corporation (JV founded 1943)	Dow Chemical	Manufactures silicone products including implants, silicone-based materials used in bathtub caulks, aircraft adhesives and electronic products.	The invention of silicone in the 1930s.
Owens Corning Fiberglas[a] (JV founded 1935)	Owens–Illinois Glass Company	Invented fiberglas and manufactures products made from glass fibers.	Knowledge of glass formulations.
Siecor (formerly Siecor Optical Cables, Inc.) (JV founded 1977)	Siemens AG of Munich	Develops and manufactures optical fiber and copper communications products for voice, data, and video applications. Major supplier for telephone companies, cable television operating companies, customer premises communications, and utility applications.	Corning is a leader in fiber optic technology.
Biccor (equity venture) (JV founded 1977)	BICC Cables Asia–Pacific Pte	Holding company to manage optical fiber cable plants in the Asia-Pacific region, principally in Southeast Asia and China.	Expertise in optical fiber technology.
Samara Optical Cable Company, Ltd.	Samara Cable Company[b]	Manufacture optical fiber cables for telecommunication applications, to be sold primarily in Russia and to a lesser extent to other countries in the region.	Optical fiber, nearly three decades of optical fiber expertise and the manufacturing capability to meet customer needs.
Corning Asahi Video Products Company	Asahi Glass of America	Tube components for television sets, including face plates, funnels, necks and neck tubing, electron gun mounts, and frit used for sealing glass parts.	Corning was the innovator and is a worldwide leader in TV tubes, necks tubing, and frit.

Samsung Corning Company Ltd. (JV founded 1973)	Samsung Group	Produces glass panels and funnels for television and display monitors, ITO coated glass, and rotary transformers used in VTR head drums.
Cormetech	Mitsubishi Heavy Industries Ltd. and Mitsubishi Chemical Corp	Produces titania-based ceramic honeycomb catalyst used by utilities, refineries, and chemical manufacturers in Germany and the United States to eliminate up to 90 percent of the nitrous-oxide emissions produced by coal, oil, and gas-fired boilers. Corning is the worldwide leader in honeycomb ceramic for automotive catalysts.
Samcor Galss (JV founded 1993)	Samtel group (JV set up 1993)	Manufactures glass parts for black-and-white picture tubes at a facility in Kota, Rajasthan, India. (JV set up a new line for manufacturing color glass shells in the country with exclusive investment from the U.S. partner.)

[a] Ownership divested in 1986.
[b] Largest telecommunications cabler in Russia.

resources. This advantage contributed to AT&T's early competitive edge and was an important resource. Similar brand equity resides in GE's and DuPont's corporate logos. In addition to considerable technical resources and other capabilities, both are desirable partners by virtue of the strength of their brand.

Cobranding alliances have increased in recent years because consumers have demonstrated that they are attracted by the combined brand equity. Through these alliances, each partner can leverage the reputation of the other and also realize cost reductions. American Express is alleged to have in excess of 1,500 such agreements. Other partnerships have been formed between Barnes & Noble's bookstores and Starbucks coffee. McDonald's has formed alliances with gas retailers (e.g., Shell, Amoco, Texaco) to share locations offering added convenience to people on the go. Financial service companies have begun to rely on cobranding to offer a bundled set of products and services. One example is the alliance between Fidelity Investments and Salomon Brothers. From Fidelity's perspective, this alliance provides a wider array of financial services to its customers, potentially results in greater share of wallet, and, allows Fidelity to truly expand its market reach with little additional investment.

With the recent deregulation in the electric utility market, alliances aimed at gaining a stronger market presence are expected to accelerate. Here, an industry that has enjoyed a monopoly position has begun to look to alliance formation to improve or protect its consumer franchise and to capture a greater share of the value chain dedicated to the generation, transmission, and distribution of electric power. Two questions lie at the core of this anticipated alliance buildup:

1. How can the local electric utility better utilize its current position to gain a stronger market presence with its retail and commercial customers?
2. If a strong market presence is partly linked to leveraging the capabilities and resources of partners, what kinds of skills and attributes become important?

That is, what capabilities does the company bring to the market and what complementary resources can be leveraged to maintain a competitive advantage? The objective is to compete beyond cost since only a few electric utilities have the resource base to produce electric power at competitive prices. Figure 1.2 presents one likely response to deregulation by

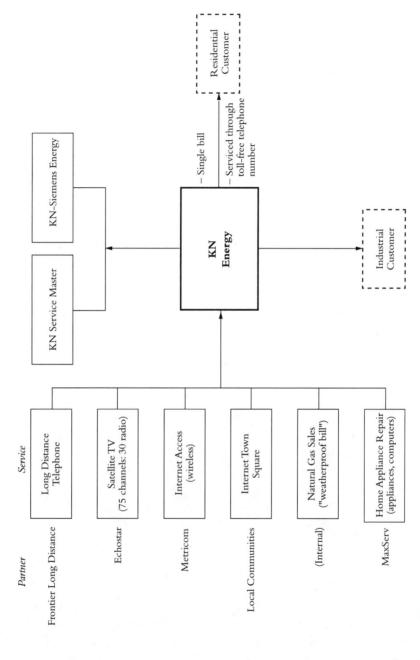

Figure 1.2 Profile: KN energy and retail bundling. (*Source: The Alliance Analyst, 2/1997*)

an electric utility. The assumption here is that key segments of retail customers are likely to seek "one-stop" shopping for an array of services that extend beyond providing electric power. Cable TV, security monitoring, Internet services, and so on can be bundled and offered to the customer through a set of alliances managed by the electric utility.

Resource Capability Is Not Enough

However, the level of resources brought to the alliance is not sufficient to explain how alliances develop and maintain a competitive advantage. Partners might bring unique and complementary resources to the alliance but be unable to work together or lack the same perspective for acceptable alliance behavior. Alliance partners should also have skills and capabilities that facilitate and foster alliance-like behavior. In the best of situations, potential partners would seek them out because they are seen as a good company with whom to partner. It is essential to consider both the resource base of the partners *and* the relationship between the partners. Alliances that have a "healthy" relationship are better able to leverage the skills each brings to the relationship. These partners are able to reduce the barriers and costs associated with managing the alliance over time.

Alliances Carry Certain Costs and Concerns

Despite the advantages gained from alliance formation, there are costs associated with managing these relationships. Transaction costs are embedded in any relationship and ensure that the relationship runs smoothly.[6] For example, if Motorola partners with a select set of highly committed suppliers to ensure that parts are shipped to its pager production facilities with zero defects, there are immediate cost reductions because the incoming components do not have to be inspected. Similarly, if early in the relationship, partners determine what technical information is jointly owned and what information is proprietary, it will reduce the need to monitor flows of information. Again, there are costs associated with monitoring behavior and setting up processes and procedures to minimize the probability of expropriation of technology. When Boeing started working its Japanese subcontractors on the 767 and 777, it needed to draw explicit boundaries around activities that were part of the relationship and those that were "out of bounds."

To establish and police procedures to ensure the smooth integration of workflows and the like between partners also has associated costs. To the extent that partners have clear roles and understand their respective responsibilities, alliance management should reduce costs by reducing the probability of duplication, or missed "hand-offs." In alliances where the objective is to combine forces to present one face to the customer, anything less than a seamless operation adds to the costs associated with running that relationship. If you take an international flight involving partner airlines, upon arriving at your destination you do not want to discover that your baggage has been lost because one partner did not transfer the suitcase—so much for seamless delivery.

Autonomy Breeds Tension

Alliances are formed among independent companies that cooperate to achieve mutually beneficial goals; yet, the partners remain autonomous. Herein lies one of the tensions facing managers charged with alliance responsibility. While an alliance affords many of the advantages gained through vertical integration without the added cost burden, decision-making processes are shared and often are a source of discomfort to those used to exercising complete control. Another tension between the partners is balancing their self-interests with the common good of the alliance. Costs are associated with opportunism and the risk that one partner will act in its own self-interest to the detriment of the other. Management processes become strained since there is no formal mechanism for exercising control. One cannot control what one does not own. Consensus between partners regarding the direction and mission of the alliance and clearly understood roles for the partners can reduce the costs associated with managing the alliance. One of the notable dichotomies that alliance managers must balance is the distinction between *shared control* and *having control*.

Alliances Require a Change in Mindset

For many companies, the change in mind-set that must accompany alliance management is difficult to achieve. It has caused considerable problems in achieving the stated goals of proposed alliances. The failure rate among alliances is high; it is often reported to exceed 60 percent.[7] Figure 1.3 summarizes data collected from a survey of CEOs by the

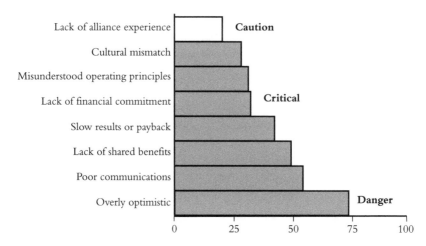

Figure 1.3 Reasons for failure: Results of 455 CEO interviews. (*Source:* Data Quest)

Conference Board suggesting reasons why alliances might fail. To some degree, failure can be attributed to a lack of alliance experience and the inability to appreciate that alliance management differs from traditional management. For management to enter into an alliance and expect a quick fix or fast results is naïve. Also, to expect that alliance management is no different from managing one's own company and that problems can be addressed through administrative fiat is, at best, an exercise in poor judgment. Moreover, to think that alliances can be managed as a side-activity with few resources and little attention ignores the reality that alliance management takes a great deal of management time and resources. It also takes practice!

Alliance Experience Is Valuable

Partners who have alliance experience and have developed an alliance acumen tend to be willing teachers and bring a highly valued skill to the alliance. These skills contribute to the alliance's competitive advantage. It is a catalyst that leverages the pooled resources of the partners. A skilled alliance partner can guide the alliance through the rough waters, accelerate its passage through the calm, and can impart valuable alliance-based knowledge to its partner so that it can improve its own alliance skills. Chapter 2 will develop further the notion of alliance-based competence. Questions that begin the process of understanding those attributes that are associated with an alliance competence include:[8]

- Does the firm have extensive alliance experience?
- Does the corporate culture support and reinforce alliance-like qualities?
- Is their senior management committed to the use of alliances as a strategic tool?
- Does an alliance infrastructure support the alliance efforts?
- How well does the firm select and negotiate with potential partners?
- Does the firm demonstrate commitment to its alliances?
- Does a process exist for developing alliance management talent?
- Does the company have mechanisms for learning from its alliance experiences?

Companies that possess these qualities are highly desirable partners and tend to have higher rates of alliance success. In addition, managers who have positive alliance experiences are more receptive to other alliance opportunities.

The opposite is also true—the corporate memory around failure is long. A recent conversation with a director in a newly formed alliance management business unit in a large U.S.-based multinational revealed that one of his problems is the resistance of senior managers to the entire notion of alliances. In addition to the company's tradition of vertical integration and the inherent bias to do work internally, there remained the memory of a failed alliance. His challenge was both to change the prevailing negative alliance attitude and to gain executive commitment to the need for alliances. There should be no surprise that many of their recent alliance attempts had fallen on tough times and were in need of repair.

A company with a high level of alliance-related skills and capabilities will understand better how alliances fit into its strategic thinking and is less likely to be swept away by the tide of alliance activity in its industry. Too often we hear, "My competitors are forming alliances, I want some!" The more capable firms often minimize the potential effects of dysfunctional behavior through prudent partner screening and selection, thoughtful planning, and negotiation that signals a win–win philosophy. Throughout the early stages of alliance development, these firms work hard to build trust and foster a joint commitment to the goals of the alliances as well as to the principles that will sustain the alliance over its lifecycle.

Alliance Competence: A Healthcare Example

The U.S. healthcare market is changing at a very fast pace. In addition to increased governmental intervention, there has been a boom of consolidation throughout the health delivery system including mergers and acquisitions between healthcare providers (e.g., hospitals, HMOs, PPOs), insurance carriers, suppliers, distributors, and wholesalers. Table 1.3 provides an example of this consolidation. The activity has spread to different levels of the value chain with acquisitions between Merck and MEDCO, Aetna and US Healthcare, to mention only two major acquisitions. Not only have the big become bigger through merger and acquisition, there has been an increase in alliance activity at all levels of the value chain.

As Table 1.3 illustrates, alliances range from buying consortia, to buyer supplier relationships, to outsourcing of nonessential services, to alliances based on technology access. They also may be a vehicle to increase both market presence and patient flow. As part of our work with a large university-based medical center, we have assessed its alliance competency. This medical center has already formed a number of alliances and has acknowledged that alliance activity is important to its continued success. At the same time, some of their alliances have proven to be time consuming and difficult to manage.

To help the executive management team better understand its alliance strategy, we surveyed the senior management to determine the medical center's current level of alliance competency. The data suggest that they have a long way to go before they demonstrate a alliance competency that would contribute to high levels of success and make them desirable to other potential partners. Despite the collective agreement

Table 1.3 Alliance Activity in the U.S. Healthcare Market

Alliance (Year Formed)	Partners	Scope of Agreement
DiaDexus (1997)	SmithKline Beecham PLC/ Incyte Pharmaceuticals, Inc.	Provides access to two of the world's largest repositories of genetic information and patents. Gene-based diagnostic tests are anticipated to be its first products.
Premier, Inc. (1995)	215 owner organizations operating 818 hospitals and affiliated with 940 other hospitals or health care organizations	The largest hospital alliance in the United States. One of its major programs involves group purchasing of supplies and pharmaceuticals. A wholly-owned subsidiary of Premier operates a physician management group.
Astra Merck (1994)	Merck & Co./Astra AB	Enhances Astra's U.S. presence and gives Merck access to Astra's research. The joint venture has U.S. rights to most of Astra AB's future discoveries.
HMO-USA (1983)	Blue Cross and Blue Shield HMOs	This national network links independent Blue Cross and Blue Shield contractors and provides multistate capability, which benefits those traveling outside of care area or multistate employers.
CVS Health Connection Center (1997)	Pfizer/CVS Corp.	Provides health education and disease management services within a drugstore. Managed care programs may contract to offer this service to members.
Metrahealth (1995)	Travelers Corp./Metropolitan Life Insurance Co.	This joint venture creates one of the biggest health insurance and managed care operations in the country.
South Valley Health Campus (1993)	Allina Health System/ Benedictine Health System/ Health System Minnesota	Three competitor care providers invested in a single-location, jointly owned health care facility with shared services to upgrade services and manage costs.

* Astra bought Merck's interest in 1998.

(Continued)

Table 1.3 *(Continued)*

Alliance (Year Formed)	Partners	Scope of Agreement
Kinetra (1998)	Eli Lilly & Co./ Electronic Data Systems Corp.	The company will create integrated networks to link insurers, physicians, pharmacies, laboratories, and hospitals.
Cell City, LLC (1998)	Cell Therapeutics, Inc./ City of Hope National Medical Ctr.	Provides for joint research to identify possible treatments for diabetes, an area of expertise for both organizations.

among the executive management of the importance of an integrated alliance strategy, results from the survey of senior mangers reveal that:

- Roles and responsibilities among alliance partners are poorly understood.
- Little faith and trust are extended to their current partners.
- They do not see their partners as equals.
- There is little sense of a win–win orientation.
- Information among alliance partners is not easily shared.
- Managers acknowledge that, in most instances, they engage in self-serving behavior.

The alliance profile captured through these preliminary results implies that an alliance based on a solid business proposition might not reap its full benefit due to the medical center's lack of alliance competence. Management does not appear to engage in, nor do they have internal processes that facilitate or reinforce alliance-like behavior. There are also second-order effects; a poor outcome in one alliance can adversely affect senior management's view toward future alliance activity and signal to potential partners that this medical center might not be a good candidate for future consideration. This does not bode well for an organization that espouses the importance of alliances to its future growth.

Alliance Competencies: A Wake-Up Call

In a recent interview,[9] John Brown, CEO of British Petroleum, describes the characteristics that define distinctive organizations. Among these characteristics is proficiency in forging close and selective relationships with major stakeholders (partners, suppliers, customers, countries) to maximize joint value. Fundamental to the success of these relationships is an ability to:

- Work toward joint goals.
- Deliver on promises.
- Be open and flexible.
- Be humble.
- Think long term.

Mr. Brown's comments shed light on some of the qualities that define a company's alliance competency. Managers cannot develop this competency overnight or by reading a book, even this book. Developing the requisite alliance skills, supportive infrastructure, and enabling processes takes time and cannot easily be transferred from company to company. While alliances facilitate learning from one's partner, alliance-related skills are often part of the company's tacit knowledge. This information is embedded in the culture of the firm and is part of its fabric. Therefore, it is difficult to observe, let alone copy.

Firms like Corning, Hewlett Packard, and Honda, with reputations for being good partners, have well-documented procedures and have institutionalized many of processes that enable good alliance practices. Each company has taken a different approach to inculcating alliance-like behavior firmwide. Certainly, one can rely on best practices[10] to learn from the successes of others. However, the ability to execute is far more difficult than the ability to understand what needs to be done. Embedding alliance-like thinking in the minds of managers is not a trivial task.

Companies with a high degree of alliance competency do not necessarily have cultures that cannot be replicated. They are, however, managed differently, have a culture that supports all elements of alliance-like behavior, and have embedded systems and processes to nurture their alliances as well as to develop the talent needed to manage their portfolio of alliances. Alliance thinking is part of the fabric of the firm; it is not the in-vogue, quick-fix solution. For many managers, the changes in thinking and in working required to become more alliance-facile is a major transformation. We are witnessing a shift from ownership and vertical integration, to partnership. In its extreme, one can easily envision a virtual corporation linked globally to a network of independent companies seamlessly providing goods and/or services to its customers.

A central premise here is that successful managers in the twenty-first century will have, in addition to functional and general management experience, alliance management capabilities. If the numbers are correct, or even close, one alliance is formed every hour. Add to those numbers the anticipated failures and the potential to squander scarce and valuable resources. The waste of time, talent, and money is mind-numbing. Have we gotten your attention? Throughout this book, we develop many principles and tenets that result in alliance competence.

Trends in Alliance Activity

A recent study by Coopers and Lybrand[11] of the CEO of firms identified as the fastest growing businesses in the U.S. in 1995–1996 reveals a number of reasons for partnering (Table 1.4). These reasons suggest trends in the explosion of alliance activity. Although the study is based on a U.S. sample, our experience suggests that these reasons are not unique to the United States and, in fact, can be extended globally.

More and more, alliance activity is driven by market-facing factors that impinge directly on a firm's competitive position. Potential partners are beginning to ask how an alliance affects its competitive position. Cost considerations are important still but are less the single driving force. Too often alliances were focused on achieving back room efficiency and improved economies of scale, or gaining additional clout through the combination of procurement activity. Many of these cost savings are very real but can be described as "low hanging fruit" because they are relatively easy to achieve. Examples of cost savings from joint procurement activities are many and can run into the tens of millions of dollars per year. In their first year, Northwest Airlines and KLM announced joint procurement savings of close to $30 million. However important these cost savings are, they tend not to be sufficient to convey a long-term competitive advantage. For buyer-supplier alliances or different forms of outsourcing alliances, true leverage is based on an understanding of what resources and/or capabilities, beyond a cost advantage, can be leveraged to support the partners' strategic intent. Outsourcing contracts based on cost reduction alone tend not to achieve their stated goals. There is an increasing

Table 1.4   U.S. CEOs' Top Reasons for Partnering in 1996

Reasons Given for Partnering	Frequency of Response (%)
Decrease cost of existing operations	44
Improve employee skills	48
Improve operations or technology	71
Create more new products or lines of business	76
Increase sales of existing products	77
Improve competitive position	77

recognition that shifting a fixed cost to a variable cost often does not compensate for inability to show significant downstream advantages in the marketplace.

Beyond Cost Reduction

Expectations are beginning to emerge for partners to take alliance thinking and its potential advantages far beyond the immediate cost savings opportunities. As a logical next step, one would try to achieve quality improvements in products and processes. This, too, is alone not sufficient and does not fully leverage the potential gains that can be achieved through an alliance. To achieve maximum benefit, partners have to change the basic manner in which they interact and relate. Through joint planning and extensive information sharing, committed partners would strive to leverage design, manufacturing, technological, and market information. The goal would be for the alliance to deliver a competitive advantage relative to other constellations of competing alliances.

Market-Focused Alliances

It is estimated that almost all the Fortune 1000 companies have designated alliances as a key strategic initiative. Some estimate that by the year 2000, alliances will account for better than 20 percent of the average company's revenue.[12] There is a notable shift to a more market-focused view of alliance activity and a search for partners who can contribute to a firm's revenue-producing assets and capabilities. For a company like United Technologies (UTC), this shift in emphasis is revealing and presents many challenges. Management has successfully managed the cost side of the business and now must also look to the marketplace for its next opportunities. Not only will partnerships help UTC companies gain access to new markets and technologies, using alliances as a vehicle allows them to become less dependent on past key customers such as the U.S. military. Now their search for partners entails criteria that provide added capabilities and skills to pursue commercial sales. As might be imagined, in the three defense-related divisions, their entire business processes and structures were developed to dovetail with procurement as conducted by the Department of Defense. Moving into the twenty-first century, these businesses cannot afford such singular focus. Alliances facilitate "bifocal vision;" now companies can focus on existing customers while pursing opportunities with new customers.

A Shift to Alliance Management from Alliance Formation

Despite the positive press and glowing estimates regarding the growth of alliance activity, one fact remains—the failure rate associated with alliances exceeds 60 percent. In addition, the rate of failure has not dropped significantly in recent years although the number of alliances formed has skyrocketed. Why haven't managers gotten better at managing alliances? Understanding the reason for the alliance and being able to achieve alignment between partners regarding objectives and goals is one thing; sustaining the momentum of the alliance over time is quite another. Our focus will shift from alliance formation and the problems inherent in getting the alliance off the ground to a greater concern for the activities, structures, and processes fundamental to ensuring alliance success over time. While understanding questions related to strategic fit, partner selection, due diligence, and alliance negotiation remain important; senior managers are beginning to appreciate better the complexities associated with creating an enabling environment for the alliances to prosper and grow. They acknowledge that the resource commitment required is far more than anticipated. Most managers do not have enough time or attention to devote to nurturing and sustaining alliances over time.

A Shift from Traditional Management Models

Traditional management practices based on principles of hierarchy and chains of command need to be unlearned and new models for managing need to be developed. Many firms have begun both formal and informal processes to develop alliance skills and capabilities among its management ranks. Not only have firms begun to formalize processes to capture and disseminate the lessons learned from alliance successes and failures, the more alliance savvy companies have begun to recognize that significant alliance experience should be a part of all high-potential manager's development plans. We hear all too often that firms are limited in their alliance activities because they lack sufficient management talent to dedicate to their partnerships. Two points become salient here:

1. There is increasing recognition that alliances are about relationships and people and that having skilled alliance managers contributes to the probability of a successful outcome.

2. Developing an alliance competency is emerging as an acknowledged core skill and many firms are struggling with the mechanisms for nurturing these skills and spreading them throughout the ranks of management.

Building Alliance Skills Throughout the Organization

The challenge is how to inculcate alliance thinking within the ranks of managers who, in the past, have been rewarded and promoted on processes and outcomes that are based on concepts that are irrelevant, and often detrimental, to alliance success. Energy devoted to creating a logical and systematic approach to alliance management lessens the errors made. An assumption here is that managers can learn from both alliance successes and failures and that the firm can facilitate that learning. In some instances, this is a very big assumption. (These issues are explicitly addressed in Chapters 8 and 9.) By understanding the complexity of alliance-related issues, managers can minimize the pitfalls of partnership failures, save both time and energy, and pass that knowledge on to succeeding generations of managers. Firms require far more than an ability to create a repository of alliance knowledge and best practices. They must adapt their processes and structures to be more alliance compatible. Alliances cannot be managed as a side-activity. Given the intensity of alliance development expected, we anticipate greater corporate attention will be devoted to remediating alliance deficits throughout the company.

Alliances as an Option on the Future

An alliance failure rate of 60 percent might appear quite high. Some might think the number is low. Placing this percentage in context helps reveal the true magnitude of the problem associated with alliance failure. The more important issue is to understand just what the failure rate represents. Alliances aid companies in adapting to the future and in leveraging the skills of their partners to better manage an uncertain world. In many situations, an alliance is a mechanism for betting on a future outcome. If one examines the range of alliances that emerged during the development of multimedia software, it becomes apparent that many of these alliances were options taken on the development of new technology. From Figure 1.4, it is possible to envision the extent of AT&T's alliance activity and to realize that for a small investment (relative to its sales) they could have access to nascent technology and be able to incorporate it in its development of this new market.

In this manner, AT&T hedges its bets and takes options on competing designs and technologies. It can wait to see which one emerges as the dominant technology. Their alliance strategy allows them to play with competing designs, learn from each of its partners, contribute to their partners' learning, and emerge from the development effort as a member of the winning coalition. Thus, alliance with a number of firms in the evolution of a market helps guarantee survival. In the development of new technology standards, a firm that is not a member of the dominant coalition might never be considered a "player," or it

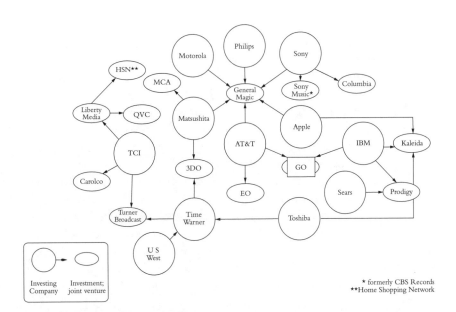

Figure 1.4 Making the connection: Multimedia's equity alliances. Some of the major equity investments by computer and communications companies in the burgeoning field of multimedia technology. (*Source: The Wall Street Journal,* July 14, 1993. Republished by permission of Dow Jones, Inc. via Copyright Clearance Center, Inc. [© 1993] Dow Jones and Company, Inc. All rights reserved worldwide.)

might enter the market late thereby losing any advantages that accrue to the first mover.

Thus, if AT&T invested in three different technologies and assumed that only one would emerge as the winner, it takes a calculated risk and estimates that 1 of 3 "bets" (alliances) will emerge. The cost of investing in all three is much lower than allocating its funds to develop these technologies internally. The result is that AT&T could gain insight into other competing technologies at a fairly low investment in time, resources, and people. However, since only one venture emerged as the winner, the failure rate (if taken literally) was ⅔ or 66 percent. To help make the point about taking an option on the future, think about an oil-drilling analogy. Typically, seven of ten holes drilled come up dry. Unless you are extremely skilled and lucky, you often must drill the seven holes to get an oil-producing well. Even the nonproducing holes provide rich information to the geologist who learns from the seismic readings and other pieces of scientific data.

To a certain extent, failure is built into the process by virtue of the degree of uncertainty associated with future events. In the world of new product development, it is often cited that one commercial success results from 100 new product ideas generated.[13] Figure 1.5 illustrates the risk and return assessment associated with alliance development. Comparing alliance development with the new product development process gives one a better appreciation for the degree of failure and the associated costs. The lines illustrate the risk and reward dilemma. In the pharmaceutical industry, the options price for a phase one alliance is far lower than a phase 2 alliance. A phase 1 project is a very early stage in the development of a new drug. Phase 2 is much further along in the development cycle where the concerns are less focused on the basic chemistry and more on clinical trials and commercialization. In a phase 2 project, there is more information known to the researcher and the probability of failure is lower. Phase 1 projects cost less but carry far more risk as the probability of discovery and clearing the regulatory hurdles are both uncertain.

Bain and Company extends the new product process analogy and concludes that two out of 100 alliances last more than four years and that most alliance overtures fail to pass the negotiation stage. Again, the picture painted here suggests that failure comes with the territory! However, caution is urged regarding the use of measures of longevity as a measure of success. While the length of the alliance speaks to the potential robustness of the relationship and the vitality of the business proposition, it is not

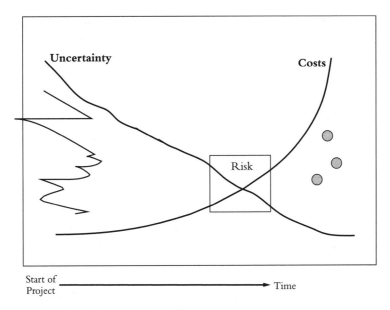

Figure 1.5   Evaluating potential alliances.

a good proxy for success. An alliance that lasts four months can be as successful as an alliance that lasts four years if both have accomplished their stated mission and objectives, and learning has occurred. The notion of long term varies and is industry specific. In mining businesses, long term tends to be 15 plus years since mines can be productive for long periods. In the world of the Internet and its burgeoning technology, 18 months is extremely long term and 15 years just does not compute! If one were to compare alliance longevity across industries, it becomes clear that length of time does not adequately capture the idea of success.

Firms in industries in which there is a high degree of technological change tend to form shorter term and less formal alliances. When the market is in transition, there often is less joint venture activity since one's ability to uncouple the venture becomes more tedious in light of the amount of comingled joint resources. Alliances based on shared technology that can be more easily separated and circumscribed into what is part of the alliance and what remains in the hands of the individual partners are more commonplace.[14] As uncertainty diminishes, alliances become more intertwined, and acquisitions or mergers often occur as a vehicle to gain closer control over the relationship. Under conditions of discontinuous technological change, ownership of assets via acquisition is risky. The risk factors center on the problem of buying either the wrong technology (i.e., not the dominant design) or paying for assets that bring no incremental value to the purchase.

Summary

The title of this chapter suggests that alliances represent a set of complex interactions. The reasons for alliance formation are well-documented and, for the most part, managers have improved their ability to build a compelling business case for why a particular alliance makes sense. However, there still exists a feeding frenzy around alliance formation and some firms are drawn to the alliance because it is the "thing to do." As a consequence, they have not fully cultivated their ability to articulate the rationale for the alliance or even to formulate criteria for partner selection. The need to develop a strategic alliance should be supplanted by a concern to develop an alliance strategy. It is far more difficult to develop a cogent alliance strategy. This chapter started down the path of viewing an alliance less from its economic derivation and has begun to articulate a theme that captures the intricate set of interactions that must exist between partners and be aligned on different levels.

Alliances are a value-adding activity in that partners are driven to achieve goals that would have been difficult to accomplish alone. The stated goals of these alliances should converge on the alliance's ability to gain a sustainable competitive advantage. Complexity enters the process as partners must engage each other on two separate, but highly interdependent levels. On one level, each brings resources (competencies, skills, capabilities) that contribute to and complement the resource base of the other. To the extent that these resources are unique, alliances achieve a greater potential gain. Processes and criteria must be developed to assess what overall set of resources is valued, what resources should be retained, and what resources one should seek in a prospective partner. However, resource richness is not sufficient. Having access to markets, technical know-how, and the like do contribute to competitive advantage. The inability to engage in alliance-like behavior, however, is likely to decrease the full benefits of the alliance despite technical know-how.

The second level of interaction encompasses the manner in which partners behave, the rules of engagement that set the tone of the alliance, and the skills each bring to the alliance that helps shape how well the alliance is nurtured over time. These skills are referred to as a partner's alliance competence. The notion of alliance competence is a central theme in this book. Partners' understanding of what it truly means to ally, their ability to both live the ideals of the alliance spirit, and pass that knowledge to others in their own firm as well as across organizational boundaries to their partner is what distinguishes a potentially strong alliance from a weak one. Such competencies are difficult to acquire since they require a change in mindset and behavior that force management from the comfort of a command and control environment.

Hierarchy establishes a chain of command in which it is clear who is responsible for what and who makes decisions and who implements them. Alliance structures tend to be less clear since partners retain their autonomy and share decision making. There is an inherent tension that is balanced by trust and a sense of fair dealing that grows, over time, through the partners' interactions. To trust one's partner to act in the interest of the alliance rather than to act in his own self-interest requires a significant change in thinking. Chapter 2 first introduces the range of changes that alliance-like thinking requires. Beyond these critical changes, many organizations do not have structures or processes that enable such alliance-like thinking and actions to emerge. Moreover, there are even fewer firms that have established processes for institutionalizing the skills and competencies we will advocate throughout this book.

The objective in this chapter has been to begin building the argument for the importance of the alliance competence. Alliances should not be viewed as an end in themselves; they represent a journey from the monolithic view of the hierarchical organization to a world in which firms are part of larger constellations of companies that compete globally. The journey includes a change from the view of an alliance as a business deal in which skills and resources alone lead to success to a recognition that alliances are also about relationships. They intertwine and both are critical to success of the partnership. Typically, the business side of the alliance is easier for managers; they have experience, a vocabulary, metrics for understanding performance. However, alliances fail for reasons other than the soundness of the business plan or the ability to execute according to that plan. The remaining chapters bridge the gap between managing the business of the alliance and attending to all aspects of its complex interactions when it comes to making the alliance work every day. The journey begins!

2

Building Alliance Competence

New Rules and
New Approaches

What Is an Alliance?

Chapter 1 alluded to the definition of an alliance; here an alliance will be formally defined. Managers often refer to certain relationships as alliances that on closer scrutiny fail the litmus test. Chapter 2 develops the framework for the definition of an alliance and discusses those characteristics that separate alliances from other kinds of interfirm relationships. In addition, the similarities across alliance types will be discussed. While different alliance types exist, each must have certain common fundamental characteristics. Merck, for example, engages in a comarketing alliance with DuPont whereby each markets the other's drugs. At the same time, Merck might form a joint venture with a small biotech company to explore the commercial viability of a new drug. And, in a third instance, Merck might have a close relationship with a key supplier to provide certain feed stock compounds for a production of one of their pharmaceutical products. These relationships all serve a different purpose, probably have different performance expectations, and require different levels of management time and resources. However, if each is truly an alliance, a certain degree of commonality should exist among them. One of the objectives here is to discuss those commonalities that are fundamental to all alliances, not to focus on the differences that distinguish them. Figure 2.1 presents types of alliances and positions them between mergers and open-market transactions.

To understand the importance of an alliance litmus test, consider that to defer the cost of oil exploration, a foreign energy company will lease certain plots to a "partner" who pays a fee for the right to explore for oil. In effect, this investor takes an option to drill for oil. The risks are borne entirely by the partner who invests his own capital and equipment. If oil is found, the partner pays royalties to the energy company who maintains exclusive ownership of the well and reaps the majority of the profits. National law states clearly that all ventures that "touch" a natural resource, such as oil, are the property of the state. Although the venture creates value for both partners, one partner bears most of the risks and the rewards are shared disproportionately. Also, the majority of control resides with the energy company since the government has the final word in all aspects of oil production and maintains a "golden share" in any joint venture that results once oil is found. While the relationship is a cooperative one in which partners share similar objectives, these so-called alliances fail other aspects of the litmus test. The following sections describe the criteria against which we judge a relationship to be an alliance.

Alliances Create Value

Alliances exist to create value. Companies join forces to reap benefits that neither partner could easily achieve alone. This mutual need drives companies to search for partners with complementary skills and resources that help both companies improve their competitive positions. Competitive advantage might lie in reduced costs, access to new markets, natural resources, and technology, or an ability to leverage the expertise of one partner to improve one's practices and processes. Alliances can focus on either offensive or defensive opportunities. Partners join together to exploit a new market or explore a new technology. Defensively, partners form alliances to combat, or preempt, the efforts of other companies or other alliances. The ever-changing set of alliances in the airline industry has both offensive and defensive components. British Air and American, along with Quantas and BA's other partners, are aligned to offer a global alternative to United's Star™ alliance that includes Thai Airlines, Varig, Air Canada, Lufthansa, and SAS. These alliances are only two of several that have global constellations, some of which share partners

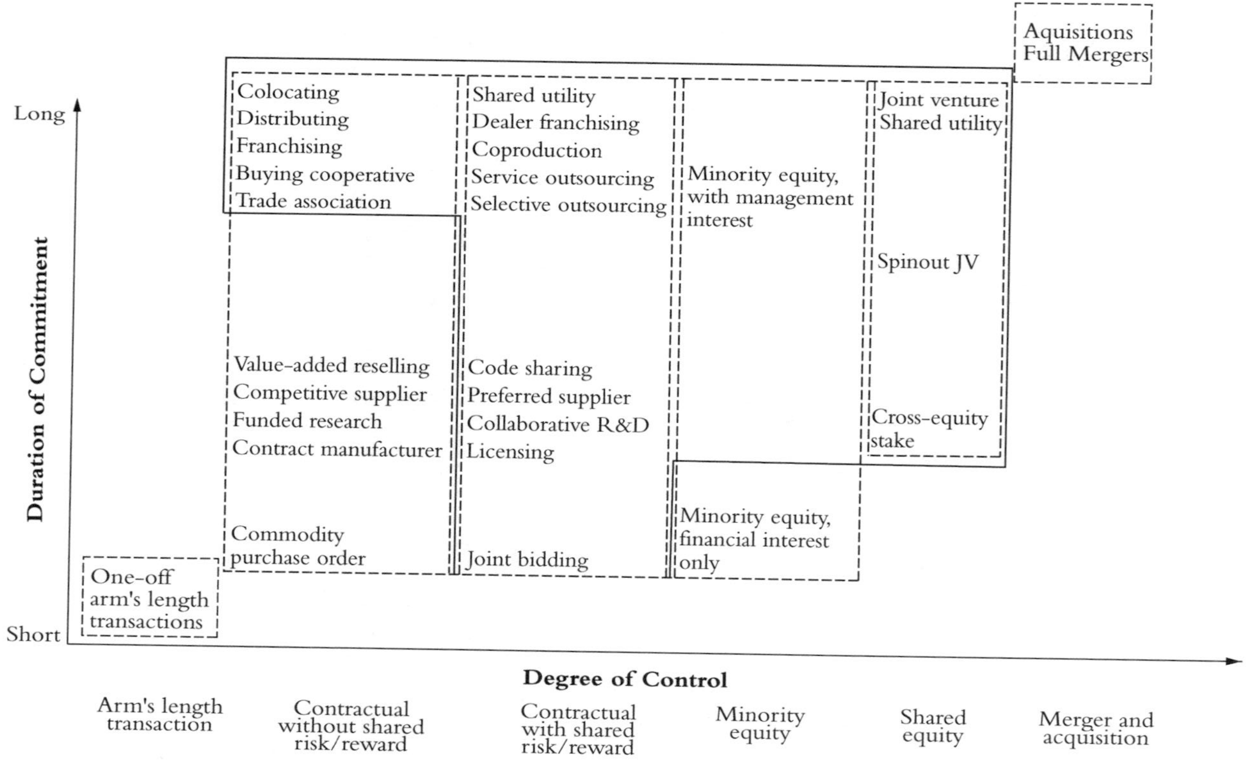

Aquisitions
Full Mergers

Joint venture
Shared utility

Spinout JV

Cross-equity
stake

Shared utility
Dealer franchising
Coproduction
Service outsourcing
Selective outsourcing

Minority equity,
with management
interest

Minority equity,
financial interest
only

Colocating
Distributing
Franchising
Buying cooperative
Trade association

Code sharing
Preferred supplier
Collaborative R&D
Licensing

Value-added reselling
Competitive supplier
Funded research
Contract manufacturer

Joint bidding

Commodity
purchase order

One-off
arm's length
transactions

Duration of Commitment

Long

Short

Degree of Control

| Arm's length transaction | Contractual without shared risk/reward | Contractual with shared risk/reward | Minority equity | Shared equity | Merger and acquisition |

Figure 2.1 Types of alliances. (Adapted from: *The Alliance Analyst*, University of Virginia.)

across alliances. For example, American has recently formed an alliance with U.S. Airways in which frequent flyers can exchange their mileage to travel on both airlines.

Alliances: A Definition

An alliance is *a close, collaborative relationship between two, or more, firms with the intent of accomplishing mutually compatible goals that would be difficult for each to accomplish alone.* Some key words emerge from this definition that warrant closer attention:

- *Collaborative* implies that a set of operating norms exists among partners such that each partner will not act in self-interest to the detriment of the others. Implied here also are the notions of voluntary involvement rather than coercion, and the expectation of reciprocal behavior.
- *Mutually compatible* suggests that there is alignment among partners such that each can accomplish its objectives within the framework of the alliance.
- *Difficult to achieve alone* recognizes that each partner is not only dependent on the other but acknowledges that their individual fates are linked. Each admits, for example, that costs are prohibitive, time too precious, expertise too limited, or management time and other resources too scarce to attempt to achieve the goals of the alliance without a partner.

Also, implied by the definition is that an alliance represents an open-ended contract between separate firms that must share decision making and control. The open-ended nature of an alliance contract reflects that alliances are formed partly as a response to an uncertain world and that the benefits can be achieved only through collaboration. In some situations, alliances can be viewed as experimental probes—a vehicle by which a firm can explore a new market, emerging technology, a burgeoning channel of distribution without fully committing resources. Also, captured here is the notion that alliances are partly utilized as a learning tool. The concept of learning through an alliance will be discussed in greater detail later in this chapter.

Shared Decision Making and Shared Control: The Heart of the Issue and a Source of Tension

Joint decision making and shared control are important and deserve attention since alliances present unique challenges to managers who are more comfortable in an environment with clearly drawn lines of authority. Authority allows those in power to control behavior and influence outcomes. Alliances are hybrid organizations[1] in that separate and independent companies combine resources and governance structures to achieve a common goal. Alliances are a paradox in that control tends not to be centralized in one firm and authority is distributed, to varying degrees, among the alliance partners. In a joint venture, where partners take equity positions, it is possible to know the relative authority of the partners. A proxy measure might be the number of board seats held by each partner. On the surface, it would appear that the majority stakeholder would have more authority and control than the minority partner(s). Legally, this might be true; practically, it can lead to a false sense of power.

In nonequity alliances, the allocation of authority is less easily understood since the partners have comingled assets and/or people, but each set of resources is ultimately tied back to the partner company. The notion of control is less meaningful since there is no joint ownership—there is nothing to control. The partners remain separate entities. Control, at one level, simply means that there will be no surprises; it ensures (certainly raises the probability) of predictable behavior among alliance partners.[2] Problems can surface because the lack of control makes many managers uncomfortable and they do not have an alternative framework through which to gain cooperation from their partners.

Shared decision making and control in alliances can be compared with similar expectations in either a merger or acquisition. Both are alternatives to alliances. Sometimes alliances are used as a precursor to a merger.[3] Similar to the growth in alliance activity in recent years, the number of mergers and acquisitions has also increased at an exponential rate. As with alliances, despite the M&A activity recorded, there appears to be some debate regarding their performance.[4] In the long term, 50 to 80 percent of all mergers and takeovers are considered to be financially unsuccessful. The British Institute of Management identifies 16 factors associated with unsuccessful M&A activity.[5] Mergers and acquisitions share problems related to people and relationships; management problems are universal. Many of the following factors apply to alliances as well:

- Underestimation of the problems of skills transfer.
- Demotivation of employees of acquired company.
- Departure of key people in the acquired company.
- Too much energy devoted to doing the deal, not enough to postacquisition planning and integration.
- Decision making delayed by unclear responsibility and conflicts.
- Neglecting the existing business due to the attention needed to manage the acquired company.
- Insufficient research about the acquired company.

In mergers and acquisitions, the concept of control and shared decision making differs from that of an alliance. An acquisition occurs when one firm accumulates sufficient shares to gain control or ownership of another organization. These takeovers can be considered friendly or hostile; however, the outcome is the same in that the two firms become one, with clear lines of control and decision-making authority. There is a "winner" and the power held by the acquirer tends not to be negotiable. When Oracle acquires a company, there is no question where the seat of power lies.

In a merger, firms agree to join together often through an exchange of stock. While there is often a winner, it is not immediately obvious. Typically, there is a period during which management positions are sorted out, the distribution of power often ebbs and flows as managers jockey for position, and the ability to control the destiny of the newly formed company remains uncertain for a period of time. Close examination of the 1997 merger between Bell Atlantic and NYNEX reveals that Bell Atlantic personnel hold more key positions in the newly formed company although the heir apparent to Ray Smith is Ivan Seidenberg, the former chairman of NYNEX. Nonetheless, in a merger, a new company emerges from the combined companies; one company loses its autonomy and, often, its identity, and the lines of authority/control and power are eventually sorted out.

In an alliance, the blending of the two (or more) separate companies does not occur. Partners (even joint venture partners) maintain their autonomy, are compelled to share decision making, and cannot truly execute their will without the cooperation of the other partners. Control, as in command and control, is difficult to achieve because the individual partners retain ownership. Herein lies the tension. Alliance partners who join forces to pursue separate goals and need to gain alignment in the direction of their goals might find that their mutual goals are at odds. To pursue one's own interests is to act opportunistically and such self-serving behavior is dysfunctional; yet, opportunistic behavior seems to be individually rational.[6] It is difficult for one partner to work its will. Since there is no hierarchy or chain of command to reference, partners must educate, influence, compromise and, above all, trust the other's motivations. It is easy to see how potentially awkward such relationships can be. In nonequity alliances, the ability to make quick decisions is likely to suffer at the hands of consensus building.

A source of frustration for managers at Renault in their alliance with Volvo was the tedious and slow decision-making process in which consensus was needed before each party could act. The initial agreement was an alliance of equals with each partner having an equal say in the joint activities. A merger was suggested to break the logjam and permit a more streamlined and purposive decision-making process. During interviews with senior managers at Renault, speed and determination were referenced as a key motivating factor. In the merged company (where initially Renault held 65% of the stock), it was felt that decision making could move faster and would not get bogged down in committee. In the proposed new company, there was a clear chain of command and lines of authority were fixed. One senior manager at Renault commented that everyone knows that time is money!

Dimensions of Alliances: Searching for Common Characteristics

As Figure 2.1 suggests, there is a range of relationships in which firms can join forces to achieve objectives. Running the gamut from arm's length transactions to wholly-owned subsidiaries, companies have alternatives for exchanging goods and services, sharing technology and research, and providing value to their customers. Some suggest[7] that while alliances are a viable and mutually beneficial strategy under certain conditions, there is an inherent fickle and tentative nature to how partners cooperate and get work done. Others go so far as to proclaim that alliances tend to be unstable and transitional; certainly they lack the stability that exists in a more traditional organization form.[8]

Figure 2.2 shows a range of alliance forms that may appear distinct and unrelated to some readers. To focus on the differences is, to some degree, counterproductive since the similarities among alliance forms provide insight into the essential ingredients that give alliances the stability to survive the inherent instability that seems to exist. Borrowing a biological framework helps to differentiate alliance types in the same way that a biologist attempts to sort out the differences and similarities among animals. Figure 2.3 presents the alliance continuum using an approach common to those who study comparative anatomy. The different alliance forms represent species. Species are groups of individuals that resemble one another and are separated from other groups by variation in structure and form. Genus is a group of species; for example, mammals. There are many species of mammals ranging from humans, to horses, to whales. They do not often look the same but all mammals have common characteristics: mammals are warm blooded, produce live young, have

Figure 2.2 Range of alliance activities. (Adapted from: *The Alliance Analyst,* University of Virginia.)

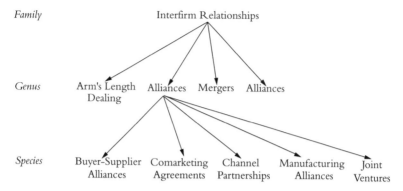

Figure 2.3   Understanding alliance forms.

hair, suckle their young, breathe air, and have seven neck bones. These characteristics distinguish mammals from other animals such as birds and fish *and* also show how mammals are related.

The question now becomes what common characteristics link the various alliance forms so that when the term *alliance* is used, there is a common reference point. A common reference allows a shared set of expectations regarding certain norm-governed behaviors. Wilson[9] refers to these dimensions as *relationship variables* that guide the interaction of partners in an alliance. If a manager of a joint venture now must work with a key buyer in an supply chain alliance, the manager should expect that certain behaviors are deemed acceptable and that other actions would violate the manager's sense of alliance-like behavior. Several characteristics contribute to the stability of the alliance. Each is necessary but not alone sufficient to enhance the ability of the alliance partners to accomplish their goals.

The term *stability* describes a desired alliance state. Alliances are "unnatural organizational forms" in that firms cooperate to achieve joint goals while simultaneously pursuing their self-interests. Balancing this inherent tension contributes to the instability. It probably is safe to say that alliances are neither stable nor unstable but require effort to maintain their purpose. An alliance is subject to many forces that cause it to stray from its intended course. The strength of the desired characteristics enables the alliance to maintain its course and heading. If any of these characteristics are absent, or if a certain minimal level on each characteristic is not achieved, the stability of the alliance is at risk. Unlike our biological analogy, mammals either have hair or do not, are warm-blooded or not; whereas alliances can demonstrate different degrees of intensity on each dimension and there might exist a minimal level to qualify as an alliance. The key dimensions follow.

Goal Compatibility

Alliance partners must share mutually achievable goals although the goals do not have to be the same. It would be unrealistic to expect that partners would share the same goals as each probably has different business objectives and performance targets. If partners ally in different parts of the value chain, such as to source product exclusively from a certain key supplier, it is likely that both share the goal of better meeting the needs of the end-use customers. Given the economics of the different levels of the supply chain, one partner might focus on reducing the total cost of ownership and leveraging technology as primary goals. The other might look at achieving economies of scale in manufacturing and accessing a new market segment as its major goals.

During the later half of 1998, Sumitomo Bank and Daiwa Securities announced joint ventures in which they will merge large parts of their investment banking operations. There is no question that some of the motivation can be attributed to the financial crisis in Japan. The objectives of the alliance are partly defensive as a move against foreign banks gaining a stronger presence in Japan. For Daiwa, it is also partly offensive in that as a holding company with smaller specialized units, foreign investors can then purchase shares in the business units and not in the holding company. For Sumitomo, the consolidation reduces its exposure and frees up some of its capital. It also repositions the bank as more of a full-service financial institution. The objectives for the alliance and for the individual partners are aligned but are not congruent. Alignment is essential and problems will arise when the goals are misaligned such that the partners cannot accomplish their goals simultaneously. Goal misalignment is an obvious place for conflict to emerge.

Trust and Commitment

These two characteristics are the sine qua non of alliances for without trust and commitment, there can be no alliance. Trust is truly the cornerstone of any alliance as it is the foundation for social order. In today's complex world, it is not uncommon for firms to partner with their competitors to meet the challenges of a global marketplace. In this instance trust takes on a new meaning. Research devoted to trust in organizations has a 40-year history[10] and the definition of trust converges on a confidence in others' intentions and motivations. Trust is the belief that one's alliance partner will act in a predictable manner, will keep his or her word, and will not behave in a way that negatively affects the other. This last point is particularly salient under conditions where one partner might feel vulnerable due to a heightened dependence on the other.

In many alliances, partners are compelled to share information/ knowledge that lies near, if not at, the core of their business. Trust diminishes the concern that this knowledge might be expropriated and used later to compete against the partner. This fear is very real among managers of small companies that seek alliances with larger companies (e.g., the biotech, information technology, and telecommunications industries). The fear exists also among many multinational alliances based on technology sharing. There exists always the fear that the larger firm is a "pirate in a partner suit" and is using the alliance to gain knowledge for its own benefit.

If this fear is real, the question is, how does one build a foundation of trust? Trust is partly engendered by one's reputation. Corning Incorporated, for example, enjoys a positive reputation as an alliance partner. A potentially new alliance partner is more likely to enter a relationship with Corning assuming a certain level of trust. Reputation extends to past dealings with individuals and the expectation that past behaviors will continue into the future.

Many of the fast-paced, short-term alliances (to be discussed in detail in Chapter 10) found in Silicon Valley can be traced to the personal relationship people developed when they either worked for the same company or had past dealings. In both instances, one partner has confidence in the intentions of the other and has no reason to question his or her motivations or to be suspect. The tangled web of interpersonal relationships extends beyond the managers and founders of these high-tech start-ups to include the venture capitalists who provide the funds for these ventures. Figure 2.4 depicts one such set of relationships in Silicon Valley. Note the extensive ties among the members of boards of directors. It is through this network that the basis for trust grows.

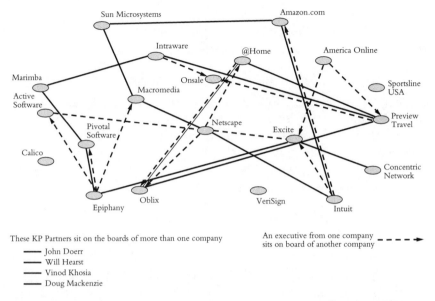

Figure 2.4   The directors in Silicon Valley. (*Source: Fortune,* October 26, 1998.)

When the risks associated with miscalculating the motivations of the other have very negative consequences, it is possible to set limits around the areas in which trust guides one's behavior. This is referred to as bounded trust. When Boeing started to work with the Japanese on the 777, it realized that it must protect core competencies such as project management and wings and lift. During its interactions, despite the technical information that Boeing and Japanese engineers shared, Boeing proactively managed its vulnerability by denying access to certain secure areas and proprietary information that was considered too sensitive to share. Here, trust was confined to certain parts of the relationship, and in other parts of the relationship the degree of interaction was minimal. Tension exists when partners in the relationship appear in conflict and the potential for distrust affects one's willingness to trust. In part, this tension is managed by setting expectations at the outset and determining what is in bounds and what is out of bounds.

As alliances move from a relationship with one partner to a network of alliance partners, the ability to compartmentalize trust becomes tenuous, at best. The social context of the industry often establishes a de facto set of operating norms in which certain kinds of behavior are acceptable and others are not. Many industries engage in clanlike behavior,[11] and the rules of engagement for certain businesses are such that a certain level of trusting behavior exists simply because blatant self-serving behavior on the part of one alliance partner violates the norms of the industry. In burgeoning industries (e.g., e-commerce), there are often sets of norms and accepted values that guide the behavior of firms. To violate these norms can result in ostracism. It is not uncommon to hear "that in this business one would never behave that way!"

Although managers are naturally suspicious and question the motivations of their partners, trust holds such suspicion in check so that the work of the alliance can move forward untethered.[12] Trust is the glue that binds the alliance and serves also to regulate the alliance-like behavior. Trust lowers the transaction costs associated with running an alliance and can substitute for a contract in its ability to induce (guarantee might be too strong) desirable behavior. Because hierarchies are less meaningful and are often irrelevant in the management of an alliance, trust can be a replacement for more formal, or legal, remedies. Trust and formal control are not substitutable; however, they do complement each other.[13] One's confidence in the other partner's ability to act in a predictable fashion is predicated on factors that include a partner's risk profile. Trust building has a cost and partners must appreciate both the costs of building trust and the costs of failing to do so. When the ties between partners in an alliance are many and the need for trust is high, the partners must take time to invest in the relationship, despite the high cost of maintaining sound relationships.

Trust building. In non-equity-sharing alliances; there is relatively low embeddedness.[14] The ability to exit the relationship is less cumbersome; the risks of unintended resource transfer are low; and the degree of alliance-specific investments is minimal. Trust takes the place of more formal control mechanisms and helps shape the nature and scope of partner interaction. Trust building, like other norm-building activities, takes time and involves several techniques.

One technique involves *risk taking*. Trust and risk taking form a reciprocal relationship—one partner takes a risk and trusts the other and the other tends to be motivated to behave in a trustworthy manner.[15] Although taking risks breeds trust, companies do not willingly take these risks. The process is gradual: a small risk leads to some level of trust and soon the partner takes a more significant risk and over time trust builds. An implication is that large-scale alliances either should follow a series of smaller, more manageable alliances or that partners should engage in large alliances in a measured, iterative manner. Logic dictates that managers should spend time together at the very early stages of an alliance to "test" and build their mutual trust.

A second technique is to establish a basis of *fair dealing* in which profits, rewards, and other benefits that accrue from the alliance are distributed fairly. The issue is not one of equality; rather, the important consideration is to treat partners equitably, so they do not feel taken advantage of. Fair dealing breeds trust.

A third technique is based on *communication* and the willingness of partners to share information in an open and timely fashion. Such an exchange leads to greater credibility and helps establish common norms and values. Equally important is the belief that information sharing leads to a more trusting environment. Opportunistic behavior is the result of asymmetries in information.

A fourth mechanism for trust building is related to the extent to which each partner is willing and able to *adapt to the changing needs* of the environment. Flexibility in one's approach to the alliance sends a signal of trust and encourages partners to focus on their mutual interests. Such adaptation suggests that partners are willing to see the alliance weather the winds of change. In one alliance, a partner willingly adapted its approach to a technical problem because the initial alliance agreement no longer made sense due to changes in the marketplace. This partner acted unilaterally without the suggestion of the other partner. Since the alliance was important to both partners, one was willing to demonstrate its ability to accommodate changing environmental conditions.

To concentrate only on the initial contract and not acknowledge that as the alliance matures unforeseen circumstances might alter the stated intent of the alliance is to question both the motivation of one's partner and implicit value of the alliance. Neither reaction bodes well for building trust. Certainly, one would question the degree of commitment to the alliance. Outsourcing contracts tend to breed problems in the second or third year since as the environment changes, one party (usually the party to whom the operations have been outsourced) has little incentive to adapt and often cites the terms of the contract as the default option.[16]

Commitment is a virtuous cycle. Related to trust is the notion of commitment and there appears to be a virtuous cycle. When one partner demonstrates commitment, there is often a similar response from the other. Commitment is simply one partner's willingness to devote time, energy, and/or resources to the alliance. In part, alliance failure is attributable to management neglect and an inability to understand those factors that engender cooperative behavior. A Coopers & Lybrand[17] study reported that while executives spend 23 percent of their time developing alliance plans and 19 percent of their time on drafting legal documents, only 8 percent of their time is devoted to managing alliances. Captured here is more than alliance management; relevant alliance activities include relationship development as well. Commitment includes spending the time (i.e., investing the effort) in managing the alliance; as the investment grows larger, the probability of alliance success increases.

If one views alliance management within a game theoretic perspective, it is likely that resources will flow to the alliance in a "tit-for-tat" manner. One company does this and the other does that; resources are committed in kind, no more and no less. One possible problem affecting the flow of resources is the manner in which the partners value assets. If one company brings hard assets and the other intellectual capability to the alliance, the accounting can be messy as the appropriate exchange rate is difficult to assess. It is not wise to get bogged down in the accounting, as will be discussed in detail in Chapter 7.

Commitment as a Signal

Commitment to an alliance signals both a sense of trust and a belief that the alliance has merit (i.e., creates value for both) and warrants support. When one partner shares sensitive information in advance of the alliance, this action is a positive signal that may result in a similar response by the partner. Dedicating assets to the alliance bolsters the partners' overall commitment making it harder for them to leave it. The unilateral commitment of resources is a risk-taking behavior and illustrates again how trust can be built. This added commitment often results in partners working together to solve problems and resolve conflicts because both recognize that they have a great deal at stake.

As a matter of policy, M&M Mars, a privately held company, does not divulge to the press much about its business. The Mars family's position is that corporate information is private and will be shared on a need-to-know basis only. A prospective alliance partner conducting a computer search would not find a great deal of information available; corporate policy has been to minimize media exposure. Management has found that, in certain instances, it has approached possible alliance partners and has willingly, albeit cautiously, shared information in advance of the alliance to reveal useful information that the partner might use as part of its own due diligence. By sharing sensitive information with a potential partner, Mars demonstrates both trust and commitment through its risk-taking behavior. Such efforts are positive and serve to decrease the guarded reaction a partner might have absent other information about the company. More important is the signal Mars sends to its potential partner. Their overture shows that they think enough of the potential alliance to share sensitive information, and they imply that they trust that the potential partner will not exploit this opportunity.

Interdependence

The notion of recognized interdependence flows directly from the definition of an alliance. Partners cannot act alone and require the cooperation and collaborative efforts of others to achieve their goals. Without such recognition, partners would engage in opportunistic behavior and would attempt to further their own agenda without consideration for their partner. At one extreme, left to their own devices, people will act "opportunistically with guile."[18] At the other, certain people have a disposition to trust and believe that people are generally well meaning and reliable.[19] These positions are diametrically opposed and highlight part of the tension that exists in alliances. In stable alliances, one partner will not act in self-interest to the detriment of the other. Hurting one's alliance partner damages the alliance. Why would one do that? What long-term advantage is gained? Remember that at the outset the alliance was built on a solid business proposition in which partners accomplish goals that neither would easily attain separately.

A buyer-supplier alliance in which the buyer extracts costs concessions to the point that the supplier cannot earn a fair return makes no sense. First, quality is likely to suffer. These relationships should not have a singular focus on price but instead should concentrate on the total cost of ownership. Second, forcing the supplier to cut price fails to acknowledge the value-added capability that a world-class supplier base can bring to the relationship. The worst example of self-serving behavior can be associated with the Lopez affair at GM. In the interest of cost reduction, GM asked its key suppliers for proprietary designs and technology to be considered for newer models. In violation of any measure of trust, GM then shopped these designs with the suppliers' competition. Such behavior cannot be condoned and is among the worst examples of self-serving behavior. The fallout from such opportunism remains, and to this day a number of key automotive suppliers do not bring innovations to GM first. Among the big three, they first go to Ford and Chrysler whose reputation for dealing with suppliers is more "win-win" than "win-lose." At the opposite extreme, there is Honda, which will invest resources in its key suppliers to improve their processes so they can better serve Honda. Honda and its suppliers recognize their interdependence; their processes are linked; technical information is shared across the boundaries of the partner firms; and all benefit from Honda's market success.

Symmetry

The term *symmetry* has multiple meanings, all of which contribute positively to the alliance. One meaning relates to the notion of size and suggests that large firms should ally with large firms and small firms with small firms. The rationale is that firms of similar size understand each other better and can appreciate better the pressures and concerns each face. In addition, management styles are quite similar and tend to vary by size. Moreover, the size differences can lead to distrust on the part of both partners. Small firms feel that they will be gobbled up and big firms feel that the small firm will "take the money and run." Despite the face validity of such thinking, it is not realistic. Such a request does not mirror reality. Big firms and small firms partner all the time. In many industries, this mismatch of size is more the rule than the exception: big pharmaceuticals and small biotechs collaborate through joint ventures and licensing arrangements to bring new drugs to market; large telecommunications equipment makers and large service providers all partner with small companies to gain access to new Internet and/or multimedia technology as well as to gain access to niche markets through specialized knowledge and specific applications.

Symmetry as information access. Symmetry also relates to the partners' willingness to share information. Numerous studies show that communication is key to alliance success. Without equal access to information, partners can more easily engage in self-serving behavior. Information asymmetry is one of the conditions in which opportunism flourishes. With access to information, partners make certain assumptions about behavior that might lead to the wrong conclusions and could seriously damage the relationship. An alliance between a U.S. and a German manufacturer was fraught with problems partly as a result of a downturn in the market to which the alliance sold. The U.S. company replaced the first alliance manager, with whom the German alliance manager had a long relationship, with a new manager who had a reputation for cost cutting. The new U.S. alliance manager waited for several months before he made personal contact with his German colleague. In the interim, the Germans did not fully appreciate the cost pressures facing their U.S. partner and, as a result, they felt that the U.S. firm was making unreasonable demands. To make matters worse, they believed that the partner was acting in its own self-interest demanding that the Germans take on a disproportionate share of the burden to manage their costs. Even after conversations were renewed, the Germans felt that they could not trust their U.S. partner and the relationship deteriorated further. At one point, there was an attempt by the German parent to sell this division to a competitor of the U.S. manufacturer.

Although problems could not be avoided due to the severe economic shocks that beset the industry, the relationship did not have to deteriorate to the extent that it did. The lack of communication coupled with the asymmetry of information between partners resulted in a misinterpretation of action that hastened the alliance's slide from bad to worse. Despite the strong business case for the alliance, its potential was never realized and the sought-after benefits never materialized. Even though attempts were made to rebuild the alliance and reaffirm the U.S. firm's commitment to the relationship, such overtures came too late—the damage had been done. Trust damaged is difficult to rebuild.

Symmetry as fair dealing. Symmetry conveys much more than partner size and access to information; it also captures the importance of fair dealing. Fair dealing entails the expectation that partners will be treated with respect and their contribution to the alliance will result in a commensurate share of the benefits. In an equity-based alliance, a partner that takes on 40 percent of the risk should expect 40 percent of the reward, no more, no less. This is an important point since all partners do not necessarily have to be treated equally. This does not suggest that minority partners should not have a voice in the alliance and feel that they are being heard. Also, this does not imply that partners should not be treated in a manner that acknowledges their value. When partners have questions about the possible inequities in the distribution of profits their confidence in and commitment to the alliance lessens. Partners in any social relationship, not just in an alliance, do not want to feel they have been taken advantage of.

In an alliance, equitable treatment has two dimensions. One dimension captures the sense that partners benefit in direct proportion to their contribution such that risk and reward run hand-in-hand. The second dimension has a temporal element and addresses the period during which equitable treatment is to be expected. In biology, scientists speak of homeostasis, the extent to which a system is in equilibrium. Achieving this balance in the alliance is unlikely to occur at any moment in time but must occur over time. Equilibrium in an alliance is the point at which partners feel that the relationship is a fair one. In all alliances, there is an ebb and flow in which one partner might be advantaged and the other not. It would be unrealistic to expect the alliance scorecard to balance all the time. Yet, over the course of the alliance, balance is essential so that the spirit of fair dealing is observed. Partners must resist checking the score on a regular basis to ascertain whether the relationship is in equilibrium. The spirit of the alliance should drive the partners to equilibrium. The dynamics of the alliance itself, the changing environment in which the alliance operates, and the other sources of static that affect the alliance all impact the alliance's ability to self-regulate: Self-regulate it must, and equilibrium is achieved over time. Balance is the desired state; yet, imbalance is the natural order.

Open Communication

Alliances are built on the willingness and ability of partners to share information. Information exchange is more complex than the mere flow of data from one firm to the other. Trading parties can exchange information related to production and inventory levels that are essential for a just-in-time inventory management system, or they can exchange point-of-purchase data critical to running an ECR/order replenishment system. This exchange might not be sufficient to qualify as an alliance characteristic. Open communications in an alliance context imply a greater depth and intensity of information exchange and the ability of key information to cross permeable organizational boundaries in numerous places. In addition, information flows tend to follow the informal set of ties that emerge during the evolution of the alliance and are not limited to the formal hierarchy and reporting system that exists within each of the partner firms.

Depth and intensity reflect the information shared. The depth of information captures the level in the organization from which the information originates and the intensity reflects its critical nature. Knowledge related to technology development that lies near the core of the firm is both deep and intense. Information related to future planning assumptions and long-term objectives is intense but is probably less deep. Data related to production workflow and inventory levels is, relatively speaking, less deep and less intense. It is easy to mentally construct a continuum of information that captures both the type of information[20] transferred and the critical nature of that information. Alliance partners are more likely to share knowledge not just data, are more willing to share sensitive information, and are more comfortable that the information shared will not be expropriated and used to their detriment. In addition, alliance partners are more likely to engage in activities that increase the storehouse of knowledge available to both. Alliances are a source of knowledge transfer *and* idea/knowledge creation.

British Petroleum, in its quest to be a more nimble global player, relies on its ability to create and transmit knowledge to its network of alliance partners. Not only is knowledge viewed as a corporate asset; it is shared with its partners, all of whom can use the same knowledge to work toward a common goal. Imagine the problems that can arise on a deep water drilling platform in the North Sea if partners responsible for managing the operation do not all have access to the same information at the same time. Technology is merely the enabler; it is trust and the open flows of communications among alliance partners that lead to success.

The question is often asked whether the importance of open communications implies that all information must be shared? The answer is a resounding No! Open communications does not mean sharing all secrets and giving free and unconditional access to all information. Alliance partners must decide early in the relationship what is important for the alliance partners to know and what information is proprietary. The Boeing example discussed earlier makes this point. The issue goes deeper than bounding the relevant pieces of information. It is essential that partners know prior to the setting of boundaries that certain topics will not be open to discussion. Partly, the objective is to shape expectations regarding the flow of communications so that when a request for information is denied, the partner understands what motivates the decision. Without such a framework, one partner might call into question the commitment of the other or ask, "Don't you trust me?" While communication among partners helps develop the alliance's common values and norms, it is also essential to protect one's core technology or any other highly valued information. Open flows of communication do not mean unfiltered flows of communication. In one recent alliance, conflict surfaced when one partner viewed information as a public good and the other as a private good. During the formation of the alliance, one partner's trust and commitment was called into question. This doubt affected alliance performance and personal morale. Partners had not anticipated that their different cultures would affect their work. Apparently, each had a different set of expectations regarding information sharing.

Coordination of Work

Interdependence is tied closely to the specialization of work. With recognition of their independence, alliance partners exchange valued resources, and, in many cases, specialization is viewed as an extension of the workflow. Specialization also connotes laws of comparative advantage where partners possess complementary capabilities and tasks are assigned based on the strength of a partner's abilities. Problems surface when the roles of the partners are not clearly established or when redundancy is built into the alliance to accommodate the partners' overlapping skills. For example, during the short-lived alliance between Apple and IBM, conflict arose during meetings when IBM managers felt compelled to demonstrate that their technical people were as good as the Apple group on certain aspects of development. This need to flex intellectual muscle not only diminished the overall capability of the alliance, it ran counter to the agreed-on work plan and the allocation of responsibility, and was one of many reasons why the alliance could not make inroads against the WinTel standard.

One advantage of an alliance is that the coordination of activities such as production scheduling, delivery, inventory management, and research and development can be approached at the level of functional integration without the bureaucracy and cost burden of ownership. Advanced just-in-time (JIT) systems like JITII®, joint marketing programs, shared R&D, and dedicated production facilities are examples of strategic alliances in which the linkages between two companies must be flawless for the entire system to run effectively. Programs in which suppliers provide technical assistance and/or predesign expertise are often less obviously linked but are no less important to the value chain and the efficiency of the production process. The concept of concurrent engineering is tied to the seamless coordination of partners. Boeing attributes its ability to take the 777 from the drawing board to full production partly a function of tight integration among a number of suppliers and Boeing. The plane is often referred to as tens of thousands of separate pieces flying in close formation.

The network of alliances that comprise Calyx & Corolla, the mail-order florist, links its corporate office (whose skills are relationship marketing, order fulfillment, and database management) with independent growers and FedEx. This highly coordinated and specialized network provides seamless end-to-end service that delivers flowers to the customer's door two to three days after they have been cut. Compare this system to the traditional distribution system in which ten days, or more, pass from the time the flowers are cut to the moment of purchase in a retail shop. Similarly, Motorola relies on a dedicated, albeit a reduced, set of suppliers to provide parts for its beepers such that they carry only 45 minutes of inventory! In both examples, the potential logistics problems are nontrivial and yet both systems are fine-tuned examples of highly coordinated alliances. It is an easy leap from these examples to images of the virtual corporation in which technology links global partners that provide seamless service to a demanding customer base. Companies that are successfully managing a global supply chain are well down this path.

In joint ventures, where a separate company is often formed from the parent companies, coordination is less tied to the workflow and is more a part of the governance structure. The parent companies comprise the board of directors who oversee the management of the joint venture. Coordination is more likely part of the steering committees, or different management structures, that provide guidance and support to the JV's operations. Coordination does not reflect directly on the day-to-day operations and is less involved in making sure the *trains run on time.*

Policy issues for setting strategy direction and intent are more appropriate at the board level. In other joint ventures, there are elements of both. Two companies might establish a joint venture to produce feed stock chemicals for the partners' downstream production facilities. Here, workflow coordination is essential and management oversight is expected. Many oil companies engage in such joint ventures to refine product as well as to produce intermediate petrochemicals.

Joint Planning

Joint planning is part of the shared decision-making processes in which alliance partners engage. The focus on planning brings the substance of shared decision making to a more strategic level. It is probably unrealistic to think that autonomous companies can act as solo actors in all aspects of their business. Even firms engaged in arm's length dealing probably share some decision making. In such market exchanges planning is limited to the scope of what is being exchanged. To a large degree, planning (probably a misnomer) equates to the conditions and terms of the contract between the companies. Strategic alliances are built on a belief that planning the substance of the exchange is secondary to planning its structure and processes. Alliance partners establish mechanisms and processes for addressing concerns that will affect the future direction of the alliance. The parties recognize that the future planning of substantive issues will occur naturally as a function of the structure and processes established at the beginning of the relationship, and these must also be flexible to accommodate future change. Simply, partners openly share future plans and take each other's concerns into consideration when planning. By sharing information and being knowledgeable about each other's business, partners can set compatible goals that help maintain the relationship over time. Jointly forecasting the impact of technological advances or market developments enhances the alliance's ability to evaluate its joint outcomes. In other cases, the investments required to meet projected changes in technology and markets enhance the level of commitment partners bring to the alliance.

Recently, we worked with a supplier and one of its key customers to help them form and execute a buyer-supplier alliance. As part of the agreement, they committed to better understand the drivers of each other's business, to periodically assemble communities of interest to explore jointly new technology and innovations that might impact the direction of the industry, and to engage in long-term planning. The initial motivation for the alliance was to reduce the total acquisition cost to the buyer in exchange for increased market share for the seller. Both parties recognized that cost savings and market share do not alone contribute to competitive advantage. By leveraging their skills and expertise and by bringing this shared knowledge into the joint planning process, both partner firms will be more successful. Moreover, the learning that will result from this experiment (neither company had previously engaged in such relationships) will be transferred to other relationships. The architects of the alliance work hard to extend the reach of shared decision making to include partners' involvement in more strategic level issues—here is where the true value is added. The alliance's ability to escalate the shared decision making was facilitated by senior management support from the outset. However, six months into the alliance, cultural differences between partners are beginning to affect the alliance's performance. Differences in culture were not anticipated in the formative stages of the alliance.

Long-Term Focus

In Chapter 1, managers suggested that when they think of alliances they tend to think of a long-term orientation. When we collect data from companies to understand better their alliance competence, we find that managers who are better alliance managers and whose firms demonstrate better alliance-like behavior, respond that they expect their alliances to last for a long time. Yet, there is a difference between expectations of longevity and having a long-term focus. Longevity implies that alliances that last for a long time are more successful than those that do not. If asked which alliance is more successful, one that lasts six years or one that lasts six months, the natural response is to attribute better performance to the longer lived alliance. Although Corning can point to joint ventures that are more than 30 years old, the success of these alliances might be equal to some of the alliances found in the world of e-commerce where six months is considered a lifetime. On one level, long term seems to be a function of the industry. In the oil and the mining businesses, long term is often more than 20 years. Oil fields, gold mines, coal fields, and so on often have a very long productive life. In just the past 18 months, the Internet and the industry that has grown up around it has changed several times and long term is measured in months and weeks.

Long-term focus, then, conveys a second meaning and embodies the episodic nature of alliance-like behavior. Actions on the part of one partner have implications for future actions on the part of the other partner. In market-based transactions, there are no expectations of future dealings since trading parties deal in the moment. Alliance-like behavior embodies expectations that what transpires in period 1 affects behavior in period n. The inference from the previous discussion about commitment and risk taking as a form of trust building is that partners knowingly and willfully invest for the future of the relationship. Implicit is the notion that the partnership/alliance is intended to last for a relatively long time. The key is the term *relative* and its is a function of the industry and how long term is defined; it is also a function of the time frame needed to accomplish the goals of the intended alliance.

In one alliance in which companies partnered to develop deep water oil drilling equipment, the initial alliance was focused on producing the equipment and installing it on the wellhead. The alliance could have disbanded at the time of installation because it had accomplished its goal. Yet, the oil company appreciated the importance of maintaining the alliance although the scope of the alliance was likely to change. Continuity with the alliance partner made sense; the manufacturer of the equipment should also carry the responsibility of reliability in the field. However, once oil begins to flow and the field comes "on line" another set of issues must be considered. First, the intent of the alliance shifts from a manufacturing alliance in which cost, speed to market, and technology sharing are key issues to a concern for safety and the environment, reliability, and maintenance/service. Second, the metrics for measuring performance shift to a concern for flawless operation (uptime) and issues germane to equipment failure. Third, the personnel assigned to the alliance change as the well moves from a preproduction to a postproduction status. For the oil company, these tasks are managed by different parts of the business. Fourth, the time line for the alliance shifts from a finite period of time (the equipment will be produced in, say, three months) to a less defined period of time that probably coincides with the productive life of the well. The episodic nature of the alliance relates to both the hand-off from one phase of the relationship to the other and the expectations associated with managing the new phase of the alliance through the well's productive life. If phase 1 had gone badly, and costs were out of line, time to market was delayed, and so on, there would have been no phase 2 alliance with this supplier.

Cultural Compatibility

The last characteristic relates to the degree to which partners' cultures are compatible. Cultural compatibility can be examined on two levels: There is a national culture that relates to the values and norms that are part of the society in which the partners live. There is a company culture that embodies the values and norms of the firm; and companies within the same country can easily have different cultural orientations. At one level, one often hears about the differences between entrepreneurial and bureaucratic firms. Examples in which a large partner has tried to impose its culture on its smaller partner are countless. This is frequently a recipe for disaster since the more rigid environment of the larger firm often demotivates employees, some of whom leave; the alliance then cannot achieve its full potential. Aspects of culture might affect the innovative spirit of the firm, its aggressiveness, or its customer responsiveness. The dilemma is that the alliance might have been formed partly to gain the benefits of the other's culture and values. The hope is that during the alliance, positive attributes will be transferred to the other partner. There is often regression to the mean because that the needy company is less receptive to change and does not revel in the diversity of culture as it should. In other instances, one partner might feel threatened and withdraws thereby limiting the degree of corporate osmosis.

Companies, like EDS, Microsoft, and HP, have developed cultures that can be traced directly to their founders. Here, there is almost an occultlike culture and the alliance partners might be too far apart in their orientation to accommodate each other's values and norms. The melding of cultures does not happen naturally and mechanisms should be considered to help partners appreciate better the differences between partners. For many companies, an important part of the partner selection process is focused on an assessment of the cultural differences between partners. FedEx has institutionalized the process and will avoid partners who do not share certain core values as they relate to customer service as well as other essential attributes.

Figure 2.5 illustrates the range of issues one might consider in trying to evaluate the cultural similarity between potential partners. The issue is not one of right or wrong, it is often one of distance. That is, how far apart are the partners on certain dimensions? In addition, there are two key questions: (1) Can the distance be bridged so that one partner can benefit from the culture of the other? (2) What level of resources is needed to facilitate the adaptation process? The important point here is that cultural differences will not resolve themselves and management must have a plan for acculturation.

Differences in national culture are probably more important since they cannot be avoided. For example, companies wanting to do business in India have no choice but to deal with issues of national culture. At a secondary level, one can then evaluate potential partners to assess company cultures. Differences in national cultures contributed to the problems

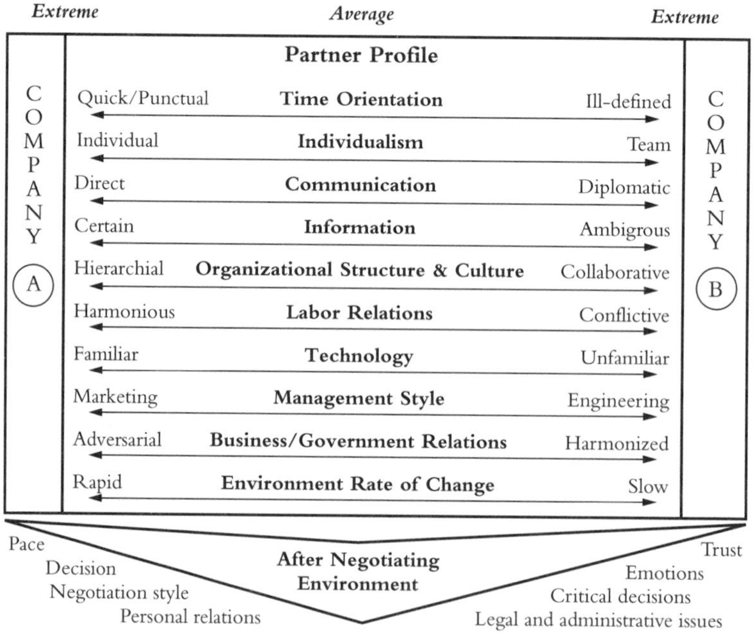

Figure 2.5 Charting the extremes of partner differences and identifying the gaps. (*Source:* Robert Porter Lynch, *Business Alliances Guide: The Hidden Competitive Weapon,* New York: John Wiley & Sons, 1993.)

experienced by Volvo and Renault both during the alliance and again as they moved to merger. Subtle differences associated with work hours, meal length, and coffee breaks all contributed to problems. The French government's attitude toward its labor unions was also a point of contention. At the firm level, Renault did not share Volvo's core value of *safety at any cost* as became apparent during the P4 project. (The P4 was a jointly developed platform on which each manufacturer would produce its own luxury vehicle. Volvo's model would have competed with the S class Mercedes Benz.) This is not to say that the merger failed because of the cultural differences alone; however, the differences were formidable and management on both sides did little to address those differences.

Working in Latin America[21] highlights the observation that North American managers tend to be more focused on the business aspects of the alliance (as opposed to building the relationship), and the Latin American manager would prefer to build the relationship prior to conducting business. Focus on the relationship side of the alliance is even more pronounced among Asian managers. The resultant tension is obvious. There are more serious issues that affect the differences in national culture relating to one's attitude toward business conduct. Some cultures place a high value on negotiation and the art of bargaining. Finalizing the deal is important but it is through the negotiation that one demonstrates business acumen. This is problematic for many U.S. managers and is a source of tension. Most serious however are the differences in the ethical standards of the partners; U.S. companies are subject to laws related to corruption and bribery. In some cultures, it is common practice to make side-payments to those who can facilitate the agreement or who can provide access to key deal makers. In a similar vein, self-serving behavior may be the norm despite the spirit and often the letter of the alliance contract that prohibits such behavior. These cultural attributes can be deal breakers that make it very difficult to conduct business.

Can these differences be avoided? Probably not. Certainly, the national cultural differences are enduring and cannot be circumvented. Companies have more options when dealing with differences in corporate cultures. In all instances, are the differences significant enough to stop the alliance? No; however, lack of alignment on core values should signal that potentially serious problems lie ahead. Cultural compatibility is a desired trait, but in many instances, it is elusive. Absent compatibility, alliance managers must acknowledge and develop a plan for promptly addressing these differences.

A Review of Alliance Characteristics

The previous characteristics distinguish alliances from other forms of interfirm relationships. More of each of the characteristics is likely to lead to more stable alliances. Managers often ask if one characteristic is more important than others or whether a low score on one can be compensated for by higher scores on other characteristics. Each trait is important, but alone cannot guarantee alliance stability. Among all of them, trust and commitment are *must have* characteristics; without them there is no substantive foundation on which to build and nurture the alliance. Trust and commitment are the mortar that hold the alliance together. As the next section will show, many of the other alliance characteristics will vary depending on the kind of alliance and its level of intensity. Joint ventures, by virtue of the degree to which resources are dedicated to the alliance, are among the more intense relationships. Nonetheless, a certain minimal level must be associated with each characteristic so that the composite profile across the full array of characteristics fits alliance-like behavior.

A Continuum of Alliance Forms

The term Alliances covers an number of different kinds of relationships that span a continuum that falls between open market transactions and hierarchy, or vertical integration. At one end are the least formal alliances, all of which are nonequity alliances. At the opposite end of the continuum are joint ventures, all of which are equity-based relationships. It is useful to understand these different alliance forms vary more in intensity and, as a result, might shape one's expectations around certain implied behaviors. To align alliance types along this continuum probably is not very productive since it detracts from understanding the characteristics that differentiate alliances from other relationships. Furthermore, it is difficult to accurately distinguish among alliance types in the abstract. The appendix to this chapter provides a short questionnaire to measure the extent to which each characteristic described here is present. Such an instrument can help partners understand how each would describe the various alliance characteristics. Any gap that might exist across the different characteristics can serve as a diagnostic and remedial tool. Knowing where differences in perceptions might exist improves one's understanding of what kinds of problems the partners might face. In addition, identifying the gaps will suggest the type of conversation partners ought to engage in to address the misalignment. However, recognizing that differences, albeit subtle ones, might exist across alliance types helps managers better align their behavior with that of their partner.

Table 2.1 portrays the range of characteristics that might exist cross alliance types. This table highlights the similarities more than the differences across alliance types. In addition, the differences found are more ones of degree than of kind. Also, this exercise demonstrates that attempts to search for profound differences in alliance types might be counterproductive. While each alliance type might organize and govern itself in a slightly different manner, to be in an alliance, certain common characteristics must exist regardless of the form taken. Differences tend to vary along a continuum. Even at the least intense end of the alliance spectrum, a certain baseline level must be present for alliance-like behavior to exist.

Issues Related to Differences in Alliance Form

Several issues emerge regarding the differences in alliance forms. First, managers' expectations regarding how the alliance will be governed will vary over alliance type. Licensing alliances in which technology and/or know-how is made available to a partner requires a far different governance structure than do joint ventures. In the former, the governance is probably set by the nature of the agreement and the partners might have very little day-to-day interaction. These alliances afford a level of flexibility in that the technology-sharing agreement can be altered relatively easily. Here, the two companies lack both the embeddedness and the degree of interdependence that might be found in a joint venture where both parties have committed personnel and hard assets to codevelop or coproduce something of mutual value.

A senior manager from Nortel described forming alliances as being like tying knots. The knot must be strong enough to handle the tough choices but also easy to untie. Joint ventures are much tougher to untie and take longer to knot together than do less intense forms of alliances,

Table 2.1 Alliance Characteristics across Alliance Forms

Alliance Characteristic	Buyer-Supplier Alliance	Codevelopment/ Comarketing Alliance	Joint Venture
	Nonequity, low intensity alliances.	Midrange alliance (might comingle assets but not jointly owned).	Equity, high-intensity alliances.
Trust	Limited to the nature of the alliance; expectation of being honest.	Partner assumed to be more trustworthy than others and treated in such a manner.	Trust built over time and established as a solid foundation; extends throughout the (two) businesses.
Commitment	Specific to the terms of the alliance; there is a tendency to test.	Longer view commitment; partners less likely to test.	Commitment focused on joint success and pervasive; measured over the life of the relationship.
Recognized interdependence	Acknowledgment exists but partners need to be reminded.	Partners sensitive to each other's worry about self-serving behavior and self-monitor.	Fate of the partners linked by alliance such that self-serving behavior is not an option.
Symmetry	Extent to which risk and reward are shared is often specified in the terms and conditions of the alliance agreement.	Sense of fair dealing that extends beyond the boundaries of the alliance.	Risk and reward shared equitably but partners tend to treat each other as equals.
Open communications	Tone and content of the exchange of information specified by the alliance agreement.	Communications more open and cross boundaries at multiple points, often extend beyond the agreement.	Tendency to speak with one voice and have less restrictions on access although certain information might remain proprietary. Partners might jointly create knowledge.

Joint planning	Limited in scope and content to the agreement.	Less tied to the specifics of the alliance agreement and will spill over to other aspects of the partners' business.	Highly linked and essential to the future of the partners' relationship.
Coordination of work	Often coordination needed because of the sequence of workflow and the need to coordinate the movement from A to B. Performance is often monitored separately.	Could be high as well but depends on the kind of alliance. Joint work could be done either in parallel or sequence. Performance is measured jointly.	Coordination of work linked to the JV and monitored by the partners. Both have input into performance outcomes and system changes.
Cultural compatibility	Some level required to agree on alliance operating principles and norms.	Higher level of compatibility useful given the degree to which partners comingle.	Without high levels of compatibility problems likely to emerge since the partners work very closely. Over time a new, joint culture might emerge.

such as a licensing agreement. Along with the differences in governance, questions related to structure, compensation, and culture must be considered. All relate to the nature of the alliance agreement and determine how strongly the knot is tied and the ease with which it can come undone.

Second, the expectations regarding performance might also vary by alliance type. In some alliances, partners bring to the alliance the skills/capabilities that will be leveraged. For example, a U.S. pharmaceutical company might bring technology and a Japanese drug company might bring a sales force and market access. Here, the skill set is predefined and the alliance should achieve its goals in a relatively short period. Figure 2.6a demonstrates that high satisfaction takes place early and that the levels of satisfaction fall over time. Once the gains from the alliance have been achieved, there is nothing more to leverage and diminishing returns often result. In other alliances, firms cooperate to develop something new. Partners have the raw material, technical know-how, or market knowledge to explore and experiment. These alliances are driven by the objective of discovery; but neither has the solution the other seeks at the start of the alliance. Here, our data suggest

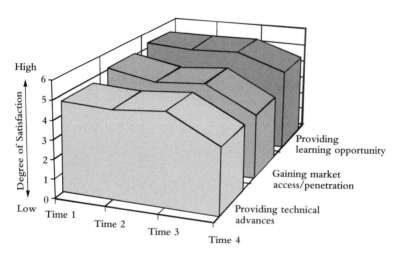

Figure 2.6a Expectations of success: Pattern 1—generally level, late decline.

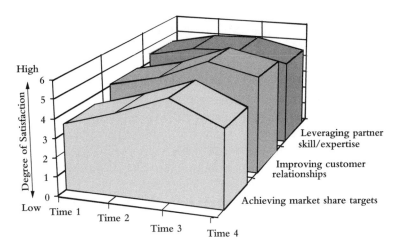

Figure 2.6b   Expectations of success: Pattern 2—increasing over time.

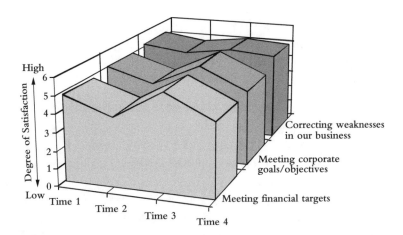

Figure 2.6c   Expectations of success: Pattern 3—decline, followed by rise.

that satisfaction with the alliance peaks later in the life cycle, and the anticipated road to value creation might take longer and might not reap the fruit achieved in the first set of alliances (see Figure 2.6b). When MasterCard and Excite allied to explore Web-based shopping, they hoped that their joint efforts would stimulate market growth. Both brought skills that they thought would be raised to another level by virtue of their joint efforts. Simply, market development is far more difficult than gaining market access through the partner's contacts.

Third, research suggests that the stock market reacts differently to the form of alliance created.[22] Findings are mixed and reward (i.e., a positive movement in stock price) for one alliance type might not lead to the positive response for another type (see Figure 2.6c). In addition, the industry in which the alliance is formed also appears to matter. In one instance, IBM was rewarded for its licensing and AT&T was not; conversely, value creation was recognized in AT&T joint ventures and not in ones orchestrated by IBM. In general, their findings suggest that licensing is rewarded most highly, followed by market and then R&D alliances. Also, joint ventures tend not to be valued as highly as other alliance forms by investors. This result also mirrors our findings as they relate to managers' self-reported measures of satisfaction. The more uncertain the outcome of the alliance, the lower the imputed value in stock price movement rewarded by the stock market. Again, our interpretation is that the licensing of technology and/or know-how brings to an alliance a known opportunity. R&D alliances and market development alliances signal that partners combine resources to gain synergy and create something that neither presently have.

Alliances as a Vehicle for Gathering Knowledge

While alliance formation can be defined as a value-creating activity, one might mistakenly focus on tangible outcomes only. There is an implicit coalignment between partners to learn and acquire skills, products, technology and knowledge that are unique to that alliance. Herein lies a challenge since each partner attempts to learn from the other while simultaneously protecting core competencies. This tension is referred to as cooperative advantage[23] and it has an impact on learning. Learning is affected by a number of factors, some of which are alliance specific such as the type of alliance formed and its stage of development. Other factors relate to the characteristics of the partner firms such as its ability to learn (e.g., absorptive capacity). For example, the criteria by which one evaluates a potential partner will impact the ability of one to learn from the other. While cultural similarity and the need to share compatible goals are key characteristics in the determination of alliance stability, these attributes also affect the ability of partners to learn from each other.

In the late 1980s, Caterpillar had sought an alliance with Daewoo to gain access to the Asian market as well as to benefit from the lower cost structure of the Korean manufacturing giant. Daewoo, on the other hand, viewed Caterpillar as a source of much needed technology that would help them enter other markets such as the Middle East. The alliance was disbanded when Caterpillar realized that it would not gain the knowledge needed to enter Asian markets and that it was going to create a new competitor in its other markets. In effect, one partner would learn and the other would not.

A firm's absorptive capacity is related to its willingness and ability to ingest knowledge from its partners. Systems that purposively rotate management through the alliance help spread knowledge through the firm; reward systems that encourage the creation of cross-functional teams, individual risk taking, and innovative approaches to problem solving also impact the firm's degree of openness. Adding to the complexity is that some knowledge is tacit and cannot easily be transferred and often is impossible to imitate because it is almost "hard wired" in the brains of the employees. Corning can join with partners to develop plants to manufacture TV picture tubes, for example, but the partner will be hard pressed to assimilate the basic glass expertise that is resident in Corning scientists and technicians. The only hope of truly gaining access to such fundamental expertise is to apprentice with the partner and it would seem that management would be reluctant to reveal such a core set of skills.

Work done in the pharmaceutical industry suggests that companies with higher absorptive capacity invested more funds in their own R&D, developed internal expertise in relevant technologies and managed the communications process with its partners and within its own organization more effectively. In Honda's supplier alliances, it is driven by best practices whereby suppliers are encouraged to work with Honda personnel to engage in "fresh thoughts," use fact-based decision processes, and apply root cause analysis to improve all aspects of the production process. Thus, management proactively and consciously attempted to leverage the knowledge base of its partners. The problem is that firms do not learn at the same rate. Such differences can affect the level of symmetry in the alliance relative to fair dealing because the slower firm might interpret the actions of the faster learner as engaging in self-serving behavior.

Alliance Life Cycles

Learning is affected by the stage of alliance development in that over time partners gain both insight and knowledge about each other. Alliances pass through a series of stages. Chapter 6 explains in detail the issues relevant to managing an alliance over time. Table 2.2 illustrates the stages of a typical alliance. Each stage is built on a changing alliance landscape as the vision for the alliance becomes a reality and then grows into a mature business. Although we portray each stage as a discrete event, the boundaries are not so clear and it is difficult to know exactly where one is along the continuum. Despite the lack of precision, each stage is intended to capture activities that account for differences in managerial behavior and thought as it applies to alliance management. Moreover, such an analysis mirrors the intent of this book. A basic theme is to depict alliances as a dynamic interplay among activities, people, and processes. The focus on this interplay begins to close the gap between merely talking about alliance formation and concentrating on the more difficult task of alliance management. A life cycle approach allows an examination of the business and the interpersonal relationships that together drive the success of the alliance. Business and relationship activities are mutually supportive, and the full strength of the alliance is dissipated when one's attention is diverted from either component.

It goes without saying that the business proposition must be viable for the alliance to continue. However, one cannot focus solely on the commercial logic of the alliance. In all social interaction (not just alliances), value is gained from cooperation that extends beyond the economics of the relationship. The interpersonal relationship braces the alliance when the business is under stress. It is the safety net that protects the alliance from self-destruction when the business is underperforming. Ironically, managers tend to underplay the importance of the relationship when the business is strong; one can easily develop a false sense

Table 2.2   Differences Found over Alliance Life Cycle Stages

	Anticipation	Engagement	Valuation	Coordination	Investment	Stabilization	Decision
Characteristics of life cycle stage	Prealliance. Competitive needs and motivation emerge.	High energy. Complementarity congruence. Strategic potential.	Financial focus. Business cases. Analysis. Internal selling.	Operational focus. Task orientation. Division of labor. Parallel activity.	Hard choices. Committing. Resource reallocation. Broadening scope.	High interdependence. Maintenance. Assessment of relative worth and contribution.	Where now?
Key business activity	Partner search.	Partner identification.	Valuation negotiation.	Coordination integration.	Expansion growth.	Adjustment.	Reevaluation.
Key relationship activity	"Dating."	Imaging.	Initiating.	Interfacing.	Committing.	Fine-tuning.	Reassessing dialoguing.
Role of alliance manager	Visionary.	Strategic sponsor.	Advocate.	Networker.	Facilitator.	Manager.	Mediator.

of security. During the bad times, there is no safety net as partners did not devote the effort to building the relation and lack the conviction to persevere. As a result, the alliance will suffer and the sought-after benefits might not be realized. In the worst case, the business downturn will lead to the demise of the alliance—had the relationship been stronger, the alliance might have survived. The importance of relationships in supporting the business proposition is discussed in Chapter 4.

Summary

This chapter has defined an alliance and has discussed the characteristics that separate alliances from other interfirm relationships. Alliances fill the space between open market, arm's length exchanges, and relationships and mergers and acquisitions where partner firms are combined and the separate entities become one. At the open market end of the continuum, the actions of the parties (not partners) are rule governed and the rights and obligations of one to the other are clearly specified. Companies interact, or chose not to, without any sense of obligation beyond the specific agreement. At the opposite end, firms are subject to a single organizational hierarchy since a single company is formed from the parts. There often exists a bureaucracy in which command and control sets the tone of behavior and establishes the rules of interaction. In an alliance, firms maintain their independence and autonomy, decision making is shared, and command and control is not a very helpful concept. Although we have presented a range of alliance types, we have described their common characteristics. Too often we hear that one alliance type is different from another; such a discussion is not terribly useful. Fundamentally, it is the similarity among alliance types that helps managers better appreciate the complex interaction among alliance partners. Joint ventures and buyer-seller alliances (to cite just two examples) share common characteristics although the intensity or strength of certain characteristics are not the same. The differences are more ones of degree than of kind. Despite the commonality that exists across alliance types, *one size does not fit all* and management must adapt to the different alliance types.

In addition, learning is an important alliance outcome in that process. This discussion expands the value-creating aspects of alliance formation to include such intangible gains. In fact, learning can be a sufficient goal for an alliance although it is sometimes difficult to measure the effects of such efforts. Market share or productions yields can be measures against plan; knowledge gained is less easily quantifiable. One's ability to learn is related to a firm's absorptive capacity. Learning happens at different rates and this differential can affect the partners' sense of fair dealing. We introduced the alliance life cycle and reinforced the premise that alliances are a dynamic interplay of activities, people, and processes.

Appendix

To what extent do the following statements describe your partnership with . . .

	Does Not Describe At All				Describes to a Very Large Extent		

Commitment

Our firm involves people from many different departments/units in this relationship.	1	2	3	4	5	6	7
Our senior management is committed to this alliance.	1	2	3	4	5	6	7
Both sides are really committing fully to this relationship.	1	2	3	4	5	6	7

Symmetry (fair dealing)

Our partner benefits greater from this relationship than does our firm.	1	2	3	4	5	6	7
We always treat our alliance partners as equals.	1	2	3	4	5	6	7
We frequently compare our costs and benefits with those of our partner, thus ensuring that the alliance is equitable.	1	2	3	4	5	6	7
Our firm contributes to this relationship as much as it is getting back.	1	2	3	4	5	6	7

Open Flows of Information

Information moves freely between partners.	1	2	3	4	5	6	7
We do not communicate very often with our partner.	1	2	3	4	5	6	7
We are very careful what we tell our partner.	1	2	3	4	5	6	7

Level of Coordination

This relationship requires extensive interaction between many people in each partner firm.	1	2	3	4	5	6	7
Partners have created face-to-face interactions among key individuals.	1	2	3	4	5	6	7
Partners agree as to who will play key roles.	1	2	3	4	5	6	7
This relationship requires a great deal of interaction between partners prior to making a decision.	1	2	3	4	5	6	7

	Does Not Describe At All					Describes to a Very Large Extent	

Long-Term Focus

Partnerships are best to achieve short-term, limited objectives.	1	2	3	4	5	6	7
We believe that this relationship will last a very long time.	1	2	3	4	5	6	7
Our firm is patient if short-term gains are not achieved	1	2	3	4	5	6	7

Joint Decision Making

Our firm feels that its partner makes decisions that are only in the partner's best interests.	1	2	3	4	5	6	7
There is agreement between partners regarding how to jointly manage aspects of the alliance.	1	2	3	4	5	6	7
Partners work hard to involve each other in decisions affecting the alliance.	1	2	3	4	5	6	7

Cultural Compatibility

The chemistry between the partners is strong.	1	2	3	4	5	6	7
The two corporate cultures are similar.	1	2	3	4	5	6	7

3

Balancing Business and Relationships

Long before strategic alliances were a popular way to conduct business, Corning and Siemens were pioneering their joint venture. In the late 1970s, then Corning Glass Works began to search for practical applications for its new fiber-optic wave-guides. Communications technology could be revolutionized if a way could be found to economically produce fiber-optic cable. Corning had worked with Siemens AG in the past, and knew that their technological expertise in cabling might provide some of the answers. The two companies agreed to form an alliance to produce and market the new technology to the telecommunications industry. Over 20 years later, that alliance, Siecor Inc., is still healthy and still a leader in world markets.

The longevity of and the value created by this alliance are truly remarkable. Far too few companies, however, realize such alliance potential. What makes Siecor unique in this regard? Corning and Siemens know a well-kept alliance secret: managing an alliance is nothing like business as usual.

Many executives bring to alliances the same mindset of management thinking they use in their internal business units. They rely on command and control, planning, executing and measuring, on deploying resources and delegating responsibility. Certainly all these techniques have their place in the alliance context, but executives in alliances need to understand what Corning and Siemens executives recognized many years ago. Alliances are simultaneously about business *and* relationships.

Business and relationship in a strategic alliance are like strands of DNA. They provide the essential building blocks of the alliance, hold the "code" for the alliance and, because they are intimately intertwined, add both strength and internal support (see Figure 3.1).

When asked about their success, two executives involved in the Siecor joint venture, the first from Siemens and the second from Corning, put it straightforwardly:

> If you were to put the process into time scales, there was a setting up phase, there was a getting to know each other phase, there was working out where the areas of opportunity were, and then a cooperative phases where we did all the things to make the operations go smoothly. And then we went to the crunch time, where we began to face the hard decisions. Now things are more or less on an even keel and our job is to keep the business running.
>
> Business changes and you have to adapt. People think that logical, rational business thinking always prevails—that is baloney! Personal issues become involved just as much.[1]

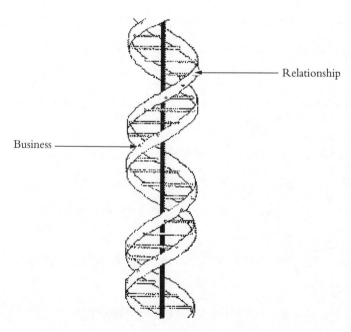

Figure 3.1 Business and relationship are intertwined.

The dual premises anchoring this chapter are equally straightforward: alliance activities change as the alliance evolves and those changing business and relationship activities need to work together. Doing so maximizes the value of the alliance. This chapter extends the business and relationship activities inherent in strategic alliances to include the skills supporting those activities. It also describes the alliance journey.

The Predictable Alliance Journey

The sheer variety and volume of activities inherent in a strategic alliance is daunting, though not unexpected or unpredictable. When working with a telecommunications company and one of their alliance partners, we asked each partner to provide a graphic representation of the journey they were on, including starting point, future destination, and stops along the way. The picture they created was telling: two cars on separate roads on separate journeys, coming together on the same road, encountering hills, detours, construction, dead ends, sometimes traveling together, sometimes separating. They seemed to instinctively understand that the journey was

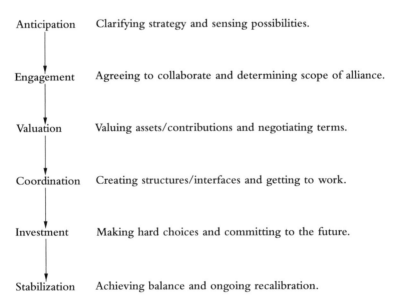

Anticipation	Clarifying strategy and sensing possibilities.
Engagement	Agreeing to collaborate and determining scope of alliance.
Valuation	Valuing assets/contributions and negotiating terms.
Coordination	Creating structures/interfaces and getting to work.
Investment	Making hard choices and committing to the future.
Stabilization	Achieving balance and ongoing recalibration.

Figure 3.2 Alliances evolve over time.

neither linear nor necessarily identical. What came into focus more sharply, however, were the common road signs along the way.

Alliances go through predictable and identifiable stages (see Figure 3.2). *Anticipation, Engagement,* and *Valuation* are the initial stages focused on creating and defining the vision of the alliance. *Coordination, Investment,* and *Stabilization* are those subsequent stages focused on turning the vision into reality. Each of these stages has a distinctive set of characteristics that represent a dynamic and constantly evolving architecture of exchange (see Table 3.1).

Closely aligned business and relationship activities form the core of this exchange. Both are aimed at building, establishing, and refining

Table 3.1 Business and Relationship Activities Change

Stage	Characteristics	Business Activity	Relationship Activity
Anticipation	Prealliance. Competitive needs and motivations emerge.	Searching	Dating
Engagement	High energy. Complementarity. Congruence. Strategic potential.	Identifying	Imaging
Valuation	Financial focus. Business cases. Analysis. Internal selling.	Valuing and negotiating	Initiating
Coordination	Operational focus. Task orientation. Division of labor. Parallel activity.	Coordinating and integrating	Interfacing
Investment	Hard choices. Committing. Resource reallocation. Broadening scope.	Clarifying and growing	Committing
Stabilization	High interdependence. Maintenance. Assessment of relative worth.	Adjusting	Fine-tuning

Table 3.2 Key Business Activities

Primary Business Activity	Typical Actions, Interactions, Activities	Key Business Skills
Searching	Looking for right partners. Surveying the field; establishing search criteria. Considering opportunities presented. Scanning, searching in a radar scan sort of way. Being constantly vigilant about the players and the changing landscape—who is networked with whom.	Visioning
Identifying	Learning what is possible with the selected partner. Identifying synergies. Beginning to craft the scope of the alliance. Identifying what is in or out of bounds—business wise; technology wise; sharing wise.	Strategic conversations
Valuing and negotiating	Making the business case. Putting values on various transaction costs in the alliance. Negotiating the formal contract and partnership agreements.	Collaborative negotiating
Coordinating and integrating	Getting down to the business of the alliance. Creating coordinating teams and work groups. Aligning work processes across partners. Seizing initial synergies and low-hanging fruit.	Collaborating in teams
Clarifying and growing	Making hard choices about the future. Leveraging synergies, planned and unplanned. Supporting choices with money, people and resources.	Managing change
Adjusting	Managing a maturing business. Readjusting or fine-tuning as needed.	Managing and growing

mechanisms that facilitate the execution of the alliance's strategic objectives. The business activities involve planning, conceptualizing, and building cases for synergistic ventures, as well as defining and operationalizing interface points across the partner organizations. These activities are outlined in Table 3.2. The relationship activities, while similar in intent, are focused primarily on creating and solidifying personal interactions that will serve as conduits for information and ideas among the partners and link the partners closely together beyond just doing business (see Table 3.3). The following sections briefly describe each stage as well as the

Table 3.3   Key Relationship Activities

Primary Relationship Activity	Typical Actions, Interactions, Activities	Key Relationship Skill
Dating	Senior executives leveraging personal networks. Wondering how to respond to inquiries. Wondering how to seek out possibilities.	Good radar; good relationship self-awareness
Imaging	Seeing the reality in possibilities. Creating a shared vision from being together. Involving trusted senior managers.	Creating intimacy
Initiating	Bringing key executives into action. Creating trust through face-to-face time. Investing in getting to know one another.	Trust building
Interfacing	Facilitating the creating of personal relationships at many levels. Traveling to partner facilities and engaging in technical conversations. Blending social and business time.	Partnering
Committing	Demonstrating that managers are fully committed to the alliance and each other. Managing the conflict inherent in making hard choices. Accepting the reality of the alliance and its relationships.	Commitment
Fine-tuning	Relying on mature and established relationships. Facilitating interaction and relationships with future successors.	Growing *with* another

business and relationship activities and underlying skills that are required. Chapter 6 expands more fully on the stages, while emphasizing the pitfalls and possibilities of each step along the alliance journey.

Anticipation: The High Hopes and Impatience of Getting Started

> We needed capital and an international dimension—our industry is highly competitive and capital intensive—so it seemed to just make more sense to have a partner. The question we didn't have an easy answer for was who?

A strategic alliance begins well before any formal documents are signed or even specific partners identified. *Anticipation* is a preliminary stage during which a company through its managers begins to envision or foresee a strategic alliance. This is a time of wrestling with possibilities, underdeveloped ideas, and snippets of dreams. It is also a time of coping with unforeseen invitations. Potential partners clarify their own strategic and competitive needs in the process of sorting through developing expectations. As a result, vision, visioning skills, and company "self-awareness" are fundamental.

Partner Search Begins with Strong Visioning Skills

In the initial stages of an alliance, the primary set of business activities involves searching for potential partners or responding to the search of a prospective partner (see Table 3.2). Search activities, however, are founded on a strategic imperative that reinforces the rationale for an alliance. Chapter 2 has already outlined perspectives on partner selection (a topic that has received considerable attention to date) and on the skills of partner assessment and potential fit. Good potential partner criteria are strongly related to how that partner fits with one's strategic intent.

In the initial activities of searching, the skills needed are those of creating a forward-thinking strategic vision and coupling that vision with partner search skills. Strong alliances form because two companies share a vision of future potential; together they can create opportunities not possible if each were to engage alone. For example, British Airways and then USAir saw a common future for airline travel: seamless passenger air travel around the globe. While plane colors or first language aloft might differ, the traveler would experience no difference in service, treatment, or ambience. That was the beginning of the global strategic alliance between the two companies: the British Airways/USAir vision. It was initially developed independently by each CEO (Sir Colin Marshall and Seth Scofield), who then "discovered" their goals were overlapping and mutually shared.

When the visioning skills are not supporting the search activities, the business activities will lack focus, clarity, and direction. One international company with which we are familiar is embarking on alliances because the chief executive officer decided "alliances will be our growth strategy." As a result, executives are furiously scrambling to ally with other companies, just to report those attachments to the CEO. While the company is getting alliances, the firm is missing any sense of purpose or strategic justification for choosing a future with those partners.

Vision and visioning are fundamental concepts in business today. Competing for the future is about identifying what will be, not what is, and thus, in many cases, requires redefining one's industry.[2] Amazon.com, FedEx, and Wal-Mart are overused examples of companies who created new space in the value chain where none had been before. While overused, they also epitomize the ability to create and dominate emerging opportunities—"to stake out new competitive space."[3]

New *alliance space* created as a result of a discernible vision can be a competitive advantage and an alliance competence. That advantage comes directly from the ability to envision and design what could be, especially if no one else has been there before. This is what Corning and Siemens did when linking fiber-optic and cabling technology. Before these technologies were combined, the competitive space was "twisted copper pairs" and coaxial cable. Today, the fiber optics industry has generated a unique set of opportunities—new alliance space—in which companies can create and leverage value.

Finding the Best Partners Requires Discerning Radar

While searching identifies a range of potential partners, another complementary set of relationship activities helps to select the most fitting partner in that range. The key relationship activity cluster in anticipation of an alliance is *Dating*. This is not a technical business term, but has been chosen for its connotations. In interpersonal relationships, dating represents a process during which individuals get to know one another to determine mutual interest, possibilities for friendship or romance, and potential for a longer term committed relationship. Similarly, in an alliance context, dating is a relationship activity in which senior executives and/or top management teams explore possibilities in the competitive landscapes. More often than not, personal relationships are the basis for the inception of an alliance (consider BA/USAIR or any number of "golf course" alliances) so the ability to date well would seem imperative. This means that managers leverage personal or professional networks, put out feelers for new business initiatives, or are receptive to outside propositions.

So what are the characteristics of a good date in alliances? Peter Shaw, former head of world alliances at British Airways, uses a model he terms "the triple A."[4] First, a potential alliance partner has to be *attractive* in terms of what the firm has to offer. An attractive partner offers strong mutual synergies, high degree of learnings, and complementary needs. Having keen awareness of what your company has to offer and what your company wants or needs is crucial to being attractive, as is knowing your strengths, weaknesses, and potential areas for growth. USAir (as it was then known) was attractive due to its route structure on the East Coast of the United States, where 40 percent of the world's air travel takes place. British Airways was attractive to USAir for its global network, premium brand image, and dollars to invest.

Second, a potential alliance partner must be *affordable*. No sense longing over a company that is financially out of reach. In the case of BA/USAir, the affordability was financial. BA had the cash and USAir's cost was in line with the investment opportunity. Affordability, however, might also mean the risk attached to not seeking a potential partner. Again, good company self-awareness can provide a strong foundation.

Finally, a partner must be *available*. In the early 1990s, airline carriers were pairing up, leaving a limited pool of unattached partners. As one executive told us, "There were not too many other potential brides in town left by the time we, BA and USAir, came together."

Engagement: After the Partner Comes the Synergistic Possibilities

> It took a couple of meetings, but I found we both had the same concept. Having recognized common understanding, we agreed that our companies together could make it happen.

So begins the stage of *Engagement,* which is characterized by high energy, enthusiasm, excitement about the strategic possibilities and potentials, and preparation for the eventualities of allying. Having agreed on the strategic intent that propels each toward the alliance, partners agree in principle to work collaboratively. Each partner accepts the other as a serious, long-term partner, and more fully explores the other's strengths and areas of expertise, the complementarity of skills, and the strategic and cultural fit. While there may be genuine areas of concern, these are often minimized, as both partners are truly captivated with the business possibilities and with one another.

Identifying Potential Synergies Needs the Skills of Strategic Conversation

As the alliance moves forward, Identifying what is really possible with that partner become the foremost business activities. There is a parallel to be drawn between the business activities of identifying and the activities of a couple about to become formally engaged. This couple would undoubtedly spend hours sharing and discussing their thoughts on their upcoming life together. In some ways, identification in an alliance context is the equivalent of those premarriage conversations. Those alliance conversations would be about the scope of the alliance, the possibilities, the restrictions, and the limits to the partnership.

Connected with the business activities of identifying is the ability to have a strategic conversation.[5] To identify the objective characteristics of a strong potential partner is one thing. But strong objective characteristics do not a good partner make. There is an element of discussion and dialogue, give and take as the partners clarify the strategic possibilities, overlap, or boundaries. Like architects who design buildings and structures, alliance executives "design" strategies.[6] Design is a metaphor that captures much about the business activities at this time in an alliance. A strategic conversation is about designing—considering possibilities, sketching and editing, drawing and erasing—until the parties craft a mutually agreeable picture. For Jack Welsh of General Electric Company and Dr. Inaba of Fanuc/Japan, the strategic conversation was literally sketched on a cocktail napkin, which hangs framed in Dr. Inaba's office in Fanuc's headquarters at the base of Mount Fuji.

Imaging Requires Skills at "Business Intimacy"

Supporting the strategic conversations of identifying are the relationship activities of *Imaging*. Imaging alliance development literally imagines the positive outcomes and future the partnership could create. Going beyond the vision, imaging adds more precision, specifics, and excitement to the alliance portrait under construction. It took only a brief time for Jack Welch at General Electric and Dr. Eng. Seiuermon Inaba of Fanuc of Japan to fully imagine the possibilities if the integrated circuitry expertise of Fanuc of Japan were to be combined with the robotic controllers of GE Automation. Such imaging is geared toward generating commitment and excitement, thinking in the future tense.[7] Learning how to build that image is critical.

Thus, a key relationship skill is the ability to build business intimacy with your partner during strategic conversations. Intimacy in an interpersonal relationship context is a process of building closeness, familiarity, and confidence with and in the other. Personal intimacy involves breadth and depth of self-disclosure and sharing increasingly more personal or private layers of information. This intimacy grows as each individual risks more personal thoughts or feelings and opens up more and more, and those expressions of connection are met with similar disclosures by the other.

Creating business familiarity in an alliance relationship is similar. One does not walk into an alliance by telling all or revealing "the family jewels." There needs to be a guarded openness, a process of reciprocal disclosure, as each partner reveals select business specifics and waits for a reaction before delivering more. This process is very much like a dance in the sense that each partner watches the moves of the other and as they learn about each other, movements become more coordinated and together they see what is possible.

Valuation: Getting Down to Business

> You could spend years arguing about transfer pricing or resource allocation or something like that. We spent six months and said "Let's really take the time to think through what the two companies' objectives are, interests are, what they're committed to, what they're willing to go along with, because once the agreement is done and this company starts, the only way we can change is to come back to the board.

Valuation is that stage in which the terms of the business exchange are formally defined. Up until this point in the evolution, emphasis was placed on ideas, possibilities and "what-ifs." The focus now is more specific, formalized, primarily financial, such as making business cases, analyzing and determining one another's worth, negotiating terms and conditions of contracts, and benchmarking each other's value added. At this time, key executives spend tremendous hours together, working in painstaking detail.

Collaborative Negotiation Requires Dialogue, Not Deal Making

The primary business activities cluster on *Valuing.* Valuation is a widely studied and researched financial tool and a substantive part of alliance formation activity. Business activities center around making the business case, putting values on various transaction costs in the alliance and negotiating the formal contract and partnership agreements. These are difficult, demanding, and exacting activities critical to the healthy development of an alliance. Thus, the associated business skill most often called on is *collaborative negotiation.*

The skills for negotiating to collaborate center on creating a relationship that benefits the alliance, not just one of the partners. Many companies are like a large energy company with which we have worked. Negotiation is taken seriously, conducted by professionals with clearly outlined objectives for the parent company. The end result is a tight agreement that often benefits that parent, not the other partner or the alliance, and that has little flexibility for change and growth. Thus, this company may find itself in an alliance in which none of the parties now want to participate, but with such tight contract stipulations that none of the parties can extricate itself.

How do negotiations in alliances distinguish themselves? They do so because the end result is not about the bargains, trades, deals, or transactions. Negotiating in alliances is more about the dialogue that occurs than it is about the end results of that dialogue. Such a process represents a double win because it expands, not divides, the pie, strives for creative solutions, and provides new pathways to and for opportunities.[8] Also, because strategic alliances are entities that will grow and change, the possibilities of anticipating every eventuality, every circumstance, and every appropriate response for that situation is simply not possible. Thus, the power of the collaborative negotiation is its ability to highlight issues, broaden perspectives, raise eventualities, and craft meaning and understanding. Negotiating in alliances requires skilled dialogue.[9] And skilled dialogue requires trust.

Initiating the Alliance Dialogue Needs Trust-Building Skills

The key relationship activities during this stage center on *initiating* activities through key executives brought in to amplify the details of the alliance even more specifically. In the case of GE-Fanuc, a team of advisers from both companies were charged with making the Welch-Inaba sketch into a viable and operational business entity. In the case of British Airways/USAir, a coordinating team of four was established to create "the blueprint of this alliance." These activities mean bringing the excitement of alliance development to others. It also means spending personal time—lots of it—with others, getting to know them and how they think.

The supporting relationship skill is trust building. Trust is built in levels, and is earned, not given. The first level of trust is built on maintaining confidences and on delivering on promises and intended actions.[10] The second level is based on knowledge shared. Only after one partner knows that information is held securely does that partner trust enough to disclose more critical pieces of technology or processes or information. The third level of trust is one of being totally assured that partners will represent another's interests. Reaching and maintaining this level of trust is fundamental to alliance success. Trust built on all too quick revelations is trust built on a shaky foundation. Creating trust slowly and steadily creates a cycle whereby sharing creates closeness, which increases trust, which encourages more sharing.[11]

Coordination: When the Tough Work Really Begins

You're engaged in direct efforts to try to achieve that vision. You are scurrying around trying to do things, you've got projects, you've got project plans, you've got skirmishes but it's all towards the goals you have set forth to accomplish. There are lots of small projects being implemented within each department.

Coordination describes the stage when the alliance goes to work. Permanent governance structures take shape. Formal interface points and processes are identified and established throughout the companies. Work teams from various functional areas within each partner's firm create cross-functional links. This is a time of multiple and connected activities occurring within and across the partner companies.

Coordination and Integration Happen through and in Teams

Once final agreements are established, *coordinating and integrating* are the business activities consuming management's attention. These activities are about getting down to the business of the alliance. Steering groups and work teams often become the infrastructure of this business activity, as steps are taken to carry out the business and functional strategies of the companies. This is a time when the operational work of the alliance takes over; results are expected.

The primary business activities, therefore, center on the skills of *teaming*. Much of the early coordination activity takes place in teams or team settings. The experience of British Airways-USAir is typical in this sense. The coordination team began its efforts by constructing steering groups and work teams deep within the two organizations. Each team was charged with bringing together their respective functional areas, and managers were chosen not only for their functional skills and representation, but also for ability to work in team and collaborative environments. BA/USAir recognized two important teaming dimensions:

1. *Team composition is critical.* The membership of a team directly impacts the decisions of that team. Who is on a team—what background or expertise they have—frames how problems are approached and which

solutions are favored. Having the "right" people and the right mix of people on an alliance coordinating team, therefore, is a pivotal teaming dynamic. Right people are found by matching skills and perspective to the alliance start-up requirements.

2. *Soft characteristics are critical.* In the British Airways/USAir alliance, members of the steering groups and work groups were picked not only for their functional expertise, but for their interpersonal and teaming abilities. The ability to work collaboratively or to work in a team environment does not come naturally to most managers. Special perspectives, orientations, and skills are needed to manage the diversity in thinking, decision making, or values within such teams, especially if team members represent different cultural backgrounds. Creating a high-performing team that brings out the best of team members is one global leadership skill[12] particularly critical in an alliance context.

Interfacing Needs Partnering Skills

With increased trust and collaborative negotiations, the primary business activity turns to *interfacing*. Interfacing activities facilitate the creation of personal relationships at many levels, oftentimes through the techno-logical dialogue getting the work done. The air of possibilities of early stages is replaced by an atmosphere of concreteness and reality. We met two engineers recently who could not have been more different—in culture, in language, in personality. Yet, they were thoroughly fascinated with building a piece of scientific testing machinery that will be a significant technological breakthrough. As we watched them engaged in the experimental activities, the language was scientific, theoretical, and often mathematical, but the tone, expressions, and general manner were friendly, collegial, and familiar. Based on their collective interest and technical interactions, they had built a partnership of scientific associates and personal friends.

Thus, the primary relationship skill at this time is one of *partnering*. Partnering is about creating results collaboratively, much as dance partners do. Independent of the music, great dance partners adjust and move with one another, lead or follow, shift fast or slow, and mirror complex or simple choreography. They have learned to adapt, to anticipate, and in partnership to create the dance. Managers are not born with partnering skills; they must learn them through practice and over time. And, as mentioned in other chapters, face-to-face time builds partnering skills.

Investment: Making the Hard Choices

> If you've done the alliance for the right reasons and you have the right attitude, there's a whole lot of leverage you can get out of it because the whole is greater than the sum of the parts. But this is when the thing can fail. . . . There comes a time when you have to make a real investment to keep the alliance healthy. It's not a simple thing to do—it becomes very complex. We're not really going to get the synergies that we could get if we were to decide between ourselves that, "well, I'm going to go out of this particular business and you take the load and put it into your factory and you get out of this other business and I'll take that load."

The excitement of the strategic vision that drove the early stages of the alliance may wane as the operational realities of moving the two companies together becomes more complex. Difficult choices can ensue. *Investment* represents the stage at which those hard choices are identified, wrestled with, and a future course decided on. Many alliances identify reaching a watershed at this stage, meaning an issue that makes or breaks forward movement of the alliance. Usually this watershed is connected to the image and identity of the alliance or either partner.

For the alliance between Corning and Siemens, investing meant acquiring a cooper cabling business in the United States and then completely changing the manufacturing operations from copper cable to fiber-optic cable. Copper represented the old technology, fiber optics meant betting on the new and taking a stand on the old to move forward. It was not an easy decision, but the positive result of this strategic watershed was continued commitment and significant investments on mutually agreed action steps.

Growth and Adjustment Is All about Change Management

As the alliance develops, the business activities of *clarifying and growing* dominate the landscape. This is a time of real productivity in the alliance. It is also a time of making hard choices about the future of the alliance, about leveraging synergies, both planned and unplanned. And it is a business time of supporting choices with money, resources, and human capital. As the competitive environment shifts, there might also be a need for strategic redefinition or adjustment.

The key business skills require *managing change*. Next to leadership, change and managing change may be one of the most researched and written about organizational phenomena.[13] Change management is crucial to today's overall corporate landscape and to alliance growth. Underrepresented and increasingly important in an alliance context, however, is the interpretive side of change management. Individuals often frame change through their interpretation of the events they experience. How those events are construed impacts the actions to be taken.[14] Understanding this cognitive side of change opens up a rich new territory in alliance management.

Committing Means Really Committing to the Alliance

Committing manifests itself in a set of relationship activities, supportive of clarification and growth. Now is the time for managers to fully commit to the alliance and to each other. It involves managing the conflict inherent in making the hard choices. And it can mean accepting the reality of the alliance and its relationships. But most of all, committing means doing what is necessary on behalf of the alliance.

The relationship skill most called up at this time is that of making commitments to the alliance and to the partner. Commitment in relationships is emotional. Its essence is making individual goals and those of the alliance the same. Such commitment carries with it a sense of obligation to acting in the best interests of the partnership, not exclusively in the sole interests of one's individual company. USAir was not able to summon the kind of commitment it needed during this crucial alliance stage (as will be discussed in Chapter 5), because USAir managers were distracted. Commitment skills focus on putting the partnership needs at least on a par with one's company's needs, as was the case in the Siecor stories within this chapter. Commitment results from an honest and genuine desire to turn "I" to "we." What the partners make at this point is a strong and real emotional commitment to the alliance.

Stabilization: The Art of Growing *With*

We are a very successful business now, but we can't stop and rest. We've got to keep moving because this business is changing fast. What is most likely to happen is that as competitive pressures grow, and at the same time the market opportunities are magnified, the partners have to figure out how they want to manage the business.

As a result of decisions taken, *Stabilization* defines the stage in which the partners attempt to achieve balance in light of changes that have occurred and continue the process of adjustment and growth. Stabilization often implies a recalibration or reassessment of the alliance and its purpose based on changes that occur over time. By this stage, both partners are actively serving markets in a way that benefits the alliance as a whole, having weathered the difficult decisions around investment, resource allocation, and parity. Interdependence is high.

Adjusting Means Just That

The primary business activity is *adjusting*—to markets and technology, to new opportunities, to continued issues or problems. In many ways, the business activities at this time in the alliance encompass all the activities that have already been discussed. Strategic and operational vigilance can make anything possible as the alliance grows and changes. At this time, managing the alliance is the business skill most needed.

Growing Old Together Doesn't Just Happen

Finally, in the last stage of alliance development, the relationship focus is on *fine-tuning*. The relationships are no doubt mature and well established. The alliance has developed a considerable history. Some of that history contains positive relationship dynamics; other aspects will be less so. Add to this history that changes in the alliance are inevitable. Thus the relationship skill most emphasized is the ability to grow *with* not against the other and to allow the alliance to adjust as each partner changes. This is not a time to fall back into routine, however. Although relationships may be mature and established, they still need attention, as Chapter 7 discusses.

As Figure 3.3 implies, each of these supporting skills represents the core building blocks of alliance development. Visioning goes hand in hand with good radar and self-awareness; strategic conversations are enhanced by skills of self-disclosure and rapport building. The collaborative negotiation process is one of trust building. Partnering happens through collaboration and teams are the modus operandi. Managing changes relies on commitment to the process and to the partnership and on growing together for the benefit of both.

As the alliance builds up, the importance of each block for support and as a foundation becomes obvious. If any block is overlooked, missing,

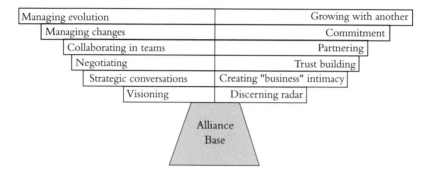

Figure 3.3   Balancing business and relationship.

or weak, the entire structure is at risk. The stronger the early foundations, the more steady the alliance can be over time. Corning and Siemens carefully built each of their building blocks over more than 20 years. Most alliances take neither the time nor devote the energy to build a solid alliance foundation.

The Key Is Balance

Alliances are all business *but the business is relationships.* Don't misunderstand. What the alliance *does* is crucial. If the business proposition is not solid, there is no reason to move forward and no amount of relationship can make a bad business better. When business is good (and especially if the alliance is financially strong and profitable), a weak relationship can be easily overlooked. We have seen this dynamic in our work with a foreign national oil company. During the times of high oil prices, a number of their joint ventures were profitable, and "working well." As long as these joint ventures were delivering on their financial commitments, managers saw no need to change. Although in one joint venture, problems were recognized and understood and relationships strained, the booming economy relative to oil made those issues seem somewhat inconsequential. However, oil prices began to drop precipitously in late 1998 and early 1999; and the worse the business got, the more the relationship issues seemed to matter. Successful alliances require strong personal relationships among the principal managers and executives.

When business gets tough, however, the strength of the relationship ensures that the partners weather the storm. Such strength of the relationship between Corning and Siemens saved the alliance from divorce on at least two occasions. There was an issue regarding building a second fiber facility in Germany in the first 10 years of the Siecor alliance. In optical fibers, cost is everything and it was inexpensive to transport fiber manufactured in the United States to Germany. There was no strategic advantage, and certainly little cost justification, to building a fiber facility in Germany. While the facility would represent only a small part of the total production volume of Corning's optical fiber business, the value-added to Germany was estimated to be 60 to 70 percent. Although there was actually a cost *dis*incentive, what motivated Corning to see beyond the cost argument?

The two key executives, who had both worked and socialized together for 10 years, took a long walk around the grounds of a castle in Germany. They talked openly and honestly, and laid bare their assumptions about the business proposition. In the end, Corning saw and accepted for the sake of the alliance Siemen's point of view. They understood that the issue was not about cost, but about doing what was best for the alliance relationship with Siemens. The strength of these two executives' personal relationship allowed them to see beyond the obvious, presenting issue—and instead address the real problems.

The key to a strong business-relationship DNA is the capacity of the alliance to *stay in the zone of balance* between business and relationships. Business demands of the alliance can easily take over. The need for tangible and immediate results ensures that the business component is on everyone's radar screen. And it can be easy to think that simply maintaining some degree of relationship ensures success.

The mix, however, is important. When the mix is disproportional, the alliance is in trouble. A telecommunications alliance with which we worked was having difficulties in moving the alliance forward. Mistrust was high; an attitude of "us versus them" prevailed. Yet, each side was working incredibly hard on alliance activities. We asked the managers to make a list of all the activities they engaged in and then classified those activities as either "business" or "relationship" oriented. They were surprised to learn that literally 80 percent of their time was being spent on business, to the detriment of their relationships. It was not intentional; it was just the way things had evolved— and therein was the problem. Faced with this reality, each partner was therefore not surprised that the alliance was not working.

It's More than 50–50

Staying in the zone, however, does not mean an equal distribution (i.e., a 50–50 distribution) of time spent on business and relationship activities. What staying in the zone does mean is that the distribution overall reflects adequate and balanced attention to both *dimensions in a meaningful proportion to that particular alliance,* enough to keep the alliance solidly anchored. However, a word of caution. While the zone of balance can be broad, there are limits. Most alliances report difficulties that directly affect the work of the alliance when the scale tips to 70–30 either way (see Figure 3.4).

Ensuring Balance Is Alliance Work

So how can alliance partners create and ensure an appropriate and proportional balance of alliance activities? Here are some bedrock principles.

Know alliance stages, issues, and requisite activities and skills. Knowing what issues an alliance might encounter can assist alliance development. That "advanced" knowledge is probably one of the reasons alliance success improves with alliance experience.

Keep management's attention in sync with stage of development. Because alliances face different challenges at different times in their development, management's role cannot be constant. The focus of management's attentions shifts with the demands of the alliance. Figure 3.5 describes the changing roles of alliance management.

In the beginning management's role is one of visionary. As visionaries, management lasers in on the strategic rationale and vision for the alliance. With that vision, management can scan the alliance landscape

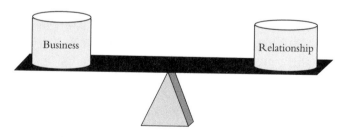

Figure 3.4   Balancing business and relationship: Where's your fulcrum?

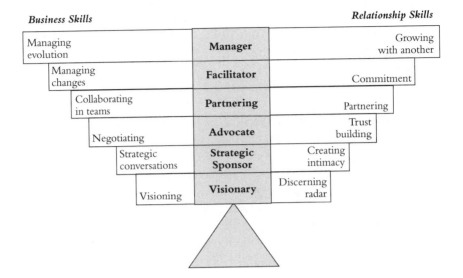

Figure 3.5 Management roles at the fulcrum.

for suitable partners. Once the alliance progresses to choosing a partner (engagement), management's role needs to shift to strategic sponsor. As strategic sponsors, management concentrates through strategic dialogue on building the business familiarity necessary for a solid alliance base. When the alliance moves to valuation, management's role becomes one of advocate, building trust through collaborative negotiation. Next, the alliance moves from vision to reality and management's role needs to shift to networker. In this role, management uses collaboration in teams and partnering skills to create coordination and integration between the partners. Then, as the alliance develops operationally, management's role gradually changes to facilitator. Alliance management then focuses on managing change and building renewed commitment to the alliance. Finally, for an alliance well underway, the role of management becomes more visibly managerial and focuses on growing the alliance.

Keep in frequent, if not daily, contact. Knowing where the alliance is in its evolution as well as its business or relationship activities and issues comes from hands-on, real time contact. Face-to-face interactions are essential. Virtual [e-mail, phone, or fax] helps, especially with time zone differences. But there is little that can replace or replicate the richness of face-to-face signals. In an alliance between a German company and a large U.S. firm, the new U.S. alliance manager was several months on the job before he contacted his counterpart in Germany. This behavior stood in stark contrast to his predecessor, who spoke with that same counterpart several times a day.

Create excessive numbers of opportunities to interact personally—in business and in more relaxed social encounters. Siecor often schedules board meetings (four per year) at resorts with time set aside for skiing, golf, hiking, and dinners with spouses. These opportunities give everyone a chance to learn who the other is, to get to know one another on a personal, one-to-one basis, so that "when you have to tell them something bad, you can do so without being afraid of World War III." This contact becomes much more important when partners are from different cultures and nationalities.

Be as vigilant about your partner's interests as your own company's. Our strongest interpersonal relationships thrive because of the emotional intelligence of both individuals, namely the willingness and commitment to be as considerate of the other as of oneself.[15] Consider a partner's interests, both business and relationship, as Corning did with Siemens in building the state-of-the-art fiber facility mentioned earlier. Or consider the actions of Asahi Glass in its JV with Corning. As part of the JV, Asahi Glass agreed to pay Corning royalties for the right to license its refractory technology. During World War II, no payments were made. Right after the war, however, an Asahi executive traveled to Corning, New York, to present a check for the accumulated royalties. When asked why, Asahi executives reportedly said: "We made a promise to Corning. They are our partner."

Avoid excessive alliance speed in building alliance foundations. Most of the construction time of a high-rise building is laying the foundation and supports for the structure. The same is true for alliances. Take sufficient time with each and every one of the business and relationship activities. Alliances are built one day at a time, individual by individual. While there can be proxies for trust, true trust takes time and effort. Building sufficient degrees of trust required in alliances cannot easily or effortlessly be turbocharged. Corning executives have long understood these facts as they create opportunities to build positive partner relationships. In the Siecor alliance, one executive describes the early history this way:

> I would make a sales call and my German counterpart never made a sales call in his life. But I dragged him in with me. In return, he takes me to the opera, which he loved . . . those are the little kinds of things. . . . the more you understand each other and are willing to learn, ask questions, ask them how their company works, you will learn a lot from your association.

As interdependence grows, so can trust, provided the foundations are solid. Remember it takes three to five years to build that alliance foundation.

Choose managers with alliance competence. Alliance managers need more than business acumen and market knowledge. Our research indicates over and over again that good alliance managers "think and see the world differently." They are diplomats, network builders, highly credible, honest brokers, cross-culturally savvy and tactful. They maintain what we call a "learning orientation,"[16] having the ability to use the past but not be constrained by it. They are flexible and have the ability to improvise. They know why and how to build successful long-term relationships. Chapter 8 expands on these characteristics of alliance managerial competence.

Summary

Alliances are about business and about relationships. Emphasis on either dimension to the retardation of the other weakens that layer of the alliance foundation. The thinner any particular layer of activities is or the more emphasis on some activities over others, the more unstable the alliance becomes. Achieving balance is the crucial role of alliance management.

The right role at the right time ensures that the alliance is getting what it needs at the proper time. What those business and relationships are and when specific interactions are critical have been outlined in this chapter. Also outlined have been the management roles and associated activities.

While many companies have legions of managers working on the business aspects of alliances, having equal relationship acumen can benefit the

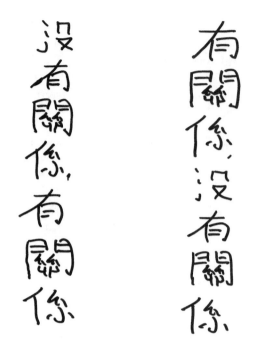

Figure 3.6   Chinese proverb.

alliance in some simple, but profound, ways. One executive shared with us an ancient Chinese saying that he felt captured the relationship dimension. As shown in Figure 3.6, the Chinese characters in the two columns are strikingly similar. The English translation reveals the reason:

Don't have relationships, have problems.

Have relationships, don't have problems.

Relationship acumen is an alliance competence.

4 | The Alliance Spirit

We are unable to conceive partnership without friendship and business relations with no sense of togetherness. Here, I think, lies one of our greatest strengths, because experience has shown that successful alliance management puts the greatest emphasis on the human side of the process. Relationship building requires a continuous effort to secure a common ground where the foundations of understanding can be laid down.

These words were spoken by the president of Bitor (Bitumenes Orinoco, S.A.) during a speech to executives in 1996.[1] Bitor is a successful and growing unit of Petroleos de Venezuela, S.A., that manufactures a patented oil derivative. The marketing of Orimulsion™, the liquified petroleum substitute for fuel oil, depends largely on the formation of alliances with other countries and markets. The product is not sexy; the business is quite fundamental. The transactions could simply be between buyer and supplier. Yet, Bitor's senior management understands that the right business disposition is as important as the product itself. Thus, the statement connotes more than the words strictly imply. The words represent an essence crucial to alliance success and an alliance competence not many companies have. Those that do are far ahead in building strong strategic alliances.

Anchoring every truly successful strategic alliance is a concept called the *alliance spirit*. Alliance spirit is not simply about cultural or value compatibility, nor is it exclusively about a sense of collaboration:

It's much more, the spirit of the alliance. . . . It really takes both partners to do it, and it truly is a partnership. If one side of the relationship is behaving in a partnership manner and the other side is behaving in a more vendor/supplier like manner, it's not going to work. Someone coming in cold who is used to being in a vendor-like environment would find an adjustment coming into a relationship like this . . . you need to think very differently when you are in a relationship like this.

Alliance spirit embodies an implicit set of assumptions *about the fundamental meaning of partnering.*

Defining Alliance Spirit

Chapter 3 compares business and relationship activities to strands in a DNA molecule. Like strands of DNA, business and relationship activities are intimately entwined with the other, difficult to isolate or separate, and most certainly working together to create the entity. But a DNA molecule is a more elaborate construction. Within the DNA

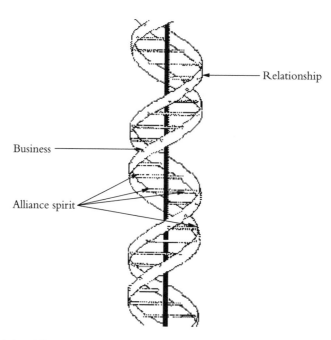

Figure 4.1   Alliance spirit is the glue.

molecule are special connectors, identifiable molecular structures (called nucleotides) that serve to fasten together the chains of DNA molecules (see Figure 4.1). Without those connectors, each of which has distinctive characteristics, DNA molecules unravel. Alternatively, any weak or missing connectors, deform or compromise the molecule's internal structural coherence. Metaphorically, alliance spirit is like the nucleic structure of an alliance.

By definition, alliance spirit is the implied *psychological contract* that exists between the partner organizations. Psychological contract[2] refers to the individual beliefs about the terms of the exchange agreement between two parties. That contract defines the expectations and anticipated interactions between the two and becomes the implicit mental model guiding those interactions. Similarly, alliance spirit defines the often unstated, but fundamental beliefs of the partnership between two companies.

There are two important aspects regarding alliance spirit of which companies need to be cognizant. The first is around how alliance spirit is defined and described by partners. The second is around the degree to which they share a common alliance spirit.

The Meaning of "To Partner"

Partnering evokes very different connotations. To some, partnering means furthering one's own agenda exclusively, sometimes with little recognition of the potential partner. The partnership is a deal. As an executive once stated: "First we hammer out the specifics of the alliance and then we look for a partner interested in agreeing to *these* terms." For others, to partner in an alliance means to share, to collaborate fully and equitably. As another executive told us:

> Partners can be bigger or smaller, have a greater or lesser equity stake, but once in the alliance, they need to be treated fairly, given voice and respected for what they bring to the alliance. Not everyone agrees with that philosophy.

Shared Meaning of Partnering Crucial

Whatever the philosophy, partners need to agree on the definition. Researchers on marriage, an analogy often evoked by managers when speaking of alliances, report that there can be different types of marriages.

These different types define at a very fundamental level the reasons for coming together of the partners and the foundation on which they interact. No one type is necessarily better than the other; each has its own strengths and weaknesses.[3] What is important is not the type of marriage, but that both partners are having *the same* marriage. So it is with strategic alliances. The partners must have a congruous alliance spirit.

Recipe for Disaster

If partners do not have the same strategic alliance, the impact can be significant, a recipe for disaster. Consider the comparison between two alliances: Ameroteck-Euroteck and USTeck-Asateck. Ameroteck is a strong and elite American player in its industry. Euroteck is younger and smaller, but an ambitious arm of a large European global entity. The alliance between them has fallen on hard times; neither side is seeing eye to eye. Alternatively, USTeck is also a strong, elite player, and industry leader in many of its markets. It competes directly with Ameroteck in one of those markets. USTeck's alliance partner, AsaTeck, is also a smaller, younger, but vibrant player in its industry, similar to Euroteck. That alliance is doing well. A shared alliance spirit makes the difference:

> I sometimes think they have not yet really understood what it means to be in an alliance. Some of their top management had to learn entirely new ways of working with a partner—they had to learn what collaborating really means. Where they were accustomed to simply deciding, now they had to talk to us, and to listen to us, which some people in Ameroteck still find hard today.
>
> Euroteck executive of Euroteck—Ameroteck alliance

> It is easy to say the word "partnership." But a true partnership can be firmly established only by cooperation based on equals. And though we are very different companies, we consider each other equals.
>
> Asateck executive of USTeck—Asateck alliance

What the principals in Euroteck *understand,* and what USTeck-Asateck *have put into practice* is this. Alliance success depends on anchors beyond the business and relationship balance discussed in

Chapter 3. Success depends on a shared alliance spirit, which is embedded in the fabric of a few companies like Euroteck, USTeck, and Asateck, but more often missing, misguided, or misdirected in others, such as in Ameroteck.

Benefits of Alliance Spirit

Alliance Spirit Gives Meaning to Alliance Actions

There is no doubt that alliance spirit has benefits to the alliance. First, alliance spirit provides the internal compass setting. That setting provides the mental model for framing and interpreting alliance actions. In one energy company, the mental model for relationships that involve oil extraction is vendor-supplier. For this company, emphasis is on formulating a tight contract, stipulating the deliverables of both parties, and outlining the roles and responsibilities of each in that quest. Thus, individual actions and decisions are seen in light of fulfilling or violating the written agreements. However, if the vendor supplier model is more partnership oriented, such as between Kodak and IBM for data outsourcing, any actions will be viewed through the lens of partnership. Like the psychological contract, alliance spirit has the "power of self-fulfilling prophecies,"[4] in that they can create the future because they frame and channel behavior in the present.

Strongest Effect during Rough Weather

A shared spirit can help the alliance ride out the bad times, thereby increasing the probability of success. Consider an instance seen as a potential "divorce item" between Corning and Siemens. Siecor wanted to build a production facility in southern Europe as a defensive move against Japanese competition. There were strong arguments on either side, but Siecor really wanted this plant. Finally Corning agreed to let Siecor move forward, not because it was necessarily good business, but because it was crucial to the partnership for Siecor to do this:

> You need each other; you rely on each other. It's like a marriage. Each partner has to go 60% of the way and the overlap is the bond. Both partners understand the position of the other. You are never in 100% strong position; we find a way to meet in the middle, sometimes more on Siemens side, sometimes more on Corning's.

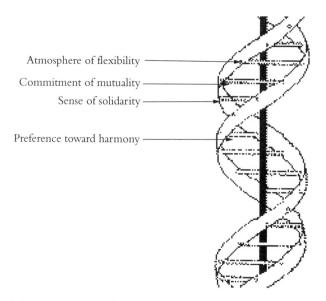

Atmosphere of flexibility

Commitment of mutuality

Sense of solidarity

Preference toward harmony

Figure 4.2   Dimensions of alliance spirit.

The shared alliance spirit made it possible for Corning and Siemens to see beyond the conflict and work through their differences with the broader benefit of the alliance in mind.

Impacts Managerial Satisfaction and Alliance Performance

Third, the alliance spirit impacts managerial satisfaction and alliance performance. Data shows that alliances that share the same view of alliance spirit essentially do better. In particular, when partners have a high degree of congruence around the characteristics listed in Figure 4.2, the alliance shows stronger levels of performance and managerial satisfaction.

Benefits Strong, but Not Easily Discussed

Despite the benefits and positive effects, alliance spirit is seldom discussed. Rare is the executive who can succinctly articulate what it means to be a partner in a given alliance—much less what is his or her company's answer to questions such as:

- Is this alliance in perpetuity (or at least long-term) or is it short-term and time bounded?
- To what degree am I/we willing to share control with the other or must I/we have all the control?
- Is my partner my "equal" (even though I am bigger or stronger or more experienced) or am I better (because I am stronger, or bigger, more experienced)?
- How do I/we feel about involving them in decision making?
- What are my views of sharing information or technology or anything else?

Why is the concept of alliance spirit so potentially powerful and beneficial, yet infrequently discussed? One reason is that the pressure for alliance results inhibits the times needed for real conversation. Also, ensuring strong alliance spirit takes time and energy, without signs of immediate impact. But, most importantly, our experience suggests that alliance spirit is little discussed primarily because managers lack a succinct framework or set of concepts for thinking about or operationalizing alliance spirit.

"Talking Points" of Alliance Spirit

We have found four fundamental "talking points" of alliance spirit:[5]

1. Atmosphere of flexibility.
2. Commitment to mutuality.
3. Sense of solidarity.
4. Preference for harmony.

A description of each dimension follows. Alliance performance improves when partners share common views:

- *About the* Criticality of frequent personal contact.
- *About the* Alliance being essential to the best interest of both partners.
- *On the statement* "Our word is our bond."

- *About the* Alliance being felt at many levels.
- *About* Information flowing freely between partners.
- *About having a* Basic understanding of each other's businesses.
- *About* Each partner adding unique value.
- *About the* Alliance crossing many functional lines.
- *About* Neither partner easily replacing the other or being easily replaced.

Atmosphere of Flexibility

Alliances require an atmosphere of flexibility and versatility. Alliances are by their very nature incomplete contracts. Not every contingency can be stipulated nor can every nuance be anticipated. Flexibility in design and execution, as well as nimbleness of strategy, facilitates coping with the normal growing pains or unforeseen problems during the alliance lifetime. Without flexibility, alliances are nothing more than defined transactions between two parties, restricted in their ability to adapt creatively or innovatively to changing circumstances. The more contractual and deal-oriented an alliance is, the more inflexible will be the spirit of its dealings with its partners. For one energy company, the closer the alliance is to extracting oil from the ground, the more structured the contractual terms and the less flexibility either partner has to conduct alliance business. Thus, when circumstances change, change becomes almost impossible.

A Commitment to Mutuality

Mutuality is another dimension of alliance spirit. Partners need to act in each other's best interest as well as their own, with equitable sharing of benefits and burdens. Mutuality does not mean a daily or even weekly balancing of accounts. At any one point in time, one partner may give more or get more from the alliance. Such unevenness is to be expected in today's fluid business climate. If lack of parity continues, however, is there an issue with mutuality. In the beginning, British Airways and USAir each benefited from their alliance. Each received commensurate financial contributions (through interest payments or direct investment) and each saw ridership increase. Parity in benefits received did not continue. USAir's 40 percent increase in ridership paled in comparison with British Airways 104 percent increase. The USAir customers were using BA to get to Europe. The BA customers, however, were much less frequently choosing USAir as their carrier within the United States. The partners did not take steps to align mutual benefits, such as financial distribution of all ridership increases to both parties, and the gap widened. This occurred even though the anticipated agreement between British Airways and American Airlines included a percent revenue distribution of ridership attributable to the alliance.

Sense of Solidarity

What keeps an alliance on track is a sense of togetherness and solidarity in the purpose and direction of the alliance. If one partner has hidden agendas, these will compromise the spirit of solidarity. For example, should one partner secretly want to position itself for a takeover, as was speculated by some in the British Airways/USAir alliance, a sense of solidarity, "we are in this together," is lacking. When solidarity is strong, alliance actions are seen as opportunities to move together, not as evidence of one partner's intent to control the other. Alliances are not about dominance or control; they are about fair dealing and shared control.

Preference for Harmony

Alliance spirit includes bias toward harmony and compatibility. Similarities are emphasized; differences leveraged or minimized. Harmony does not mean lack of conflict. Conflict in alliances can be plentiful (see Chapter 7) as well as constant background noise (see Chapter 5). What a bias toward harmony suggests, however, is a preference for rapport and repair. Early on in their alliance, USAir and British Airways both worked toward rapport. They comingled management staff to enhance idea exchange and really tried to work through issues together. However, by the time USAir filed litigation regarding BA's proposed alliance with American Airlines, all semblance of a bias toward harmony was lost and the alliance was at the breaking point.

Building Solid Alliance Spirit

Creating and ensuring a strong alliance spirit is work. No alliance benefits from a strong alliance spirit because that spirit magically appeared. Alliance spirit is built through individuals, anchored in values of trust, reciprocity, and mutuality, and woven into the fabric of the company.

Alliances develop alliance spirit and that development starts with the sense of partnering that each party brings. Building alliance spirit involves six steps.

Step 1. Accept That Alliances Are Not "Business as Usual"

Part of ensuring a viable and supportive spirit is recognizing and acknowledging that alliances require (and are built on) a different kind of logic. The foundations of alliance spirit are not necessarily the economic or traditional transactional realities of business. Alliance spirit is based on reciprocity, trust, and interdependence.

For a company like Corning, the spirit supporting alliances is woven into the fabric of the company and thus requires no targeted attention.

Table 4.1   Alliances Are a Different Way of Doing Business

	Power Game	Trust Game
Modus operandi	Create fear.	Create trust.
Guiding principle	Pursue self-interest.	Pursue what's fair.
Negotiating strategy	Avoid dependence by playing partners off against each other. Retain flexibility for self but lock partners in.	Create interdependence by limiting number of partnerships. Both parties signal commitment through specialized investments, which lock them both in.
Communication	Primarily unilateral.	Primarily bilateral.
Influence	Through coercion.	Through expertise.
Perspective	Short-term, today's view. Based on component.	Long-term, big picture. Holistic approach.
Contracts	"Closed" for formal, detailed and short term. Use competitive bidding frequently.	"Open" or informal and long term. Check market prices occasionally.
Conflict management	Reduce conflict potential through detailed contracts. Resolve conflicts through the legal system.	Reduce conflict potential by selecting partners with similar values and by increasing mutual understanding. Resolve conflicts through mediation or arbitration.

One company who attended one of our alliance workshops, however, felt its managers were just not getting the notion of alliance spirit. They created the chart in Table 4.1 to frame the different logic of strategic alliances.

This company asks its managers and its partners what "game" they want to play: the power game or the trust game. Each "game" has a different modus operandi, a unique set of guiding principles, negotiating strategy, communication pattern, influence method, and perspectives. Executives are asked to seriously consider which game their actions support.

Step 2. Discuss Your Company's Alliance Spirit

Have conversations among key managers about what it means to partner *before* entering into alliances. Normally, what partnering means does not register for most companies until they are immersed in the nitty-gritty of alliances. And then each manager is likely to have his or her own interpretation.

Using a tool like the one shown in Table 4.2 has helped alliances and alliance managers think about alliance spirit. When using this tool, one pharmaceutical firm became aware that within its alliance management team, there were vast differences in alliance spirit. Suddenly they had a

Table 4.2   Spirit Discussion Tool

We believe that an alliance is:					
	exclusively	usually	both	usually	exclusively	
short term	____	____	____	____	____	long term
an expedient solution	____	____	____	____	____	a committed relationship
about dominance	____	____	____	____	____	about equality
managed individually	____	____	____	____	____	managed together
controlling	____	____	____	____	____	sharing
rigid	____	____	____	____	____	flexible
?	____	____	____	____	____	?

new understanding of one of the expressed frustrations of their alliance partner: inconsistent and contradictory managerial actions and decisions.

The tool creates dialogue by raising the underlying dimensions of alliance spirit to a discussable level.[6] There is not necessarily a "correct" pattern of responses. Most important is the opportunity for managers to grasp their similar perspectives or raise differences for discussion. Managers within the same company can begin to discuss their rankings on the dimensions, the meaning that each dimension has, and add any other dimensions that seem relevant to them or to their company. Alternatively, managers on both sides of the alliance can complete the tool independently and use the similarity or differences in response patterns to stimulate conversation. Once the beginnings of the alliance spirit are known, work can begin to infuse that understanding into all parts of the company.

Step 3. Include Spirit as a Due Diligence Criterion for Partner Selection

A large grocery store chain in New Zealand does this. Compatible values and a partnering mindset are as important selection criteria as the viability of the business case. There have been occasions when this company did not select a specific partner because there was incompatibility of spirit, even though there was strength of the business case.

Including spirit as a due diligence criterion depends on making alliance spirit a crucial piece of the strategic conversation along with competitive dynamics, market data, and internal strengths or weaknesses. As Chapter 3 demonstrates, this ability takes skills in strategic dialogue and building business intimacy.

Some alliances use a simple series of questions, answered by each partner, as a basis for having a conversation about alliance spirit. Questions that ask about the objectives of each partner, expectations, "undiscussables," strengths, and goals can be used to explore spirit during the due diligence stage. Table 4.3 suggests a methodology that encourages each partner company to complete the questions about themselves and about the other.

Including spirit also means astutely interpreting partner actions. Sometimes spirit is not stated, but inferred from actions, decisions, or managerial behaviors. The partner who continually refers to contract specifics, the partner who voluntarily shares sensitive market data, and

Table 4.3   Starting a Spirit Conversation

Our Company	The Alliance between Us	Our Partner
What are our *objectives* in this alliance?	What should the *objectives* of the alliance be from our point of view?	What do we think are the *objectives* of our partner?
What are we *expecting* from this alliance?		What is our partner *expecting* from this alliance?
What are we *expecting from our partner* in this alliance?		What is it that we think our partner is expecting of us?
What *strengths* do we bring to this alliance?	What will be the unique *strengths* of the alliance as a result?	What *strengths* do we see our partner as bringing?
What might *prevent* the alliance from moving forward?		What do we think will *prevent* the alliance from moving forward for our partner?
What would challenge the success of the alliance?		What would challenge the success for your partner, in your view?
What are the undiscussables?		What are the undiscussables for your partner?
What topics is it too early to discuss?		What topics do you think your partner will designate as too early to discuss?
What outcomes do you want from this discussion?		What outcomes do you think your partner wants from this session?

the partner who asks questions while encouraging questions in return are all sending hints about their meaning of partnering.

Step 4. Nurture the Alliance Spirit

The alliance spirit can grow and mature as companies have more practice with one another in allying. As the alliance moves through its natural evolutionary rhythms, partners gain additional insights into the meaning of coming together. Frequently both partners need *time* and contradictory experiences to really understand what is important to them in the alliance. Sometimes it takes partnering experiences that are *not right* to help clarify *what is really right* and important.

The greater the opportunities for reflection, the better companies can do in alliance and partnership situations. Dialogue with your partner continually by finding opportunities to expand your understanding of your alliance spirit, inquire about your partners or reinforce what is important to you. There cannot be too much communication or too many times for questions or statements that encourage climbing the ladder of inference.[7] During conversations, seek opportunities to ask questions, such as:

- Why.
- What do you mean by that?
- What does that mean to you?
- Here's what that means to me.

Step 5. Use the Power of Apprenticeship

Corning creates continuity of alliance spirit through apprenticeships and mentors. Future alliance managers are brought into an alliance five to seven years before they will assume a top-level management position. Thus, there are no newcomers to the spirit of cooperation. In fact, each incoming alliance manager is intimately familiar with this spirit and its part in the culture of the company. According to Corning, one "would never put a new person in such a very important position [an alliance manager position] . . . never." Corning takes the time to provide its managers with escalating alliance experiences as part of their professional development. Chapter 8 expands these dynamics.

Apprenticeship is not just viable for large companies. Small entrepreneurial firms can use role modeling and mentors to instill the alliance spirit in employees.

Step 6. Take a Lesson from the Firefighters: Conduct Spirit Reviews

Ideally, the foundations of alliance spirit are put into place as the alliance grows and develops. Mismatches or differences never forcefully erupt because the dialogue is open and trusting enough to surface problems before they become serious issues. Even the best intentions for alliance spirit, however, do not always work as intended. The question then becomes one of recalibrating alliance spirit, not building it. One answer is drawn from an unlikely source—firefighters.

After every fire, firefighters return to the station for a "critical incident review." They sit together and systematically review the actions of each other during the fire situation. There is no judgment or blame; rank is of no consequence. All firefighters, from the battalion commander to the rookie firefighter have equal chance to comment on the actions of others and to learn from the practices and processes of fellow firefighters.

The same process can work for reviews of alliance spirit. The emphasis is on communication. Literally, communicate, communicate, communicate and then communicate more.

It is not only amount; it is type and style. The kind of communication that builds alliance spirit or that helps align spirit gone astray builds on the values of trust, reciprocity, mutuality, and respect. It is the kind of communication and interactions that emphasizes inquiry (not debate),[8] and builds relationships with a strong emotional quotient,[9] that is, relationships anchored by a firm understanding of one's self and the other.

Even though British Airways and USAir communicated a lot, British Airways realized even that level was not enough. As they were putting in place the seeds of the alliance with American Airlines, they realized they had to communicate even more, particularly about the alliance spirit.

Summary

Alliance spirit is an infrequently discussed, sometimes minimally nurtured, but powerful glue in bonding partners. As the next chapter discusses, spirit is the adhesive that strengthens the alliance against background noise that is always present within the alliance landscape. It is built on the meaning of and congruence around the following dimensions: atmosphere of flexibility, commitment to mutuality, sense of solidarity, and preference for harmony. But, alliance spirit takes time and effort.

At one of our alliance seminars, a participant ended her summary of the week's learnings with a simple drawing. She had sketched a ghost with bold black eyes and a menacing stare. Her tag line was "Don't fear your alliance spirit: embrace it. It's a good thing." We agree.

5

Alliance Static

In the early 1990s, Royal Dutch Shell and MontEdison began discussions for a possible joint venture in Italy. Among the strategic reasons for the alliance, MonteShell, were the complementary needs of the partners. MontEdison had upstream capabilities—refineries—but a retail system of stations that were losing money; Royal Dutch Shell, wanting to reenter the Italian market it left in 1973, had downstream expertise in service stations. Shell wanted market access; MontEdison wanted an efficient pipeline for its refined crude. The match looked favorable and agreements were signed. Yet, three months later, MontEdison sold the refineries, negating the very reason Shell wanted them as a partner. Asserted bluntly by a Shell executive:

> Imagine getting married, going to bed and waking up the next morning with a totally different partner. That's what MontEdison's actions felt like to us.[1]

No alliance is or will ever be flawless nor does it evolve in a context free of obstacles, diversions, and pitfalls. While alliance spirit acts like a natural adhesive keeping the alliance together, there is another force that just as naturally works to loosen the bonds (see Figure 5.1). That force is known as "static."

This chapter explores the phenomenon of alliance static. Not all static is as disruptive, undermining or noisy as that in MonteShell. In fact, some static is both predictable and manageable. This chapter discusses the three sources of static and their effect on the alliance, as well as possible mechanisms should static become disruptive.

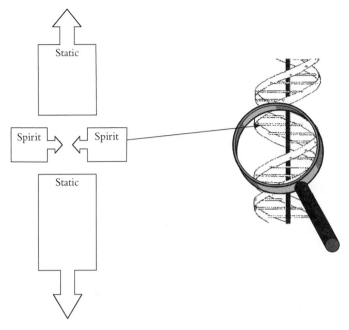

Figure 5.1 Static and spirit as countervailing forces.

Defining Alliance Static

Static is the ever-present, background noise in the alliance landscape. The term static was chosen because of the parallels to the phenomenon of electrical static. Static is an ever-present electrical disturbance in the atmosphere. It ranges from noise undetectable or unheard by the human ear (such as static picked up in the cosmos by radio telescopes), to audible but not annoying (the sound of the air conditioner), to loud and disruptive (noise when a TV station suddenly goes off the air). Electrical static can be reduced or minimized, but never eliminated completely. The same is true for alliance static.

Static is part of an alliance's landscape. In some instances, alliance static presents merely unnoticed ripples in the alliance journey. In others, alliance static makes it impossible to conduct the business of the alliance, diverting resources and attention away from alliance activity. Trying to eliminate static is not a useful exercise because static is a tangible and integral element of alliances. It is more useful to anticipate

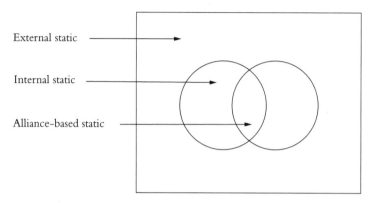

Figure 5.2   Sources of static.

where static originates from and envision strategies for predicting and managing its effects.

Sources of Static

As Figure 5.2 and Table 5.1 outline, alliance static originates from three sources. From time to time, there may be noise that comes from within one of the partner companies. This form of static is called *internal static*.

Table 5.1   Sources of Static

Static Source	Examples
External	Changes in government or government policy. Changes in the regulatory environment. Shifts in market or competitive dynamics. New and significant technological breakthroughs.
Internal	Poor financial health or financial crisis. Change in strategic intent. Company restructuring or reorganization.
Alliance-based	Breaches of faith. Time zone differences. Change in alliance managers. Lack of parity of contribution. Cross-functional/cross-cultural differences.

And then there is noise that occurs completely outside the alliance and its partners, but still has an effect. This is *external static*. Within the alliance itself there is inherent noise, called *alliance-based static*.

Internal Static: Noise from Inside Either Partner Company

During the entire life of the alliance, USAir was under increasing financial pressure, at one point losing $1 million a day. With the highest cost structure in the industry, management was trying desperately to take costs from the system, including renegotiating labor contracts with its unions. Tight money and cost-cutting pressures made management reluctant to dedicate individuals to the alliance on a full-time basis. Most of USAir's alliance managers, therefore, had dual responsibilities. Because the majority of their time was devoted to turning the airline around, the alliance had a small and, as pressures increased, even smaller share of mind. It is easy to imagine the impact on the alliance. All these sources of static were *internal* to USAir, and all had a tremendous negative impact on the alliance's momentum.

In general, there are several internal sources that managers most often cite as causing static in an alliance.[2] These include an internal reorganization, strategic shifts, financial health of the company, or other internal distractions (see Table 5.1). USAir's financial health is a vivid example of internal static and its disruptive effects. The example at the beginning of the chapter relative to MontEdison is an example of an internal shift in strategic direction of one partner that reduces or eliminates the importance of the alliance for the other or both. Finally, as one more example, shortly after the alliance began between two aerospace firms, one partner was consumed with a massive internal reorganization that created new business units and reporting structures and that redeployed personnel. This restructuring made it extremely difficult for the other partner to identify, let alone contact, their designated counterpart. Nothing changed in one partner; everything was different in the other as a result of the restructuring.

Despite the distinct points of origination, the manifestations of internal static have commonalities. These internal sources of static are company-specific, internal situations faced by one of the partners with the potential to disrupt the flow of the alliance. This includes any event that might affect the tone, duration, or interactions associated with the alliance. Though not specifically mentioned in our sample, internal sources of static could also include litigation, top management team turnover, downsizing, or the institution of a new companywide system or procedure.

External Static: It's Just in the Air

The British Airways/USAir alliance was peppered with external static. Initially, the bitter regulatory arguments and debates over the "Open Skies" agreements, which would have opened London's Heathrow airport to U.S. carriers, presented constant and loud noise with which the BA/USAir alliance had to contend. Simultaneously, all the major world airlines were beginning to form global alliances. United, Lufthansa, Air Canada, Thai, Varig, SAS were forming the *Star Alliance,* while KLM and Northwest Airlines were creating an alliance of their own. These competitor actions put increasing pressure on British Airways not to be left out in the cold. Finally, as the alliance was taking operational shape, British accounting regulations had forced British Airways in 1996 to write off its financial investment in USAir as a loss—a move that received significant and negative press attention in the United Kingdom and called into question the long-term intentions of BA.

External sources of static originate *outside* either partner. These include environmental factors embedded in the industry structure, the competitive dynamics, the technology or national governmental politics (see Table 5.1). For BA/USAir, U.S. governmental regulations, particular around forbidding foreign ownership of a U.S. carrier, represents an external static source that restricted the alliance.

Among the most problematic source of external static to strategic alliances are government regulations and restrictions. Many global, cross-border alliances, by their very nature, have such built-in external static, because of the local government's role in protecting its sovereignty and interests. These governments often set policy and laws directly affecting how the alliance competes or cooperates within its market space. Requiring *golden shares* (stipulations that allocate a percentage of the alliance revenue back to the government), maintaining ultimate veto power (as the French government did in Renault's alliance with Volvo), or simply requiring government as a partner (as in joint ventures in India and China) are all realities with which many partners have to contend. The alternative, allying with a non-government-owned or controlled partner, is commonly not an option. In many public-private partnerships government is both the rule-making body and the partner. Such partnerships range from simple outsourcing of government activities (e.g., processing welfare checks, fire and safety, or jails and schools management) to more loosely defined cooperation (e.g., efforts to enhance U.S. textile industry productivity through advanced technology linkages from the grower to the retailer).

Alternatively when competitors or competitive dynamics change, the impact on an alliance can be profound. Consider what would happen to alliances in pharmaceuticals if the chemical composition of new drugs was in the public domain. Or, consider the impact of a change in the dominant technology design standard. In industries where technology changes repeatedly, the potential for external static is a real threat with the potential to deal a hard blow.

As with internal static, the sources are many and may vary by industry. Some sources are generalizable, as discussed. Each company, nonetheless, needs to scan and assess its strategic landscape for potential external static relative to its individual alliances.

Alliance-Based Static: When Static Comes from Partner Interactions

As part of the alliance governance structure, British Airways acquired three seats on USAir's board of directors. Those directors were constantly and vociferously urging Seth Scofield, USAir's CEO, to fix the cost problems, renegotiate with the unions, and stop the flow of red ink. Equally disturbing was that a significant number of British Airways' employees never really viewed USAir as a partner with something to contribute. These British Airways employees felt that their global, premium brand image was getting tarnished by association with an airline whose name at the time was the brunt of many jokes. Numerous observers on both sides believed that the alliance was one sided. And perhaps most damaging of all, Scofield and Sir Colin Marshall, British Airways' CEO, whose interpersonal chemistry had been largely responsible for the alliance, both stepped down. The two new CEOs, Steven Wolff and Robert Ayling, brought very different perspectives on alliances in general, this alliance in particular, and especially different chemistry between them.

These examples are all ones of alliance-based static. Alliance-based static is inherent within the alliance itself, an outgrowth of the interactions and relationships between alliance partners themselves (see Table 5.1). Alliance-based static can result from the *core competencies of one partner being either unrecognized or underutilized*. For example, one alliance partner with years of project management experience believed it knew how to do the alliance project and that its partner had little if any knowledge, though that partner had its own set of comparable alliance experience. *Parity of contribution* (one partner not perceiving it receives its just due from the alliance) as well as inability or *unwillingness to make the hard strategic choices* can all contribute to alliance based static. Parity of contribution was certainly true in the alliance between British Airways and USAir, as demonstrated through the ridership inequities documented in Chapter 4. In another alliance with which we are familiar, the parties are locked financially in an alliance that none want but would cost dearly to end. To the detriment of the alliance, one partner cannot decide its strategic direction and the other is unwilling to incur huge financial losses.

Additionally, there are multiple sources of alliance-based static at the operational level. *Breaches of faith* between alliance managers, *cross-functional or cultural animosities, abrupt changes in alliance managers,* all can result in significant static. Because of the time required to build relationships, lack of adequate face-to-face time or abrupt changes in alliance management without an adjustment handoff can be particularly problematic.

The Static Top Ten and Their Effects

Our data show that static is equally likely to come from any of the three sources (see Figure 5.3). Of all the static sources cited, no one source of static stands out as more dominant or overwhelming to alliances than

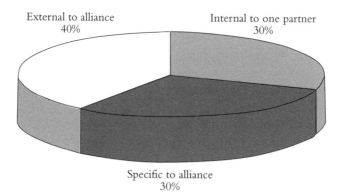

Figure 5.3   Source of top ten static factors.

another.[3] Of the top sources of static, roughly one-third is attributed to each static source: internal, alliance-based, and external sources.

While any source of static is possible, the top 10 sources of static cited as most disruptive or problematic to alliances display a different pattern. Our surveys identify the following top static-causing situations:[4]

1. Changes in marketplace dynamics.
2. Breach of faith between partners.
3. Changes in the nature of competition.
4. Shifts in partners' strategic intent.
5. Shift in one's own strategic intent.
6. Changes in the number of competitors.
7. Changes in management assigned to the alliance.
8. Differences in managerial cultures between partners.
9. Changes in the partners' allocation of resources.
10. Changes in the technology affecting the alliance.

Of those top ten, two of the three sources of static appear to be more problematic. External and alliance-based static represent a greater percentage of problem-causing static (see Figure 5.4). Thus, when markets or technologies shift, competitive dynamics change, or a breach of faith occurs, such static is bothersome to the alliance. Internal static, however, shows up much less frequently than the other sources of static. While internal static may trouble a particular partner, in many cases the alliance on the whole may be more shielded from its effects, resulting in less instances of disruptive internal static.

In the end, external and alliance-based static took the greatest toll on the alliance between BA/USAir. By 1996, British Airways announced a new alliance with larger, stronger, and financially profitable American Airlines (which later fell apart because of external static issues, too). USAir filed a lawsuit for breach of trust, and the alliance fell apart in a whirl of bad publicity.

Differing Effects of Static

To complicate this picture, static may have different effects on the alliance depending on the specific source of static and when in the life cycle of the

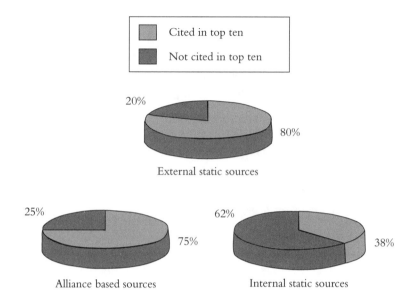

Figure 5.4 Static sources cited in top ten.

alliance this static occurs. Static interrupting a television broadcast is more problematic when the movie is at its denouement than when the credits are rolling. Figures 5.5 through 5.8 graphically depict the impact over time of specific sources of static. The height of the graph represents the degree of impact; greater height equals greater impact.

The Effects of External Static Are Constant over Time

With the exception of marketplace changes, the effects of external static seem to remain *consistent* and *persistent throughout* the evolution of the alliance (see Figure 5.5). There seems to be no time during its evolution when an alliance is more vulnerable or less vulnerable to external static. External static, probably because it is a contextual part of engaging in alliances and partnerships, is just "there" and can "hit" with equal force at any time. Alliances must exist in a context. Problems affect an alliance because the world is uncertain and static is always there.

The one exception to this pattern is changes in market dynamics, which has a more defined pattern over time (see Figure 5.5). Alliances seem most vulnerable to market changes when they are well into the

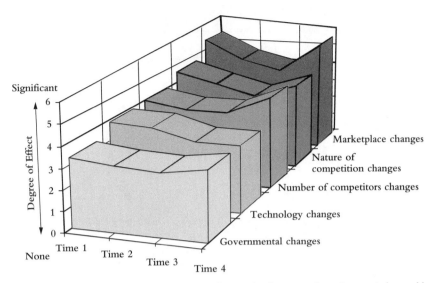

Although the figures denote time periods in alliance development, these time periods roughly equate as follows: Time 1 = Anticipation and Engagement; Time 2 = Engagement through Valuation; Time 3 = Valuation through Coordination; Time 4 = Coordination through Stabilization.

Figure 5.5   Effect of external static over time.

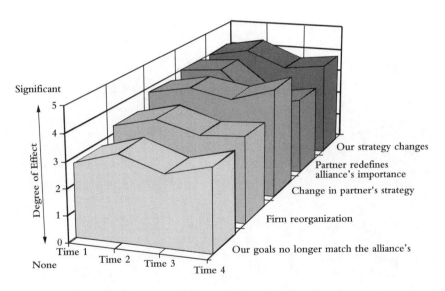

Figure 5.6   Effect of internal (strategic) static over time.

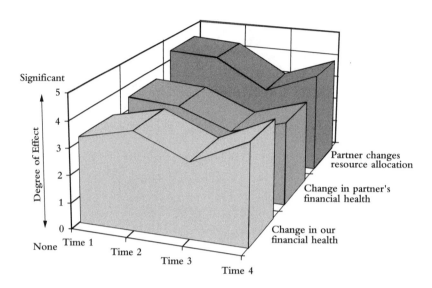

Figure 5.7   Effect of internal (financial) static over time.

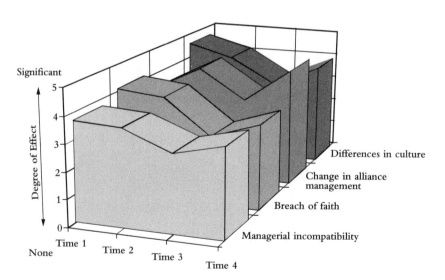

Figure 5.8   Effect of alliance-based static over time.

investment stage. When marketplace dynamics change during the mature stages of the alliance, partners must make tough choices about strategic direction, alliance image or identity, or full commitment to the strategic mission of the alliance. This process calls the raison d'être for the alliance squarely into question. No wonder this particular source of static carries so strong an impact at that particular time. It can profoundly affect assumptions, throwing off any plans for implementing the alliance strategy.

An Alliance Is Most Sensitive to Internal Static in its Formation or during a Watershed

Internal static, on the other hand, as shown in Figures 5.6 and 5.7, seems to have the greatest impact either when the alliance is just getting started in valuation or after it is moving closer toward stabilization, the time Chapter 3 describes as a watershed moment. These are times in the alliance evolution when alliances are more likely to draw heavily on the assets, physical and human, of their parent companies. Any distractions within the parent company make it difficult for that partner to commit the concentrated time and resolve demanded at critical points. Internal static diverts the collective energies of one partner away from alliance activities or diminishes the ability of managers to fully focus on the alliance.

Alliance-Based Static Is Volatile and Timeless

Alliance-based static (see Figure 5.8) seems to have the most volatile and consistently negative effect. At any time, this static can arise. Because alliances are about relationships—between companies and between managers across companies—the many points of contact create many sources for static, increasing the potential for disagreement, conflict, misunderstandings, or misinterpretations.

Identifying and Creating Awareness for Sources of Static

Awareness of the presence of static in alliances and of its potential impact is a fundamental first step in discovering ways to contend with it. Only when alliances recognize and acknowledge static as disruptive can they work to solve the problem. And, there are mechanisms to minimize static's detrimental effects.

Table 5.2   Assessing the Source and Impact of Static

Source	Degree			Effect on Alliance		
	Low	Medium	High	None	Manageable	Disruptive
Poor financial health (an internal source)	⎯⎯	⎯⎯	⎯⎯	⎯⎯	⎯⎯	⎯⎯
Constraints created by government policies (an external source)	⎯⎯	⎯⎯	⎯⎯	⎯⎯	⎯⎯	⎯⎯
Abrupt change in alliance champions (an alliance-based source)	⎯⎯	⎯⎯	⎯⎯	⎯⎯	⎯⎯	⎯⎯

Table 5.2 presents a tool to facilitate managerial and partner identification and discussion of static. Although Table 5.2 lists several rep-
resentative examples, companies are encouraged to generate their own
alliance-specific list. Partners list potential sources of static in their alliance (either experienced currently or possible in the future) and evaluate each source in terms of the disruption it is causing (or could cause)
and the degree to which that static is or could be actively managed.

This diagnostic tool helps partners identify and agree on the types of
static and level of impact. In a recent workshop, partners in a pharmaceutical alliance using this tool were startled not only by their agreement
on static but by the static experienced by one partner that was unrecognized or underacknowledged by the other. Developing a common description of static within their alliance was pivotal for them to develop
strategies for moving forward. Thus, knowing these sources of static is
key to developing strategies to anticipate it or deal with it.

Contending with Alliance Static

Static is a powerful force in the alliance environment, requiring management watchfulness and alertness. Despite the variety of static, unmistak-
ably from every direction, static can be anticipated, predicted, and
managed. The effects of internal static may be the most predictable and the
most manageable. External static is the least, and alliance-based static falls

somewhere in between. Depending on the source, there are different coping strategies.

Vigilance Is the Internal Static Watchword

Internal static requires inward management vigilance—paying attention to what is going on inside the company and constantly asking, "How is this going to affect my alliance?" Being vigilant means having a focused and targeted sense of alertness, as well as knowing instinctively when to see danger.

There is another side to the equation, however. In addition to considering the possibilities of internal static inside your own company, managers need to constantly pay attention to what is going on *inside the partner's* business. If good relationships with counterparts have been built, alliance managers will be able to readily access, discuss, and act on this information in a timely way.

We often use the analogy of sheepdogs. These animals remain on the perimeter of the flock, actively scanning the flock and the pasture for signs of trouble. They take action when the flock or a particular member is threatened or when boundaries are about to be violated. Thus, alliance management, as the "sheepdogs" for alliance static, need to recognize when a situation could lead to problems. The answer lies in their ability to think strategically and understand the potential consequences of actions taken.

Here are some ways to increase internal vigilance:

- Stay constantly informed about strategy and operational issues with your company.
- Network with others to stay in tune with what is happening in other parts of the business.
- Avoid being totally focused on only the alliance.
- Think actively and expansively about how changes at the organizational level (e.g., downsizings, cost-cutting initiatives, new processes or procedures) might affect the alliance.
- Use past experiences as guides.
- Wonder occasionally what would happen if.
- Maintain strong relationships with your partner so you know what is happening in their company that might affect the alliance.

- Take the time to ask your partner what's on the horizon in their company.
- Brainstorm together possible effects on the alliance.

Alliance-Based Static Demands
Strong Alliance Management

Coping with alliance-based static requires positive alliance management. This means alliance executives constantly advocate and build internal support for their alliances. They strive to keep business and relationship balanced. Trust and reciprocity are the foundations that minimize alliance-based static. Taking a partner's point of view, treating it fairly and watching out for its interests are expectations within the alliance. And strong alliance management does all this while continuing to meet its expectations and targets.

There is no getting around the fact that alliance-based static will occur in an alliance. Good alliance management practices, however, act like a vaccine. In the best cases, good practices prevent adverse effects. In other cases, even though trouble occurs, the difficulties are made less severe because of the strong alliance practices.

Here are some ways to ensure strong alliance management practices:

- Recognizing the criticality of managing the alliance.
- Realizing that alliances take work, attention, and management time.
- Resolving to work on the relationship side of alliances as actively as the business.
- Spending time getting to know your partner and their business.
- Creating ways to increase face-to-face communication.
- Working to establish a positive alliance spirit.

Anticipating External Static Takes Foresight

External static is the most difficult of all. It can be totally unexpected and sometimes impossible to anticipate or control for. How can one predict or control sea changes in technology, political realignments, or massive revisions of the regulatory environment? You cannot, so we look to some of the more forwarding-thinking companies for a clue on how to respond. By now, the art of scenario planning is widely understood and used.[5] At the heart of scenario planning is foresight: "the ability to *see* what is *emerging*—to understand the dynamics of the larger context and to recognize new *initial conditions* as they are forming."[6]

This technique has tremendous validity when it comes to external alliance static. Thinking through, describing, and planning for the four or five most likely sources of external disruption is the best way we know to deal with it. And those scenarios that are jointly created by the partners are the best ones. The goal is to prepare the alliance for those shocks and to develop processes to minimize the potential damage.

Static will always be there, and it always has the potential to cause serious problems, but executives, armed with a few tools and perspectives, can increase the odds that they will survive the buffeting of its forces. Sometimes, however, loud and disruptive static calls for the most serious of interventions. Chance favors the prepared mind.

Here are some ways to anticipate external static and its effects:

- Set sights outside and well beyond one's individual company and the alliance.
- Consider the logical extensions of the present: "what would happen ifs."
- Imagine the most unlikely or seemingly impossible "what-ifs," the ones that could never happen.
- Speculate about company or alliance-specific reactions to those what-ifs.
- Take personal responsibility for foresight.
- Avoid delegating foresight to others (e.g., another business unit, external company).
- Be willing and open to have assumptions, biases, and expectations challenged as a premise for new thinking.

Summary

Static is a natural and normal part of the alliance landscape. Static exists because the world is uncertain, change is a customary component of organizations, and people don't always share the same perspectives or agree. Engaging in alliance activity automatically involves exposures to static from the external environment, from dynamics or conditions within one of the partners, or from the alliance itself. Not all static is disruptive and what is disruptive to one alliance may not be to another, as interpretations of static are quite individualized to a particular alliance. It is therefore important for alliance management to understand and agree on the sources of static bombarding their alliance. If the static is internal to one of the partners, vigilance on the part of alliance management can be a successful antidote. Should static be external to the alliance, scenario planning techniques can help the alliance foreshadow consequences. If static comes from within the alliance itself, good alliance management before and during is an effective vaccination. Finally, independent of type of static, a strong alliance spirit guides the alliance through those rough waters.

6

Managing the Alliance over Time
Possibilities and Pitfalls

The evolution of a strategic alliances is a journey. The alliance itself is not a destination or a goal, but is a means to achieving a set of goals. Although no two alliances will have precisely the same journey, some strikingly similar roads can be traveled, as discussed in Chapter 3. The focus in this chapter is on the pivotal processes governing the stages through which alliances must pass, as well as the pitfalls and opportunities inherent along the journey. Chapter 3 describes somewhat of an ideal road map, the best route, where stage, business, and relationship fit together and support one another. This chapter describes the detours, problems, and pitfalls alliances can encounter, what's possible in those situations, what can go wrong, and how to fix it.

Road Maps Have Advantages

Having a road map of alliance development offers advantages. First, such an approach equips managers with a better appreciation for the complex interplay among the different elements that comprise both the business and the interpersonal components of the alliance management process. Part of the difficulty in managing alliances is that at every stage changes effect the delicate balance of business and relationship. As depicted in Figure 6.1, partners first share in the opportunity and the chance to bring a wish (or vision) to fruition. The alliance is an idea of what could be if

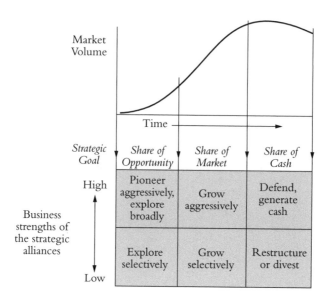

Figure 6.1   A life-cycle approach to alliance.

the partners were to combine resources. Over time, emphasis changes so that managers share in the growth of market share and then in the profits. Effort and competence will affect the speed with which an alliance progresses from an idea to "cash." Alliances tend not to fail during the planning stage. They fail during implementation. A life-cycle approach helps prepare managers to navigate implementation: to expect certain behaviors, anticipate concerns and problems, and be cognizant that certain issues are more important at one stage than at another.

Second, a life-cycle approach places emphasis on the evolutionary process and, therefore, on the anticipated activities and management roles required at each stage. Not only is there a better appreciation for the range of tasks to be performed at each stage, insight also is gained for the skill sets needed to more effectively execute these tasks. The question of fit—management role and what is needed at that time—is critical. The wrong role emphasized at the wrong time can aggravate an already complicated situation. When Shell formed its alliance in Italy with MontEdison, the skill set of the chosen manager and the role he played were adequate for the beginning of the alliance. The alliance manager was a big-picture visionary, whose charge was to help Shell reenter the Italian retail gasoline market. As the alliance progressed, however, and Shell assigned a new alliance manager, problems surfaced. The existing Shell manager was operationally focused. A financial crisis facing the MontEdison group, however, affected their view of the alliance's objectives and current focus. Conflict existed in how the alliance was to be managed, and in the expectations surrounding the projected growth and competitive viability of the venture. While a change in one's partner's objectives is a very serious problem, an effective alliance manager might more effectively navigate these rough waters.

Third, a life-cycle approach can highlight problems and pitfalls that go beyond the assignment of the wrong person to the alliance. They can be structural in nature. Problems often result when one group is responsible for early-stage alliance activity and another manages the later stages of the relationship. In many companies, business development people are responsible for finding and getting partners and others are charged with creating value. Such delineation of responsibility, as depicted in Figure 6.2, is found in some pharmaceutical companies where the business development people conduct the due diligence and negotiate the deal. The alliance is then handed off to the alliance team who works with the partner on a going-forward basis. There is potential for problems to emerge as the alliance is handed off. When the hand-off occurs abruptly, trust often needs to be reestablished and interpersonal bonds sometimes need to be rebuilt.

The most obvious problem is that the hand-off is not done smoothly and the transition from one part of the organization to another really becomes a break point causing the linkages between partners to suffer thereby causing a loss in momentum. More subtle, and probably as serious a problem, is the potential for a lack of continuity in shared values, expectations, and an understanding of the rules of engagement. Early-stage interaction often sets the tone of the alliance and serves to frame the interactions between partners. The likelihood of an alliance developing problems increases if the parts of the organization are motivated by different factors, attend to different partnerlike attributes, and do not have shared responsibility for ensuring a smooth transition. Such a stark hand-off contributes to a lack of continuity, adds to the problems inherent in managing the relationship over time, and almost ensures that the alliance will not achieve its full potential. If the business development people focus mainly on the value of the technology being pursued and

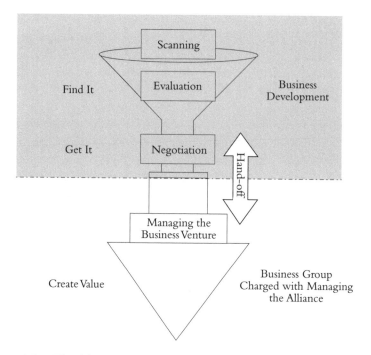

Figure 6.2   The delineation of responsibility.

neglect consideration of the partner's alliance competence, it is easy to imagine that the costs of running the alliance will be higher and the returns will be lower.

The Alliance Journey: From Birth to Maturity

Table 6.1 describes the stages through which an alliance passes from birth to death. These stages are described in the following subsections.

Anticipation

This stage represents the point at which the alliance appears as a vision in the minds of the alliance's architects. Often, these architects are the chief executive officers. For Volvo and Renault, this stage began with Mr. Levy and Mr. Gyllenhammer meeting in Belgium to discuss the possible joining of their respective car companies.[1] Gyllenhammer believed that Volvo was too small to survive as a stand-alone car company. The time was ripe

Table 6.1 Differences over Alliance Life-Cycle Stages

	Anticipation	Engagement	Valuation	Coordination	Investment	Stabilization	Decision
Characteristics of life cycle stage	Prealliance. Competitive needs and motivation emerge.	High energy. Complementarity. Congruence. Strategic potential.	Financial focus. Business cases. Analysis. Internal selling.	Operational focus. Task orientation. Division of labor. Parallel activity.	Hard choices. Committing. Resource reallocation. Broadening scope.	High interdependence. Maintenance. Assessment of relative worth and contribution.	Where now?
Key business activity	Partner search.	Partner identification.	Valuation negotiation.	Coordination integration.	Expansion. Growth.	Adjustment.	Reevaluation.
Key relationship activity	"Dating."	Imaging.	Initiating.	Interfacing.	Committing.	Fine-tuning.	Reassessing dialoguing.
Role of alliance manager	Visionary.	Strategic sponsor.	Advocate.	Networker.	Facilitator.	Manager.	Mediator.

for an alliance given the pressures facing the automobile industry, and Renault possessed a number of complementary attributes.

In the case of British Air, Sir Colin Marshall first had a vision of a global world airline that provided seamless service to the world business traveler. Similarly, the CEOs of AT&T and Sprint had competing visions of becoming a full-service global telecom provider with an ability to provide seamless global voice and data connectivity to their key multinational customers. World Partners and Global One were created to fill that need.

During the high hopes of anticipation, management's role is visionary. As visionaries, their primary responsibility at this point is to sketch the vision, to get others to see what they see on the blank canvas, and to begin gaining alignment and support for "what could be." Painting begins with the broadest strokes and the business case is only beginning to take form. At the same time, others must be able to view the canvas and understand what the final picture is intended to be. Broad strokes do not mean that one should not understand the full composition of the canvas. For Volvo and Renault, both CEOs spoke of the potential synergies and cost savings gained from the combined procurement and shared production and R&D facilities. However, others could not see what they saw.

The vision for the alliance need not reside with the CEO. A strategic alliance vision can, in fact, take shape lower in the organization. Reflecting on the joint venture between Siemens and Corning, the vision for Siecor began with a Corning scientist who was well connected with other researchers, attended a series of conferences, and had an appreciation for the potential impact gained from transmitting telephone signals as light waves over optical fibers. A small team of scientists of Corning then made the key invention of low loss optical fiber. Joined by an experienced business development manager, they soon realized that the fiber would have to be cabled to be of practical use to customers. At the same time, a Siemens scientist, learning of Corning's invention at a scientific conference, was struck by its potential for radically changing the telecommunication cable industry. Corning lacked cabling expertise and began to look for a partner; Siemens was a recognized world leader in cabling. Exploratory discussions at the business and product development level engaged upper level management in both companies and led to the formation of a small joint venture in Germany dedicated to cabling optical fiber for market exploration worldwide. As U.S. market potential increased, a commercial scale joint venture was created in the United States, Siecor Inc.

Soon after this joint venture was established, and validating the urgency for bringing Siecor up to speed was a conversation that Corning and Siecor had with MCI. MCI was just beginning to compete against AT&T in the long distance market and was about to place a significant order for fiber-optic cable. The business opportunity created by the MCI order lent credence to the vision surrounding the potential of fiber-optic cable. It all began with the vision of a small group of scientists and business development people on each side.

A future vision for the firm, however, also connotes a vision for the industry in that assumptions are made as to how industry boundaries will align, who potential competitors and new entrants will be, and what factors will drive demand.

The downside of vision. Vision without an ability to gain support for the alliance, however, can lead to failure. Visionaries cannot act in a vacuum, and support from others in the firm is essential. Wins in the "buy-in" process help build momentum and create a greater sense of purpose among those who must implement. Yet, senior managers tend to overestimate their abilities to "rally the troops" and often suffer from the illusion *that I am the boss and all will do what I say.* (Again, the fallacy of command and control surfaces.) Where an alliance might be contemplated with a competitor, it is essential that parties on both sides understand clearly the factors motivating the alliance. Absent an ability to articulate the vision, managers charged with implementation often lack an appreciation for the rationale and economic motivation for the alliance. Relationships with competitors especially raise questions in the minds of even the most loyal regarding management's true intentions. As SeaLand began to partner with its key competitor to share ships and reduce redundancy where overcapacity existed, managers understood conceptually why the partnership made sense but the emotional reaction to partnering with A.P. Møller's shipping company was another matter. Given the potential for mixed messages, lower level managers have little incentive to cooperate fully; obstacles surface, seemingly minor problems become serious, and the alliance is likely to flounder.

In part, the Volvo–Renault alliance (turned merger) failed because there was little support among the key managers and little commitment among other stakeholders to move the alliance forward. Neither Gyllenhammer nor Levy (then Schweitzer) fully understood the effort required to shape the thinking of the key people and stakeholders who would ultimately have to manage the alliance and transform it into a merged company. Pointing out the distance between the CEOs and their respective management, informed observers suggest that both CEOs focused too much on the symbols of the alliance: the opportunity to orchestrate a pan-European auto company that would be the pride of united Europe and would create the sixth largest car manufacturer in the world.

Signals sent—signals received. While the seeds for the alliance are germinating and potential partners are bring courted, signals—intended and unintended—are being sent through the business activities of search and the relationship activities of alliance building. As the visionary begins to articulate a dream for the alliance and the motivation that drives it, there is also some shaping of the problem/opportunity such that a vague set of criteria begin to emerge or a certain set of potential partners might begin to take form. In many situations, executives meet and during the conversation, a rough outline of a mutually beneficial project may emerge. Senior managers establish a dialogue whereby they jointly shape their visions of the future. In other instances, partners might not have begun to interact, although there is posturing and positioning through each party's pronouncements about their industry vision.

Such signaling behavior is not without risk. This positioning often sets the tone for how partners might engage each other. At times, such posturing may lend insight into how one potential, seemingly powerful, partner views the growth of the market and intends to manage the market's development. At a recent trade show for firms that sell enterprise software, senior management of SAP spoke about how they saw the future shape of *their* industry and the role played by alliances in their global strategy for world dominance. As reported in Fortune,[2] Mr. Plattner, co-CEO of SAP, is alleged to have said: "We're SAP. . . . We intend to control all the enterprise software our customers use. We will select a handful of partners to work with us. If our partners cross us, we will crush them into dust."

Two points are worth repeating and both relate to the overt display of power. First, management did talk about dominance. Second, SAP made very clear that it would not tolerate disloyal partners and would act swiftly to leverage its market position. There is no question about how SAP sees its role in the marketplace. Also, its pronouncement should serve to forewarn potential partners as to how SAP is likely to view the partnering process and should make potential partners quite cautious. While less bold in his comments, Oracle's Elison spoke with a similar degree of confidence. His remarks warned partners about crossing the boundary into developing software that competed with Oracle's core applications. Both firms have taken a position that reveals a great deal about their alliance-like behavior and how they view alliance management. To be sure, we gain insight into their definition of alliance spirit. Potential partners now have a sense of what to expect when dealing with both companies.

During anticipation, partners have not yet begun the formal due diligence that helps ensure compatibility among alliance partners and reduces the risks associated with selecting a partner with whom there is little in common. At the same time, the visionaries may not fully examine the extent to which the alliance fits with the firm's future goals and objectives. The business case is in a very preliminary stage where the parameters are slowly taking shape and the value proposition is beginning to emerge. If attention is given to the degree of match with the firm's core strengths, there is only an informal test of alignment: Is the proposed alliance consistent with the firm's strategic direction? It is unlikely that there has been active and purposive senior management involvement around the following kinds of questions:

- Does the alliance fit our business strategy? Long-term? Short-term?
- Will the alliance help the firm achieve its objectives faster/less expensively?
- Does the company's value system, structure, and processes support alliance-like behavior?
- Will the alliance take the firm away from its core competencies and recognized skill base?
- How will the proposed alliance create value and what does our firm bring to the value equation?

To avoid or minimize the pitfalls during anticipation, managers should address the following questions in detail:

What are the objectives and the general strategy for an alliance?

The goal is to more fully explore the degree of fit and alignment of potential partners with the firms' strategic direction and intent. It is key to understand how the proposed alliance adds to the current strategy of the firm. Often there is a feeding frenzy around alliance formation and firms are drawn to alliances because they are in vogue and their competitors have them. Alignment must exist between the partners. If a JV is formed, alignment exists also between the partners and the new JV. We have observed JVs that have attempted to encroach on the business of one of the partners! In all instances, one must first understand the *whys* and the *how comes*. The elevator test is all important: If asked how the proposed alliance fits into your current strategy when the you enter an elevator in the lobby and the doors close, you should be able to answer the question by the time the doors open again on the second floor. If a succinct and cogent response cannot be articulated in this brief period, the basic motivation for the alliance has not been well developed nor understood.

What defines a good partner?

A list of good partner attributes and characteristics can be long. Variation depends on different factors such as the kind of alliance (joint venture versus comarketing alliance), its scope, and the level of resource commitment required by each partner. However, a common feature must be that partners are attracted for positive reasons. Informal due diligence tends to center on the quantitative or objective issues related to financial health, technical competence, number of patents, marketing acumen, and the like. For the most part, data are collected that attempt to quantify partner resources or skills. Such lists often omit the tougher questions and fail to address concerns that cut to the heart of what it means to be a good partner, as discussed in Chapter 4. This qualitative information can be hard to gather, particularly if the firm has no prior experience with the proposed partner. If the potential partner has a history of alliance activity, however, this information is available.

During anticipation, the questions are basic: What is the firm's alliance readiness? And, is there a supportive environment in which an alliance can flourish? Despite the CEO's vision and desires, real structural and process-related barriers must also be addressed. Consideration, for example, should be given to staffing the alliance and understanding both the skill sets needed and the level of commitment required to support and nurture the alliance over its life. Managers speak of their span of attention (i.e., bandwidth) and their ability to juggle different tasks and responsibilities. Alliances are messy, and often take considerably more time than one might have imagined. Assign your best people to the alliance. Not only do these top managers improve the chances of alliance success; raw talent is not enough. Experience coupled with talent will ensure that your firm develops the breadth of alliance talent needed to carry your firm forward. If alliances are to be more important to companies during the new century, care should be given to developing that critical talent now. These issues relate directly to the notions of developing an alliance competence discussed fully in Chapter 9.

Engagement

This stage begins when the specific partner has been selected; they are now "engaged." With that partner, engagement forms a clearer sense of what the alliance's value proposition is, how competitive advantage will be sustained, and what the partners' mutual expectations are surrounding the alliance. The vision takes concrete form and the homework of delineating rights and responsibilities between partners begins in earnest. What the future holds through the alliance generates excitement and enthusiasm.

Previously, partners could very easily have worked in parallel, each conducting their separate analyses of the other and each conducing their own assessment of the alliance—its potential value and viability. Based on that work, partners now labor to reach a mutually beneficial agreement. While partners conceivably might continue to work separately, it is preferable for them to work together in an open discussion as they question assumptions, conduct analysis, and reach an agreement with shared input. In this way, they can avoid the gamesmanship that often accompanies the art of negotiation.

While visionaries were critical earlier, at this stage, strategic sponsors are needed to orchestrate a larger base of support for the possible alliance through the business and relationship activities of strategic conversations and dialogue. There must exist a point person who is willing to take responsibility for the alliance and is dedicated to moving it forward. A strategic sponsor need not be the CEO or a very senior manager but must have the authority to commit resources to the alliances. Position is less critical than certain key attributes. In addition, the sponsor must have respect, be highly credible, and be viewed as trustworthy. Too many alliances languish because a strategic sponsor becomes disengaged, or has never really emerged.

No alliance pairing is perfect. Strategic dialogue and conversation skills are needed to understand the gap that might exist between your company and the partner on key issues. A strategic dialogue and conversation would be incomplete without consideration of:

- *The nature of the alliance.* Partners might have traditional approaches they have become comfortable with. One might prefer joint ventures and the other has only experiences with less formal alliances. Different alliance forms carry different sets of expectations.

- *Different views of the alliance between partners.* Partners might define alliances differently. Partners should share a similar view of what an alliance is and what it is not. If there is little convergence between partners, there are potentially serious problems facing the alliance down the road. Partners who have not agreed on the basic tenets of what an alliance is probably do not share a view of what is and what is not accepted behavior.

- *Upper management's view and the view from middle management.* The issue here extends beyond the distance between managerial levels and also includes the attitudes associated with alliance activities. In an outsourcing alliance, senior management might view the motivation as an opportunity to focus on core skills while lower level managers might view these alliances as merely a chance to offload financial burdens by shifting fixed costs to variable. Since alliance activity requires multilevel interaction between partners, different interpretations at different levels could signal future problems. Our experience when working with companies is that a great deal of finger pointing goes on between the different layers of management. Do not ignore the view from the middle. It is here that the implementation occurs. Middle managers must be part of the process and must be empowered to carry out their responsibilities.

- *Expectations of results and accomplishments.* Partners need to shape expectations early so that they have the same sense of what can be accomplished through the alliance and what cannot. If one partner expects quick wins and speedy returns from their investment and the reality of alliance development is that longer periods of time are required to achieve value creation, these different expectations do not bode well.

- *What collaboration means.* In Chapter 1, we introduced the exercise, "I say alliance, you say. . . ." An ability to define collaborative behavior and to conform to the set of norms that develop over time is fundamental to understanding how partners are to behave. Understanding collaboration is key to understanding the rules of engagement during the alliance.

- *Skill assessment.* Partners should look for complementary skills when selecting among potential partners. One issue centers on correctly assessing the partners' skill base and being able to discern between what you can do and what you say you can do. As one might imagine, partnerships based on the future development of a product, or a piece of software, are intimately affected by one's ability to deliver on promises.

- *What tasks need to be done in support of the alliance?* It is easy to underestimate the amount of time and support needed to nurture an alliance. If both partners are new to the alliance game, it is likely that they will not allocate the requisite resources, nor understand the full range of activities that must be executed in support of their alliance

- *Decision-making styles.* Decision-making styles are also important in understanding the degree of compatibility among partners. If one partner is autocratic and decisions are delegated up and the other partner actively empowers its managers and encouraged (and supports) decision making at lower levels, one can easily imagine the ensuing tensions and possible problems.

- *Risk-taking profile.* Partners might differ on both their tolerance for uncertainty and the manner in which risk is managed.

Risk-taking profile can affect the manner in which firms negotiate any future investments that the alliance might require. This difference can be further exacerbated if the alliance is more central to one firm than it is to the other. Such issues arise in the alliances found between big pharma and small biotechs. For example, the larger firm may want to cut its losses early if the development of the new drug or technology is not progressing on schedule because it is managing a portfolio of products and research projects of which this is one. This alternative is better than to pursue a project that appears to be heading nowhere. For the smaller firm, this project is the whole of their business and management is more likely to be tolerant of the delays and wants to spend both the time and the funds to overcome this setback.

- *Culture, work processes, and organizational context.* Differences in culture, structures and organizational processes, and policies can kill the best alliance. Partners must not underestimate the importance of these issues and must take the time to understand the degree to which differences exist. The obvious aspects of culture include differences attributed to national and company norms and customs. Yet, cultural differences extend to other realms such as customer retention and care, employee treatment, and legal and ethical issues as well. As discussed, cultural distance can cause significant problems. The difficulties can be subtle as implied by the reference to such issues as customer care and employee relations. In one alliance we witnessed, questions of downsizing were important to control costs, and the U.S. partner was frustrated that its German counterpart was unable to move as quickly to shed workers. Culturally, it is far more difficult to lay off workers in Germany due to that country's societal norms, welfare system, and the relative strength of the labor unions.

Emphasis is given to the attributes and characteristics that affect how the partners will interact and how different roles and responsibilities will be shaped. Two questions emerge. First, should partners be perfectly aligned? And, second, if they are not in alignment, is there sufficient reason not to proceed? The answers to these two questions vary. The case could be made to seek partners where the variance in profiles is not very significant. One might compare the firms and develop mechanisms to manage the gap. Yet, there are other concerns that might be considered *show stoppers;* if so, partners should proceed very cautiously. As a general rule, the closer the issue is to the core values that determine what is means to be a good alliance partner, the greater the degree of concern. If partners do not share similar values regarding partnering and collaboration, or their sense of ethical behavior and what is "right or wrong" do not align, steer clear. Such misalignment signals only problems.

Valuation

Valuation tends to concentrate more on the financial aspects of the alliance and is tied, in part, to the negotiation process whereby partners now work together to forge the details of the alliance. While there are details related to *who does what and when,* partners often spend a great deal of energy trying to ascertain the value each brings to the alliance. Questions of fair dealing and equitable behavior become paramount, making collaborative negotiation and trust-building critical skills (see Chapter 3). One of the advantages of an alliance (over either a merger or an acquisition) is that one can "carve out" and partner with only that part of the business that adds value to the business proposition. In the acquisition, the process often entails the buyer wanting to pay as little as possible and the seller wanting to maximize the price—it is very much a zero-sum game. The process is more complicated since the buyer often must acquire the whole enterprise to get the part(s) that are of interest. After the initial transaction, the buyer then sells the parts that do not match with the intent of the alliance. In an alliance, one can estimate the worth of the essential part, not the entire firm. Despite this advantage, valuing the contribution of the partners is not an easy task. This process might be seen as a test of one's view of partnering and whether one "values" the partner as an equal or not.

Contributions large and small. When partners are of unequal size, the larger partner can significantly impact the alliance. If that partner gives equal weight to the smaller one's intellectual contribution against their "hard" assets, this gesture often bodes well for future interaction. In determining value, the following realities often surface:

- Some assets are hard to value. It is difficult to determine the value of market knowledge or other relationship-based assets such as reputation and industry presence. Tacit knowledge in general presents a challenge during the valuation process.

- Some contributions are hard to delineate and, as a result, relative contribution is hard to determine. A focus on research output may be desired, but so too is the wish to remove from consideration the cost of the infrastructure that enables the development of these products and/or ideas.

- Partner value and contribution will shift over time. The precise point in time that value is assessed could be a point of discussion. Because learning happens during the alliance, the value of a partner's unique contribution tends to diminish over time as one partner learns from the other. How this decrease in future value might affect the initial worth placed on that contribution is a serious question. For example, the net present value of the partner's contribution would decrease if one were to determine partner worth as a dollar amount discounted from the future to the present. Such an approach is likely to be used when equity stakes are being allocated in a joint venture.

A partnership of equals versus an equitable partnership? Differences often exist in how partners weigh what is important to them and, as a result, the methods by which associated value is assessed. As Chapter 4 suggests, such difference can, in subtle ways, strike at the core of what is means to partner. At the heart of this discussion is this difference: Is the alliance a partnership of equals or an equitable partnership? Chapter 2 addresses fair dealing and the importance of equitable treatment in building a basis of trust within the partnership. Partners often bring quite different skills/resources to the alliance, and these capabilities might not be equal. At the same time, discussions can become dysfunctional if partners get bogged down in an attempt to value precisely each other's contribution, thereby developing the "perfect exchange rate." Concerns affect the level of respect one has for the other; whether one sees the other as superior/subordinate; and/or, whether the espoused concern for an alliance of equals is played out in the valuation process.

Two potential partners were engaged in structuring their proposed joint venture for the delivery of medical care to the indigent population within their state. One partner was a network of rural health sites and the other was a large tertiary care medical center. The medical center had funds to invest and given its expensive high-tech medicine required a certain flow of patients to assure cost-efficient operation. The rural health sites only had access to patients; it had no cash. The alliance broke down when it became apparent that the hospital could not justify an exchange rate that had Y dollars equal X number of patients. Both had incentives to cooperate and both were encouraged to do so by the State Department of Health. Yet, the medical center's management felt that the health network was not meeting its financial obligations. The medical center's management felt also that the rural sites viewed the hospital as the "rich uncle" and that they expected the hospital to provide needed cash. First, the process of fair valuation proved to be a show stopper. The health center could not get beyond the fact that it brought hard assets to the table and the partner did not. Second, the process broke down because of both an inherent lack of trust and an inability to reach a fair settlement of each partner's key assets. Valuation is driven partly by trust and one partner's expectation of fair dealing. It should not be driven by ego.

The question of whether partners are equal or equitable is formidable. If one partner expects to have an equal voice and the other, under an attempt to fairly assess comparable worth, discounts the value, the tone of the alliance can be irreparably damaged. Not only is the spirit of the alliance called into question, but the trust-building process is adversely affected. The ability to accurately determine partner contribution is important, and of greater significance when partners have to deal with proprietary technology, sharing patents, access to tacit knowledge, and the like. Contracts are important repositories of these contributions. However, contracts and the "drama" surrounding the negotiation of the contract are revealing as well.

Contracts are important but. . . . An alliance is not predicated, nor is it built, on a contract. Its basis is the relationship among alliance partners. Use caution, therefore, during valuation; be attuned to the method for valuation and develop a sensitivity to how the other partner interprets such efforts. Simply, partners should put themselves in the shoes of the other and attempt to view the process from their partner's perspective. North American managers tend to overemphasize contract negotiation and often rely too heavily on their attorneys to help structure the "deal." (Parenthetically, the term *deal* is problematic because it sends the wrong message.) More times than not, such a heavy reliance on the legal side of the alliance results in a contract that runs counter to the alliance sponsors' intent. As alluded to previously, the negotiation process serves as a window to each partner's definition of a partnership.

Once the contract is written, put it away. Our advice would be to write the contract, place responsibility for negotiations in the hands of the managers who will run the alliance, and work with attorneys who understand the spirit of the alliance and will abide by the business proposition that is fundamental to the alliance. If circumstances require reviewing the contract, there are often serious problems between partners.

A good contract . . . Contracts and the negotiation process are inherent sources of tension. They exist for practical reasons, but they carry a great deal of symbolism. Contracts facilitate a crisp and clear understanding of the partners' intentions. The process of contracting can be a valuable addition to the negotiation and trust-building process itself. The following factors should be included in the alliance agreement:

Define clear objectives and the extent of commitment expected.

Include a specific business plan.

Articulate an organizational structure for the alliance.

Understand contribution and capability of partners.

Delineate partner rights and obligations.

Reward formulas should be tied to risks.

Link investment and compensation to performance.

Define, as best as one can, measures against which to gauge performance.

Link budgets to resources and priorities.

Try to understand tax and legal considerations.

Tie alliance leadership to contribution and expertise.

Contain provisions to recommit to the alliance.

Develop governance structures (boards, etc.).

Articulate processes to deal with conflict and problems.

Encourage the ability to accommodate change.

Ultimate value of a soft contract. Contracts are intended for problems associated with precision and valuation. Also, they help set the rights and obligations of the alliance partners; and they articulate roles and processes, rights and responsibilities. The future, however, tends not to unfold as precisely as a contract may state. Thus, a contract is only an *incomplete agreement* that cannot delineate with precision and detail future behavior. To rely heavily on a contract ignores the key point about alliances made in Chapter 3: one does not manage a contract, one manages relationships. Do not confuse the two: at the end of the day alliances are about relationships. Although a contract attempts to fix the value of assets partners bring to the alliance, these assets have a market value that rises and falls over time. This is a weakness of *hard* contracts that attempt to set a precise value to future assets. Instead, we encourage the use of *soft* contracts that rely on mechanisms and processes to determine future value. Such contracts acknowledge that future uncertainty will affect the value ascribed to the partners and that one cannot know in advance the exact nature of these contingencies. Valuation is a fluid process and is subject to uncertainties; to think that a contract will eliminate these uncertainties is to rely to heavily, and naïvely, on the letter of the contract.

Coordination

Coordination describes the stage at which the joint work between alliance partners begins. Partners begin to design the processes and structures of integration through the collaborating and partnering activities. They also attempt to organize their activities: to achieve espoused leverage, to realize scale and/or scope, and to facilitate the seamless flow of materials and information between and among part of the business in support of the work of the alliance. The hard work of alliance management begins since now partners must plan and execute the reality of their vision. Integrating activities and processes among functionally separate entities is a challenge under a single hierarchy. Trying to do so while maintaining separate organizational structures and reporting systems adds an element of complexity.

Issues of complementarity. If truly complementary activities exist among partners, parsing responsibility can be fairly routine. The decision heuristic becomes one of laws of comparative advantage. A high overlap in skills/competence is likely to create some conflict over which partner will play which role and may engender unnecessary waste and duplication. Such issues detract from the benefits of the alliance and will lead to underperformance. Yet, partners sometimes overestimate their skills or want to participate in other parts of the value chain so they can expand their repertoire or attempt to capture more of the value chain. From a value chain perspective, it is best to objectively assess each partner's capabilities early on and assign responsibilities accordingly. If the partner skills are highly substitutable, the rationale for the alliance should be questioned as such overlap often results in problems.

Tandem or sequential. Whether the shared activities are to be performed in tandem or in sequence has coordination implications. Activities conducted in sequence can face problems of timing and coordination as they relate to hand-offs and bottlenecks. Like the problems of a production process, the issues are often ones of staging, coordination, and ensuring that the workflow moves according to plan and that information is shared in a timely manner. A supply chain partnership in which certain partners perform certain roles is the most obvious example. If a tier 1 supplier is to deliver subassemblies to the manufacturer who carries 45 minutes' worth of inventory, it is clear how the partners must interact. To miss a delivery window or to ship parts with defects will cause the entire process to break down.

When partners must work in tandem, work is shared (i.e., pooled) between partners and different problems can surface. Problems relate to sharing the workload; issues surface regarding the joint development of both tangible and intangible assets and the rights associated with intellectual property and of ownership; and there may be concerns about how to evaluate the contribution of each partner. If partners comingle researchers in a jointly funded laboratory where the alliance is charged to discover a new compound, to solve a technical problem, or to write a software application, one can envision a discussion regarding the direction of the work, the timeliness of deliverables, property rights, patents, and the like. For example, Lucent and Philips recently canceled their telecommunications JV to develop technology for cellular phones. Philips was to employ Lucent's new technology in its next generation cellular phones. Philips claimed that Lucent was unable to deliver on its technology and Lucent claimed that changes in management caused the venture to lose focus.

Problems unique to joint ventures. Unique to the joint venture are problems related to how the parents govern the JV and its permitted

Table 6.2   Potential Problem Areas in Alliance Design

Alliance Type	Sequencing Problems	Working in Tandem Problems	Governance Problems
Nonequity alliances	Workflow bottlenecks. Timing and coordination. Transfer pricing.	Protecting proprietary information. Patents and other property rights.	Shared decision making. Management continuity. Oversight and performance criteria.
Equity alliances	Same as above. Capturing share of value chain. Ensuring equitable sharing of gains.	Same as above. Determining value contributed. Reconciling difference in contribution with ownership.	Same as above. Resolving questions of equal voice with equity stake.
Joint ventures	Same as above. Managing problems between parents and JV.	Same as above.	Same as above. Matching oversight to skills. Alignment of goals between parents and JV.

scope of work. Usually, parents do not like the JV to infringe on what they consider to be their domain. This demarcation can be defined by either products or markets, or both. Dow Chemical and LG Chemical have established a petrochemical joint venture in Korea to produce polycarbonate, a plastic used in compact disks, cars, and computers. Conflicts might arise, for example, if the JV had been charged with coverage of the Asian marketplace and over time it began to infringe on markets and/or customers presently served by either of the parents. The potential conflict is obvious. These potential problems are summarized in Table 6.2.

Governance and structure issues. As partners struggle with the design of the alliance, the question of governance and its structure is also important. First and foremost, the alliance should be structured to meet its needs and not the needs of the partners. While the primary intent of structure is to enable the alliance to accomplish its goals through the effective allocation of partner resources, it serves also to encourage personal accountability and it seeks to permit partners to act quickly and responsively to factors that affect the alliance (i.e., static). Partners should consider four issues as they plan how to govern the alliance:

1. *Attempt to ensure continuity among key alliance personnel.*
Many alliances take up to three years before they are fully functioning.
Yet, companies tend to rotate their managers every 18 months, or so.
When these cycles are out of sync, personnel changes affect the nature
of interaction, expectations and how norms are developed. Should the
rotation of key managers be unavoidable, time should be taken to ensure
that hand-offs to the new managers are made in a purposive and deliberate manner. In both the IBM-Microsoft and AT&T-Olivetti alliances
changes in the champions affected the tone and the effectiveness of the
alliances. In one case, change was unavoidable; Estridge, a key IBM
manager, was killed in a plane crash. In the AT&T alliance, Cassoni was
asked to return to Italy. In both instances, the loss of these sponsors had
a negative effect on the relationships.

2. *Tie incentive schemes to the performance of the alliance.* A frequent question is whether to keep managers on their respective company's payroll or tie their pay and incentives to the alliance. It is better
to link pay and incentives to the alliances because it shows commitment
to the activities of the alliance; it guarantees that managers will work to
further the goals of the alliance rather than act in the self-interest of the
partners; it decreases the appearance of conflicts of interest; and it fosters accountability. Incentives attached to alliance performance should
exist at all levels of the organization and must be linked to the reward
structure of those involved. A sensitive point, however, is the difference
in pay scales between the alliance partners. Imagine a U.S. firm and a
Chinese partner attempting to calibrate the pay scale between their respective alliance managers in light of the significant difference in salary
structure and standard of living between the two countries.

3. *Encourage multiple layers of contact between partners.* Alliances operate at three levels: strategic, operational, and project specific. Contact should exist at all three levels and should not be reserved
for CEO to CEO, or project managers to project managers information exchanges only. Flows of information should be both up and
down as well as across each of the levels, as shown in Figure 6.3. The
point is to place information and decision-making authority at the
right spot in the alliance as well as to ensure that information does not
get lost between levels or committees. We have witnessed the effective
use of steering committees, operating committees, and joint task forces
(work teams) both to inculcate the values and operating principles of

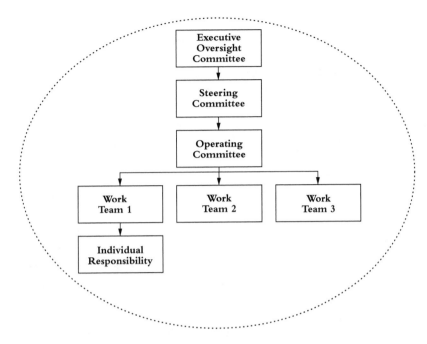

Figure 6.3   An example of an alliance structure.

the alliances and to manage the coordination and integration of the work of the alliance.

4. *Recognize that governance systems change over time.* In the earlier stages of the alliance, attention is drawn to the steering committee and the need to orchestrate the future interaction among partners. As would be expected, over time the concerns become more operational and the steering committee takes on more of an advisory role. Nonetheless, it is important to consider how changes will affect governance by boards or steering committees. Alliance champions should be placed on boards/steering committees early and should continue until the alliance is fully functional. This ensures momentum, and the focus will tend to be more strategic. Next the board should consist of managers with relevant skills and experience. As a final consideration, as the alliance attempts to adapt to change, it is far easier to replace board/steering committee members than it is to add either another level of committees. The alliance can drown under the weight of its own bureaucracy and can lose any semblance of speed and responsiveness. Governance in the

Volvo-Renault alliance was in the hands of 21 operating committees—no wonder management was concerned about decision-making speed!

Also, partners should begin to establish performance outcomes. Initially, they might focus measures internally as attempts are made to co-ordinate activities. Milestones might emphasize coordination and integration issues. Soon, however, these performance indicators will shift to external metrics that reflect the stated intent of the alliance. After in-stituting metrics associated with ensuring coordination and integration between partners, managers might emphasize cost savings and the elim-ination of redundancy and waste. Over time, and certainly, through sta-bilization, performance measures will highlight standard performance measures such as sales, market share, penetration and/or ROI.

Investment

At this stage partners have fully committed to the ongoing maintenance of the alliance and allocate the resources needed to sustain and, if needed, grow the alliance. Previous estimates of the resources needed to manage the alliance were developed during the development of the business case. In many instances, this stage runs smoothly as both partners remain equally committed to the goals and purpose of the alliance. However, plans can derail because change is likely during the development of the business case and the time at which full commitment is needed. For ex-ample, Hoechst and Mobile recently canceled a 50–50 joint venture for the production of polypropylene film having signed a letter of intent six months earlier. The JV would have controlled close to 16 percent of the world's production. The agreement began to break down when it be-came clear that Hoechst would not be contributing an equal share of as-sets to the venture and the two firms could not resolve this discrepancy. It would appear that investment is partly a function of expectations set earlier in the alliance and when these expectations are disconfirmed, managers often must reconsider the level and type of investment required to sustain the alliance.

In other instances, the alliance could be progressing according to plan or is doing better than expected and one partner wants to increase its stake in the alliance to further enhance the alliance's development. The other partner is content with the status quo, however, and does not re-gard the alliance with the same sense of importance. As a result, it is un-willing to make the same level of investment. The investment decision hinges to some degree on the alliance being considered more central to the future strategy of one partner than the other. Ciba Geigy and Corning faced such a problem with their medical diagnostics joint venture—Ciba Corning Diagnostics. Simply, what was considered a small investment to Ciba was a large investment to Corning. This is particularly true given that the diagnostics business was positioned by Ciba to be a complement to its core pharmaceutical business and that the business was not a core business to Corning. As a result, the JV had to unilaterally meet Corning's financial goals. Tension grew as a result of the lack of alignment in goals although the relationship between the alliance partners was excellent. Tension is natural because priorities can change over time and each partner is subject to different kinds of static and pressures. In fact, the discussion of static in Chapter 5 suggests that changes in circumstances and strategic direction are not uncommon.

Stabilization

This final stage suggests that the alliance has passed through major crises and is on track. Through this stage there are minor adjustments needed to maintain both speed and direction as alliance managers navigate the alliance's course. Again, measuring the performance of the alliance against targets and milestones becomes a major concern of managers. It is well known that what is measured is important and what is important gets done. It is essential that the metrics reflect both quantitative and qualitative aspects of performance. While we advocate hard measures like sales, return on assets, or market share, we know that alliances also are vehicles by which companies learn and there should be a set of outcomes associated with learning. At the same time, although these measures are softer, they are no less important. Beyond these softer measures, one must address issues related to our belief that alliances are open-ended contracts. Metrics should be adaptable because it is likely that aspects of the alliance will change. Also, there is an ebb and flow to the outcomes used to calibrate success. Partners might not share equally in the bounty of the alliance at any moment in time but over time there should be equitable treatment based on the initial alliance agreement. Again, the incentive structure should reflect the objectives and intent of the alliance. If the goal is to gain market presence, performance metrics should reflect market penetration and numbers of new customers, or market share and bonuses should be tied to the same set of metrics. A final issue is the

Table 6.3   How Alliances End★

Termination of an alliance	Planned vs. unplanned.
	Friendly vs. unfriendly.
	Both agree vs. one objects.
Outcome of the termination	Termination by acquisition.
	Termination by dissolution.
	Termination by reorganization or restructuring.

★ Adapted from Serapio and Cascio, 1996.

duration of time at which measures should be taken. If the equilibrium point is longer to reach than the measurement cycle allows, it might appear that one partner is advantaged over the other simply because the timing was wrong.

This stage carries the alliance through maturity and into decline. Alliances fall or become less productive and managers must decide whether to continue to invest in a declining venture. Alliances end for several reasons:[3] (1) The alliance was not successful; (2) There were differences between partners (e.g., objectives, values, management incompatibility); (3) Limits were stated in the breadth of agreement; (4) The alliance is no longer aligned with partners' objectives; (5) Other opportunities exist or resources need to be reallocated; and (6) The alliance has met its goals. In all cases, alliances can end according to three scenarios and can have three possible outcomes. These are summarized in Table 6.3.

As would be expected, partners should consider certain legal issues such as those captured in most exit clauses: conditions of termination, dispositions of assets and liabilities, and dispute resolution mechanisms. We will address issues relative to decline and exit in Chapter 7. Our rationale is that it is the process that leads to exit that is important and warrants a separate discussion. We will subsume that discussion under the *No Blame Review*© that follows in Chapter 7.

Summary

This chapter has traced the different stages through which alliances pass during their development. These stages are independent of the productive life of the alliance. Built on a biological metaphor, all alliances must pass through each stage as they progress from birth to death. In general, we believe there is value gained by understanding the complex set of interactions at each stage. We have presented the key activities performed as well as the key concerns that surface during each stage. There is a interplay of business activities, people, and processes. Through this presentation we have provided a more robust picture of that complex interaction and have narrowed the gap between alliance formation and alliance management. Our position is that alliances tend to fail at least as much because of poor management as because of flawed strategy.

In addition, we demonstrate that one cannot focus exclusively on the business logic of the alliance to the exclusion of the relationship. After all, alliances are about people and relationships. In the next chapter, we discuss how to address problems that arise. Conflict and tension among alliance partners are natural occurrences and exist even in the best of alliances. The question is not whether there is conflict; the real question is whether the level of conflict is detrimental to the future success of the relationship. Chapter 7 presents a mechanism for resolving conflict.

APPENDIX

Thinking Critically about Alliances: Important Questions for Alliance Partners

Anticipating

- How will we draw in and motivate people who are critical to the alliance's success?
- How can the strategic sponsors of the alliance demonstrate their enthusiasm for (and commitment to) the alliance?
- Are we doing the alliance for sound business reasons, for emotional reasons, or for other reasons?
- Do we start small and build up, or do we go for the whole thing at once?
- What rumors are making the rounds, and how do we manage them?
- Is our rationale commonly understood and shared?

Engaging

- Will there be external lawyers, consultants, or others involved in the alliance? What will their role be? Who are they working for?
- Can we find early wins to build momentum?
- What kind of training will people need?
- What are the key roles that we will need people to play? Who will fill those roles?

Valuing

- How can we create face-to-face time for key individuals from all partner companies?
- How can we create cross-functional participation?
- Do we really trust our partners' expertise enough to let them control some things?

- How can we involve the people "in the trenches"?
- If it takes longer than we expect, are we willing to wait for this to come together?
- How can we ensure that critical issues don't get hidden or ignored?

Coordinating

- Have we created strong interface points? Are we communicating regularly?
- Are people spending face-to-face time together?
- Are people from many different functions involved?
- What are we doing to rally the people "in the trenches?"
- Do we have enough energy to face difficult times?
- Does the company "buy in" to this alliance?
- Are we giving relationships enough time to develop?
- Do we have the trust of our partner?
- Are we regularly reviewing our progress?

Investing

- Are we willing to make hard choices? Are we communicating those choices to our partners? Do we know the choices they are facing?
- Can we live with the choices we must make? Can our partners?
- Assuming some will win and some will lose with these choices, have we planned how to manage their reactions?
- Are we willing to compromise for the sake of this alliance?
- Are we contributing as much as we are getting back?
- How fast will we expand? Are we poised to build on the alliance capabilities?
- How do investments in this alliance affect other alliances in our portfolio?

Stabilizing

- How does this alliance fit in with our company's business? Are we maintaining it for cash? For technology? For market access?

- Are we making the most of the trust and interdependence we have built with our partners?
- Are we addressing issues as they arise?
- Should this alliance be a stand-alone business?
- Are we letting our alliance managers run the business?

7

Conflict Resolution and the No Blame Review

Strategic alliances are a paradox: considerable effort is needed to generate strong returns on the investment, but the odds of achieving those results are poor. Alliances take a great deal of hard work, often in excess of any-one's expectations. If done well, the effort pays off. Alliances are profitable ventures, earning at a rate higher than comparable U.S. industry averages, such as the overall Fortune 500, and having a higher rate of success than do either mergers or acquisitions.[1] To further build the case, more experienced alliance firms earn at a rate twice that of their inexperienced counterparts.[2] However, the probability of achieving success in an alliance is low. High failure rates in alliances have already been discussed in previous chapters. How does a manager make sense of this paradox? The answer is simple and endemic to the nature of alliances. The natural tensions facing partners must be tackled through joint efforts for the good of the alliance; yet, the natural tendency is for firms to act in their own self-interest. Conflict is a natural part of the process.

Nothing ensures that an alliance will be conflict-free over its life-time. Fitting and aligning goals and objectives, screening for the right partner, and developing a mutually agreed-to plan of action, are all important steps of the alliance-building process, but only go so far. Pressures may arise from partners' attempts, even unwittingly, to further their own self-interests; the environment continues to change, and this change often challenges the basic premise/business proposition on which the

163

alliance was based. Thus, the issue is not whether conflict exists. The issue is how serious is the conflict and will it lead to a suboptimal outcome?

The purpose of this chapter is to explore the causes of conflict and to help managers appreciate better those mechanisms that facilitate conflict resolution. From the outset, one should realize that conflict resolution does not ensure a sustained relationship. Successful resolution might be alliance dissolution. One often does not recognize that since potential partners stand in the wings, ready to draw conclusions from one's past actions in other alliances, the process of conflict resolution is far more important than the outcome. Others watch how alliances unfold and draw conclusions about the desirability of potential partners. Future decisions to partner are made on the observation of past behavior.

This chapter presents processes to help manage conflict and achieve those outcomes both desired by both partners and optimal for the alliance. Before discussing steps at conflict resolution, conflict needs to be understood, specifically, what it is, what it does, and what its sources in an alliance context might be. Then, different approaches to conflict resolution are discussed, compared, and contrasted. Special attention is given to the No Blame Review©, a process through which partners tackle the most serious issues. Finally, the chapter raises the issues associated with exit clauses and the use of these *prenuptial* agreements as part of the alliance negotiation process.

The Different Sides of Conflict

Conflict is a multifaceted phenomenon, especially in an alliance context. At its best, conflict in alliances can be beneficial, by propelling the alliance positively forward and by building stronger foundations. Conflict achieves this purpose because it raises issues, encourages innovative problem-solving, points out significant differences of opinion, or clarifies true goals and objectives. In this way, conflict encourages and supports the identification and resolution of potentially devisive issues.

When approached with caution, conflict can:

- Bring problems to light where they can be discussed.
- Bring a fresh perspective to an old problem.
- Generate new ideas and creative approaches.

- Allow alliance members to clear the air.
- Lead to greater harmony and productivity.
- Cause alliance members to self-examine and reflect on their actions, motivations, goals.
- Bring better clarity to the problems facing one's partners.

At its worst, conflict is damaging to alliance stability and performance. Conflict can easily render one rival network of companies less competitive relative to other networks.[3] The productive benefits derived from conflict diminish and the results of conflict become severe, putting at risk both the performance and continued well-being of the alliance.

While there are no guarantees, a careful and systematic approach to conflict encourages the benefits to emerge.[4] The inverted "U"-shaped relationship between conflict and performance means that there is a vast area in which conflict can be beneficial, not detrimental. Said another way, conflict is to be expected, but its damaging effects need not come into play immediately. When two autonomous firms agree to share decision making, thereby relinquishing some of their independence and sovereignty, conflict is a likely outcome. Because change is likely to occur as the alliance matures, it is natural to expect that partners will not be affected to the same degree or with the same level of severity. At the same time, partners' goals and objectives change over time, and it is not uncommon to find misalignment in the future needs and direction of the alliance partners. Conflict is difficult to avoid, what becomes most important is how to manage it.

The No Blame Review

While alliances partners ordinarily have regular board meetings and progress/status reviews, there are occasions in which something more is needed. Situations arise where standard review processes are not adequate and a more specific and orchestrated review process is required. That special process is called the No Blame Review (NBR). As the name implies, the NBR is a collaborative process of conflict resolution, during which fault or blame is completely absent. The goal is to create an objective, nonthreatening, and non-value-laden opportunity for alliance managers and sponsors on both sides to raise, explore, and review serious issues and dilemmas. Think of it as an elaborate pulse check that spans both strategic and tactical issues. It is a state-of-the-alliance review.

The No Blame Review Is Not . . .

There are two things the No Blame Review is not. First of all, the review is not the time or the place to raise accusations, introduce disarming surprises, and judge or evaluate actions or outcomes. It is not an opportunity to raise challenges or present ultimatums. It involves clear, precise, and nonevaluative conversation with the emphasis on listening, understanding, and exploring. Second, a NBR is not business as usual or a routine event. Done too often, the NBR loses its impact and becomes just another one of the alliance conversations. The NBR is most effective before a crisis reaches a head and is ready to erupt. During crisis, pressures can be too great, the temptation for a quick fix too strong, and the tendency to focus on the symptoms and not the root cause of the conflict too likely.

Beyond crisis situations, the NBR is intended for periods when significant challenges, either positive or negative, are apparent. Both crisis and severe challenges are likely to impact the future course and scope of the relationship. The NBR is a normal, albeit special, part of the alliance management process. Knowing when the time is ripe for a No Blame Review becomes a critical determination. Experienced alliance managers understand the whys, whens, whos, and how of this review. It is a periodic guide to the alliance; a process to correct the course of the alliance; and a mechanism for change. It offers the opportunity to check the alliance's vital signs and to make a determination that all systems are in alignment. Table 7.1 outlines the key dimensions of the No Blame Review.

Indications for a No Blame Review

There are no typical times or reasons to conduct the No Blame Review. Any sources of static, areas of disagreement cited, or unexplained or unexplainable internal actions on the part of alliance personnel might prompt this type of review. Independent of a particular incident, an NBR might be warranted if some of these signs and signals are present:

- One partner is talking more *about* the other than *to* the other.
- One partner believes strongly that hidden agendas are behind the activities and actions of their partner.

Table 7.1   A No-Blame Review: Purpose and Process

What is it?	Joint review by alliance managers on behalf of sponsors. Simple, direct, candid, objective discussions of the alliance.
When?	At critical event times. Times that mark significant change in the direction of the alliance. Events that are either an opportunity or a threat.
Who?	Alliance managers only (sponsors might attend). Staff, consultants, counsel, facilitators are available but do not attend.
Where?	Neutral, off-site location. Atmosphere conducive to both work and social time.
Before the meeting consider	Alliance progress to date and how it tracks with original strategy and objectives. What is important to you, the alliance manager. What is important to your company, your partner's company. Alliance's shortcomings, successes. What issues concern you about the alliance. Where you would like the alliance to be heading.
Ground rules	Accept that there is no blame here. Establish an atmosphere of confidentiality. Engage in simple, direct, objective conversation. Process and outcome are both important. Lay cards face up on the table—no hidden agenda. Listen without judgment. Identify open issues. Celebrate success and failure—this is an opportunity to learn.
Possible outcomes	Validate current strategy. Readjust strategy. Agree on how the relationship should work. Recommit to the business goals and objectives. Recommit to the relationship goals and objectives. Identify key milestones moving forward. Agree to termination and the process for dissolving the alliance.

- One or both sides of the alliance experience a general sense of malaise.

- The alliance is experiencing an unexpected strategic shift, strong and unmanageable static, or upheaval beyond its usual ebbs and flows.

- Alliance managers are not meeting regularly, are engaged in serious interpersonal conflict themselves, or are not communicating well enough.

- Either partner is dissatisfied with the results of the collaboration, particularly if one partner is consistently extracting more value than the other.

- The strategic intent on the part of either or both the partners has significantly changed. There is a feeling that goals are no longer compatible.

- One partner actively begins to court other alliance partners to do the same work.

While this list is not exhaustive, it suggests that the underlying need for an NBR is a perceived or felt sense that "something is not right or about to not be right in the alliance." One natural time for an NBR is when partners face investment decisions or must commit additional assets and feel that the alliance might be facing a watershed or turning point. There exists an uneasiness about future events and there exists a need to recommit to the relationship. The ensuing discomfort might signal the need for an NBR.

The Setting of the NBR Matters

Because the NBR is a discussion with a serious purpose, every step needs to be orchestrated to ensure open and honest dialogue and keep both partners "at ease." This begins with *where* the meetings are held and *who* is in attendance. First of all, a neutral, off-site location is best. Partners need to be away from pressures that might bias the objective nature of the process and/or might distract their attention. Conducting the review at either partner's headquarters, a location associated with other alliance meetings, or a setting inconvenient or uncomfortable to one of the partners, in a very subtle way, can create the wrong atmosphere. In addition, conducting the review where there are few opportunities for social as well as business time increases the likelihood for disaster. Especially in highly charged situations, alliance managers need time to relax and see each other in more personal settings. These occasions contribute greatly to trust, or allow partners to partly bridge the gap that results from a breach of trust. Alliances are about relationships, not just business.

Second, the NBR is for the alliance principals only; the key alliance managers. This does not include extra staff, lawyers, consultants, or outsiders. Sponsors might attend parts of the meeting if endorsements and/or corporate commitments are needed beyond that for which the alliance manager is responsible or can muster the requisite resources. The reason is simple. The individuals involved, by conducting the conversation without assistance, have to struggle with understanding and be accountable for what they say and do. At some point, the two individuals who are ultimately responsible for the alliance need to close the door and talk alone. Additional people bring additional agendas and perspectives that could work against, rather than for, the communication between the principals. If, in the end, the alliance managers cannot communicate with one another and be understood, the alliance has a very serious problem; relationship is the glue that holds the alliance together. However, staff and others can help prepare each of their respective principals although they do not participate in the actual meetings.

Preparation Is Essential

Although the NBR is designed to encourage spontaneous conversation, such conversation cannot happen unless both partners clarify first their own issues and concerns. Each must first understand what is happening in their own organization. Reviewing alliance progress to date vis-à-vis your company, and comparing that progress to expectations is each partner's first preparation step. Part of realizing whether the alliance is offcourse is knowing the intended course set at the start of the alliance. This includes a full disclosure of current issues and concerns, as well as favored desires for the direction of the future of the alliance. One goal is to make the discussion as fact based as possible. Sharing information so that both parties have the same access to information is an NBR hallmark.

Another aspect of preparation is a candid assessment of your company's strengths and weaknesses as a partner in this alliance. Reassessing congruence with the original strategic intent means knowing what each partner does well, fails to do well, needs, or is managing for the alliance. Only under these circumstances does a comparison to what is received, desired, actually given, or received make sense. Although the actual NBR has limited participation, the gathering of information and data can and should include others in the alliance. Staff can, and should, assist in preparation but should not participate in the actual meetings.

To the extent that corporate politics exist, they should be excluded from the discussion. All organizations of any significant size naturally have complex political interactions. Managers and staff people have somewhat different agendas as well as turfs and powerbases to protect. To limit the NBR to those who have direct responsibility for the alliance removes extraneous noise and corporate politics from the true issues affecting the alliance. Whenever possible, internal politics should be addressed offline. These issues can be a distraction and can easily derail the focus of the NBR.

Part of the process must attend to the alliance managers' own aspirations and goals. Many times, actions taken (or interpreted) in an alliance reflect the career development of the alliance managers. Should either manager need this alliance to succeed for promotion, or have a career stake in the outcome, or be "under the gun" to produce or not fail, these motives can directly affect the alliance. It would be naïve to ignore these personal factors and believe that political and personal agendas are not part of the process. Having each partner knowledgeable, if not understanding of the meaning of the alliance position to their colleague, may not ameliorate difficulties, but it may shed additional light on actions and preferences.

The Meeting Is About Facts and Feelings

The meeting itself needs ground rules. The NBR is not a cause for either partner to dredge up long-held grudges. It is not "who did what to whom when." The simple, direct and objective conversation, based on facts not innuendoes and suppositions, depends on strict confidentiality. What is said in the meeting and how it is said remain there. As much as possible, this is a time to surface all issues and to strive to be open and honest. With that comes the responsibility of the listening partner not to jump prematurely to conclusions. Especially if one partner is raising issues that threaten the other, staying nonjudgmental is essential, hard work, and energy draining. Staying fact based and allowing emotional release helps ensure full disclosure of information.

Many Results Are Possible

Just as the NBR is as much about process as content, the results are more about what was discussed than what was decided. However, the outcome of the NBR is important. Many results are conceivable, depending on the desire of the partners and the outcome of the process. One outcome is revalidation or slight readjustment of the alliance strategy. There might also be minor refinements in how the partners work together. They might affect changes in infrastructure or governance. Both might affect alignment between partners to achieve better results. On the other hand, the final decision could include an agreement to terminate the relationship. The difficulties may be beyond repair, or the strategic rationale may be so changed or undermined that moving forward is senseless. This could be a positive outcome since, in its current state, opportunities were lost and dollars squandered trying to salvage a poor, ineffective alliance. Ending an alliance is not a bad thing—it makes no sense to spend good money after bad. Simply, the range of outcomes are many and often the outcome becomes known only after the process begins. Having a preconceived idea of outcomes will shortchange the process and limit an open and honest exchange.

NBR Ground Rules Have Broader Relevance

Although the NBR is reserved for critical alliance events, the spirit in which the NBR is conducted can be used to frame other discussions of a more targeted nature when problems of a more specific nature occur during the alliance. Recently, we worked with partners who were experiencing difficulty in one project of a multifaceted buyer-supplier alliance. These firms were engaged in projects aimed at both reducing the total cost of ownership and leveraging each other's skills to improve both firms' competitive position. Problems in one project were affecting the level of trust in the larger relationship because of the corporate attention received and the overlap in people assigned to the project. The basic tenets of the NBR serve as the guide for their discussion. By establishing the same nonevaluative ground rules, the partners were better able to engage each other, talk more honestly, and move beyond the name calling to realize that both had different sets of expectations regarding the other's involvement in the project.

Trust Anchors the NBR and Any Conflict Resolution

Trust is fundamental to the context of effective conflict resolution[5] and especially the No Blame Review. Trust represents one partner's willingness to risk increased vulnerability to another because of confidence that the other will not exploit the situation. Expectations of such fair treatment help partners enter the conflict resolution process feeling safe in arguing a win-win solution.

When trust is strong, there is a natural tendency for each partner to understand and take the perspective of the other. Shared values and a sense of interdependence, characteristic of heightened levels of trust, encourage the risk-taking behavior often required for the creative solutions to some alliance issues. Risk-taking behavior might entail a willingness to make concessions for the well-being of the alliance, share information in the spirit of attaining a win-win solution, or forfeit an opportunity to compete. Without trust, any actions such as those above could be considered conciliatory and interpreted as a sign of weakness. With trust, however, each partner knows that the actions are being made in the interest of the alliance.

Trust is important between partners and trust is also critical between the alliance manager (AM) and other key company stakeholders. Alliance managers, as individuals, have to be seen as credible and trustworthy if they are to be effective in their boundary-spanning role. Credibility must exist both within the firm and with one's partners. Alliance managers must be seen as honest brokers. Without a strong foundation of trust, others can question an alliance manager's motivation and loyalty.

It is not uncommon for people internal to the firm to ask where the loyalty of the alliance manager lies—does he side with the company or with the alliance. This dynamic can be especially salient if the alliance is a joint venture. Partners without trust tend to monitor and attempt to control the actions of the alliance team. Not only do these actions decrease the credibility of the alliance manager, they have the potential to adversely affect the alliance itself. Also, such monitoring adds to the costs of running the alliance—it could diminish its effectiveness.

The alliance manager (AM) works for the parent company and is responsible to the parent for the performance of the alliance. The AM is committed to the performance of the alliance as part of the parent's strategy. The general manager of a JV is 100 percent responsible for the performance of the JV as directed by the parents through the alliance managers.

In Conflict Resolution There Are Better and Worse Ways

The actions taken to resolve conflict matter. Table 7.2 summarizes conflict resolution techniques most frequently cited by our global alliance sample. Those approaches used successfully most often require a basis of trust and a desire to reach an even-handed resolution. Joint problem-solving based on equal access to information is a desirable approach to conflict resolution. At the opposite extreme, the least frequently used and least effective conflict resolution techniques involve lawyers and rely on the contract to reach resolution.

While contract negotiation is an important part of the alliance formulation process, relying on those contractual stipulations to resolve conflicts is not helpful in the long term. Alliances are about business and relationships, not about contracts. Once the contract is pulled from the file drawer, the alliance is in serious straits. The alliance is also in trouble if principals are using harsh words or veiled threats.

Finally, using mediators can hurt, not help, alliance conflict resolution. Although mediators are extremely valuable in many conflictual situations, their use within an alliance context adds an element of complexity because of the introduction of a third party to the alliance. That involvement could be sufficient to change the dynamics of the relationship. Equally as important is the symbolism associated with using mediators. Their

Table 7.2   Conflict Resolution Techniques

Most Effective Techniques	Least Effective Techniques
Working hard to resolve problems.	Using external mediators.
Talking openly and honestly.	Resorting to harsh words.
Joint problem solving.	Having lawyers craft solutions.
Trying to convince partners.	Referring to contracts for remedy.

involvement might be seen as taking responsibility for conflict resolution out of the hands of those directly responsible for managing the alliance. Alliance managers must take responsibility for conflict resolution; they cannot abrogate that responsibility. Successful alliance management takes hard work and requires the commitment of the partners; the manner in which conflicts are resolved should be consistent with this perspective. Relying on the recommendations/input of a mediator removes the much needed conversation that is a hallmark of the NBR.

Areas of Disagreement Are Many

The areas of potential disagreement in alliances are many. The following list summarizes our findings regarding the reasons for disagreement among alliance partners:[6]

- One partner competes with the alliance.
- Partner is acting in self-interest.
- Resources are not shared equally.
- Partner does not see from our perspective.
- Benefits are not shared equally.
- Partner does not focus beyond own problems.
- Goals are incompatible in scale and scope.
- One partner gives poor support to the alliance.

These sources of conflict have the potential to strike the very heart of the alliance's core values—its spirit. Self-serving behavior and the absence of fair dealing diminish commitment and undermine trust in a way that may be beyond repair. It should not be surprising, therefore, that across these reasons, alliance managers report lower levels of satisfaction with their alliance's performance when these are the areas of disagreement. Opportunism lies at the heart of these sources of conflict and violate a fundamental understanding of what it means to partner.

Alliances Thrive on Diversity but Diversity Breeds Conflict

A major tenet for partner selection is to select a partner who has different, or complementary skills. An overlap, or redundancy, in value-adding capability will detract from the advantages of the alliance. By combining complementary skills, the alliance is likely to be more competitive and sustainable. Yet, within this diversity might lie the seeds for conflict based, in part, on these sought-after differences. These differences provide the raison d'être of the alliance and the resultant interdependence becomes the foundation for alliance development and growth. Often this form of diversity can be inventoried and partners can be evaluated on the extent to which they complement one another. Over time, however, one partner can learn and acquire some of the skills/competence of the other thereby destabilizing the alliance. One's attractiveness as an alliance partner erodes in direct proportion to the other's ability to learn. If both partners do not invest in continually strengthening their skills and competencies, the alliance will languish and the synergies will become less attractive. Alliance management is a dynamic process, and both partners must work to sustain its growth.

The second form of diversity relates to the innate differences that exist between partners. These differences often relate to differences in culture and are acute as one engages in global alliances and joint ventures. The differences in national cultures are profound and have become the topic of many a seminar titled "Doing Business in . . . [insert the country of your choice]." Here, the effects of time are positive. At the outset, these differences tend to pull partners apart. However, the learning (and the tolerance) that occurs over time tends to strengthen the partnership. Partners develop better coping skills, understand each other better over time, become more adaptive to the unique differences that partners potentially bring to the relationship, and develop greater trust. All these behaviors are essential to improving the performance of the alliance. Certainly, all contribute to the longevity of the relationship, but longevity is not a surrogate for performance.

Diversity among global partners exists on several levels as summarized in Table 7.3. While each can be discussed separately, they are interrelated. For example, societal norms permeate each of the other forms of culture and comprise the bedrock of how people interact and interpret the world. Diversity can be found at the operating level and often relates to structural and process-related factors. Management styles, decision-making processes, the extent to which planning is done formally, all can affect the nature of the alliance. An obvious example is the joint venture between GM and Toyota, NUMMI, where cars are jointly produced in the United States for domestic sales. The differences

Table 7.3 Dimensions of Diversity between Companies*

Dimension of Diversity	Definition	Example
Societal	Basic cultural differences found between cultures that affect norms, values, and beliefs.	Certain cultures value the individual over the group (e.g., U.S. vs. Japan) and such norms set the tone for all interactions.
National	Differences relating to laws, regulations, the manner in which firms compete and cooperate.	In Europe, cooperation has been hampered by cultural and linguistic differences. More serious is the protectionist and nationalistic views of many governments.
Corporate	Differences relating to the firm and its unique properties. The impact of societal and national factors cannot be isolated.	If one compares U.S. and Asian firms, a notable difference is the consideration of time. U.S. managers are notoriously impatient: Building relations takes time and let's get on with it. The need for short-term results drives decision making more than it does Asian expectations for alliance results.
Operating level	Issues affecting implementation and the processes by which the alliance would operate. Planning, control, decision-making styles are all important.	Questions of rewards, compensation, and decision-making responsibility often highlight differences across global alliances. Other cultures are far more egalitarian than that in the U.S. Differences in compensation between senior managers and line workers are but one indication.

* Adapted from Arvind Parkhe, "Interfirm Diversity, Organizational Learning, and Longevity in Global Strategic Alliances," *Journal of International Business Studies 22,* 4 (1991): 579–602.

between the Japanese and U.S. management styles have been well documented as is the dissimilarity in the two cultures. Yet, this diversity was pursued as a opportunity for each company to learn from the other. The results have been mixed in that the Japanese, by most accounts, have gained from the experience more than GM.

The relationship between diversity and performance is complex. Diversity encourages firms to unite because of the complementarity of skills; yet, these differences pull the alliance apart. Performance, and the health of the alliance, can improve over time as partners learn more about each other's unique culture and grow to appreciate and value these differences. Cross-cultural training and other means for learning to adapt to diversity help build bridges between partners. Flexibility in how partners shape the direction of the alliance reduces potential conflict situations because it shows both commitment and trust. At the same time, managing diversity between partners is a significant challenge and requires hard work and senior management attention.

Small-scale alliance projects that have a finite life and purpose tend to minimize conflict as the objective of the alliance is built on the current skills and capabilities of both partners. It is possible that by the time learning has occurred, the alliance has run its course, and there is little or no negative impact on the alliance. The point to be made is that learning can have both a positive and negative impact on the performance of an alliance. The advantages of learning about the culture, norms, and values of one's global partner far outweigh the possibility that technical capability transfers from one partner to the other thereby diminishing the impact of the alliance. If companies can become more knowledgeable of, sensitive to, and accepting of the diversity that is part of global work, companies become better alliance partners and ultimately are likely to be more successful competitors.

Lewis[7] classifies cultures into different categories and suggests that these differences both affect how managers from these countries view the world and interact. Task-oriented cultures emphasize planning, organizing, and linear thinking. The adage of "time is money" is typical of how these western European and North American managers approach business dealings. These managers fly in for the alliance meeting, want to ink the deal, and fly back to the United States. People-oriented cultures, like those found in the Arab world and Latin America, stress personal relationships and tend to be more emotional in their business dealings. Respect oriented cultures, illustrated by China and Japan, are characterized by conflict avoidance, listening, saving face, and displaying patience. These Asian cultures view time as being in unlimited supply and disagreements are to be avoided. Think about the U.S. manager who jets in and out and the potential clash with these other cultures. A manager who is aware of the differences among cultural types, can more easily navigate the potential problems and often can reach mutually beneficial agreements.

When there is similarity between cultures, conflict situations can be avoided. In fact, similarity does lead to a more cooperative and integrative approach to problem solving. Absent similarity, parties tend to rely more on formal mechanisms, such as contracts, which would indicate a breakdown in trust. Forcing a more legalistic solution diminishes the information exchanged, often leads to lower performance, and could aggravate, not solve, the problem. A study of U.S. and Chinese joint ventures revealed that similarity in cultures improved problem solving; however, power differences between parties resulted in a more one-sided solution and forced a compromise (often as a consequence of more legalistic approaches).[8] Both compromise and a one-sided solution had a negative effect on JV performance.

Our data, summarized in Figure 7.1, indicates that longer lived alliances are less prone to conflict in general. The findings show an interesting effect that might occur over time; engaging in self-serving behavior is the highest area for potential conflict independent of the age of the alliance. Opportunism is followed very closely by factors related to the allocation of resources and the assignment of risk/reward. In both instances, these factors are more serious in longer term alliances than

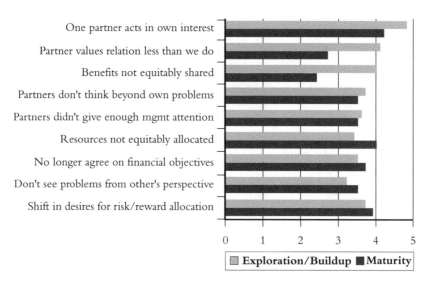

Figure 7.1   Stages by conflict areas.

they are in shorter lived alliances. One explanation is that in mature relationships, where the opportunity for growth is less, partners might begin to quarrel over how to slice the remaining pie and the decision rule for one partner might change once the alliance is in the mature stages. As long as rising tides raise all ships, conflict is probably held in check.

Conflict in the previous example stems from a feeling that one partner is benefiting from the alliance in excess to its contribution or that a sense of fair dealing has been violated. The diversity that breeds global alliances and joint ventures also is subject to problems in governance that can lead to heightened conflict. The shared decision-making model under which the joint venture must operate adds tension and bargaining costs to the process for resolving disputes. Unless a unified command and control mechanism is used for making decisions by fiat and authority relationships, JVs rely both on the alliance agreement and on the ability to resolve conflicts harmoniously.

The challenge facing alliance managers is to avoid the "us versus them" factionalism that can so naturally occur when managers attempt to solve problems in the JV. One cannot ignore the political realities of working in a joint venture and the conflict that can result. Carried to their extreme, political pressure and power attempts to reduce conflict run counter to the fundamental principles of alliances. Given the tendency for such situations to polarize, the costs are high and managers will revert to hard influence tactics (i.e., power attempts are manipulative in nature) that might lead to compliance but never commitment.[9] These attempts may fuel the conflict and are less likely to result in long-lasting positive outcomes. The following list highlights the generally accepted approaches for conflict resolution:

- Be aware of cultural differences, beliefs, and values.
- Hold one-on-one discussions early to encourage positive interaction.
- Set ground rules for an open dialogue.
- Listen carefully and don't get defensive.
- Focus on the problem not the person.
- Do not use inflammatory language.
- Keep a record of the discussion.
- Focus on the common ground, goals, and areas of agreement.

- Try to reach consensus on a solution.
- Communicate, communicate, communicate.

To let conflict go unresolved will affect the level of trust between partners. Since the harder influence tactics are less focused on reciprocity, open communications, and other strategies that enhance high-quality decisions, the conflict can spiral and damage the overall effectiveness of the venture. Conflicts spiral[10] when an attempt at resolution fails and contentious communications from one party are repeated by the other and so on. Since these events often have a core of hostility, the thought of mutually beneficial gain, or a win-win solution is far from the minds of the alliance players. Although no agreement may be reached, when one does occur it tends to be one sided. If such a solution is reached, it is likely to inflict long-term damage. This kind of damage is never fully repaired since the underlying basis of trust has been questioned.

The question is then how to avoid a conflict spiral. First, do not start; partner should not respond to contentious communications in kind. Easy to say; not easy to do; the natural inclination is to respond in kind. Acting out of emotion does little to cool the embers of conflict. Once the spiral has started, what can be done to stop its continuation? Brett and her colleagues suggest that it is prudent to force the discussion away from the dysfunctional behavior that gave rise to the conflict. Refocusing the discussion neutralizes conflictual behavior because parties begin to emphasize commonalities rather than differences. Without a fundamental level of trust between parties, any attempt to resolve conflict will be suboptimal. Conflict and conflict resolution cannot be discussed independent of trust; it plays a central role in managing conflict.

Termination of the Alliance and the Use of Exit Clauses

Alliances end at some point. Anticipated benefits are unattained or no longer available. Other alliances meet and achieve goals and objectives, reducing the needs of partners for the relationship. Similarly, priorities change, new markets or technology fail to develop, or conflict in the alliance reaches a counterproductive level and the alliance derails. While the reasons are many, termination is as natural to alliances as is their inception. The point is not that alliances may end or dissolve. The relevant issue is preparation for such an eventuality.

The decision to consider dissolution is often not easy or straightforward nor is it taken without considerable thought. The following list summarizes the types of questions to be considered when and if termination of the alliance becomes *the* option of choice:

- What assets and resources did each being to the alliance?
- What was the fair market value of these resources?
- What is the present value of each partner's contribution?
- How will future value be determined?
- Have we developed a process to ensure that assets have been distribute fairly?
- What happens if partners have not contributed equally to future gains?
- What proprietary knowledge, assets, skills did each bring to the alliance?
- Who owns what now? What contribution has each made?
- Have patents, copyrights, licenses been protected?
- Are royalty or licensing fees in order? For what?
- Have markets/customers/geography been allocated fairly?
- Is there a need for noncompete, nondisclosure, or other agreements to protect partners from expropriation, free-riding, or using learning to own advantage?
- Is there a concern for employees to move between firms? Should it be limited?
- What will be the consequence of my former partner allying with a key competitor?

The purpose of such questions is to ensure each partner independently understands the potential consequences and ramifications of unbundling the alliance. Ideally, these questions would have been formulated, asked, and addressed during periodic review sessions, especially during a No Blame Review. Perhaps the result of an NBR is the decision to terminate the alliance. Whatever the precipitating motivation, thinking through strategies and implications is wise, and it may even be wise *before* the alliance forms.

The Case for Exit Clauses

Establishing exit clauses (often referred to as prenuptial agreements) as part of the initial alliance agreement has merits. The first is the potential to establish ground rules and the terms of exit at the outset, thereby avoiding any messy, time consuming conflict when the alliance ends and the "spoils" are divided. Despite the admonition that alliance managers commit to the relationship for the long term, the harsh reality is that alliances end and partners must ensure the protection of their interests. It would be naïve to assume otherwise and such preparation is just good planning. Establishing a process to dissolve the alliance in the midst of conflict and unrest is likely to result in an emotionally charged, self-serving effort by the partners. Therefore, thinking through collaboratively and agreeing unilaterally to circumstances and procedures under which the alliance would terminate makes sense. Without the bitter reality of exit, partners could be better able to establish ownership rights/obligations, the value of assets and other property, and the disposal of patents, copyrights, and the like. To settle claims while partners are still in the honeymoon phase of the alliance removes the tension of having to deal in the moment.

Another reason supporting exit clauses involves protection. Some partners may want to protect what they contribute to the alliance from the very beginning. If partners are concerned about preserving their intellectual capital, patents, and other forms of tacit knowledge, the inclusion of a noncompete clause, should the alliance dissolve, makes good business sense. Engaging in such a conversation provides the opportunity for each partner to leverage capabilities and to set limits and expectations. Corporate lawyers will argue that exit clauses can avoid costly litigation later on, thereby minimizing the downside risk of the alliance. Certainly, the element of surprise is eliminated.

The Case against Exit Clauses

While clear-headed and advanced thinking is laudable, exit clauses have their downsides. Often not enough information is available to be objective and open about. It is impossible to know in advance the circumstances affecting the value of assets or the intellectual content of projects yet to be enacted. When the alliance is an experimental probe into a new technology, forecasting becomes more of an art, fraught with assumptions that render the exercise ultimately flawed. Under these circumstances, searching for a precise solution to a yet undetermined problem seems pointless. More beneficial and useful might be the establishment of mechanisms and processes for determining value or for assigning ownership to intellectual property. In fact, committing to processes to dissolve the alliance is far more consistent with the principles of alliance management than attempting to assign a specific value to a future event or outcome.

Another compelling argument against exit clauses exists. Such effort and attention at the start of the alliance sends signals—potentially the wrong ones. After partners have selected each other based on extensive due diligence, built a sound business case, and started to build trust and commitment, an exit clause can introduce a sour note. Exit clauses are intended to protect each partner's interests and resources; yet, exit clauses can signify a lack of trust, raise the question of partners' future commitment, and suggest that future benefits and gains might not be distributed in accordance with the alliance spirit. The symbolism of the exit clause is important and should not be ignored. Contradictory messages are being sent that can affect the alliance's forward momentum and could have the unintended consequence of calling into question partners' true intent. If partners spend a great deal of effort on determining the future worth and the value attributed to each partner's contribution, the exercise can diminish the positive feelings both have regarding the alliance.

Finally, having exit clauses provides an immediate and acknowledged way out for the partners. It could become the default option. Rather than working hard to resolve conflicts, and committing to the maintenance and growth of the alliance, knowing there is a way out might, in some cases, encourage partners to exercise this option. The exit option could limit the partners' willingness to commit to the alliance. Cortés sent a strong message to his troops when he landed in the New World—there was no turning back, he burned his ships! Since commitment is a self-renewing process, any behavior that casts doubt on partners' willingness to work hard on behalf of the alliance could detract from the alliance's goals. The a priori development of an exit strategy can become a self-fulfilling prophecy.

The Case for Exit Processes

Exit processes (outlining and agreeing to a process of how to dissolve), focus on the best approach to the problem of exit clauses. Processes for managing alliance dissolution are more effective since precise valuation is a moving target and is dependent on many factors. If the assumptions employed at the outset are invalid and the partners attempt to use these assumptions to affix a specific value to a future outcome as part of the alliance contract, such efforts are misplaced. Rather, exit processes develop methodology to assign value to which all partners can agree. By agreeing to a process, partners acknowledge that uncertainty is a reality and cannot be easily controlled. Moreover, they are willing to jointly work to resolve what can become an emotionally and legally charged confrontation.

The exercise of thinking through future events, as part of the contracting processes, helps partners articulate and consider certain issues that might not surface normally during the process of alliance formation. If partners bring nothing but enthusiasm to the alliance, commit no hard assets, and join to develop a new technology or exploit a new market, there is nothing to protect. Having no baggage or prior commitment diminishes the need for exit clauses. An exit clause forces a decision on how to share and allocate the future rewards of the alliance. The calculus for determining future rewards is partially a function of the partners' risk profile and their future expectations. Certain issues do not become salient until one considers the worst-case scenario.

The No Blame Review Can Shape the Tone of the Decision

Concerns about exit clauses as part of the initial alliance agreement are bolstered by the power of the No Blame Review. Yes, there are potential problems associated with negotiating alliance dissolution in the heat of the moment. However, the NBR process sets the tone for the objective, open, and candid resolution of problems. Within the NBR framework, that alliance termination can be managed effectively. Partners can value assets and determine each one's contribution, and during the NBR partners can fairly calculate and articulate dissolution processes and mechanisms. There is less uncertainty, partners are not dealing with hypothetical events and allocations can be more fairly determined.

In general, exit clauses attempt to shape or control the element of risk partners face on alliance termination. There are second-order effects to consider as well. Attempts to mitigate risk can have unplanned and negative consequences. For example, the attempt to fix prices to minimize exposure could also affect the level of innovation generated in the alliance. A low price stifles innovation. Often, we do not think about whether the exit clauses carry unanticipated expectations that run counter to the intended purpose of the alliance. Alliances that are built to leverage the skills of partners could suboptimize their value if the exit clauses carries heavy restrictions about what is considered proprietary and what can and cannot be used by the individual partners on termination.

The debate continues and both positions have merit. The key points are summarized in Table 7.4. The negative signals can overwhelm the win-win philosophy of a strong alliance spirit. If partners are focused on setting exit clauses at the start of the alliance, why would they also not engage in self-serving behavior? Expectations are set early in the life of the alliance. Exit clauses set the stage for ease of exit, present a rationale for not committing to the alliance, and tend to detract from the partners' willingness to trust and invest for the long term.

Table 7.4   Exit Clauses or Not: Reasons For and Against

Reasons for Exit Clauses	Reasons Against
1. It is important to protect one's assets going into the relationship.	1. It sends the wrong signal.
2. Set value while partners are not at risk and are still committed to the alliance.	2. It gives partners a way out before they engage in the hard work of building the alliance.
3. The alliance will end; set expectations for dissolution early. It removes the element of surprise.	3. It demonstrates distrust and emphasizes the worst-case scenario.
4. It is just good planning.	4. In a subtle way, it takes responsibility away from the business people and gives power to the attorneys.
5. Our lawyers want us to do it!	5. It could sour the relationship at a stage when it is fragile and just building.
6. It minimizes the downside risk of the alliance.	6. It is impossible to calculate future value and worth in a changing, highly turbulent world.
7. It avoids costly litigation later.	7. Attempts to control risk affect commitment.

Summary

The alliance phenomenon cannot be addressed without a chapter on conflict. Conflict is inherent in the alliance management process. Independent companies do not always act selflessly *and* will revert to behaviors that promote their self-interests. Although conflict is always present, its impact can be positive. To air differences with the intent of solving problems or reaching a better solution is a benefit of conflict. The difficulty is that one cannot know the exact level of conflict and may not work to keep it in the "safe" zone. Disagreements escalate, and when differences become severe or when self-serving behavior overwhelms the spirit of the alliance, conflict becomes pathological and must be resolved if the alliance is to survive.

The No Blame Review captures the most positive approach to conflict resolution. Its principles and its process support our vision of what an alliance should be, and it re-affirms the tenets established by the spirit of the alliance. While the outcome of the NBR might be termination of the alliance, the process encourages the partners to examine the whole of the alliance, in an objective fashion, to jointly assess and deal with areas of concern and disagreement.

Much debate often surrounds exit clauses as part of the alliance contract. Although the arguments in support of exit clauses are compelling, the unintended consequences and the negative signals communicated, in many instances, outweigh the benefits. If exit clauses are employed, effort should focus on processes to allocate assets committed to or developed as part of the alliance. It makes little sense, nor is it a good use of managerial time, to attempt to assign a specific value or percentage ownership to an uncertain future event or outcome. If exit clauses are unavoidable, in the spirit of fair dealing, partners should develop processes for resolving disputes. Exit clauses have a self-fulfilling prophecy aspect to them and provide an easy way out should trouble arise.

8 | Alliance Managers:

Thinking and Seeing the World Differently

When Samuel Hearne[1] took over as alliance manager for a major joint venture between a European multinational and an Italian conglomerate, the alliance was in serious trouble. There were industry upheavals in the petrochemical business and market difficulties in Europe, particularly in Italy. The Italian conglomerate MontEdison was riddled with internal scandal and was experiencing a financial crisis so severe that the banks had essentially assumed control. The other partner, Royal Dutch Shell represented through Shell Italia, dealt with the consequences provoked by the alliance manager Hearne was replacing. MonteShell, the joint venture, had reached an impasse. Neither side was willing to give in; the joint venture was not moving forward. Shell was committed to making long-term investments in Italy, while MontEdison resisted investments because it needed all the cash MonteShell was throwing off. The business was in trouble and the relationship between the partners was even worse. If there ever was a time for a strong alliance manager, the time was now!

Not enough attention is given to selecting just the right person to manage alliances. In all the books that have been written on strategic alliances, the weight of discussion and words of wisdom falls decidedly *away from* discussions of managing the alliance over time. In all the books published in the past 5 years on alliances, a small percentage *significantly* address alliance management; even fewer discuss the managerial and leadership characteristics of an effective alliance manager. The operating assumption seems to be that getting the business in order automatically leads to adequate alliance management.

Table 8.1 Management Roles and Responsibilities

Primary Management Roles	Role Responsibilities
Visionary	Serves as the driving force behind the alliance's creation. Paints a picture of the possibilities an alliance creates. Maintains a broad perspective spanning inside and outside the company. Understands the compatability of strategic intents.
Strategic sponsor	Sells the concept of strategic alliances inside company and beyond. Has authority to commit resources and key personnel to the alliance. Is "in" the alliance, not peripheral to it. Puts in motion alliance opportunities. Creates an atmosphere that fosters high energy and personal compatibility. Builds an organization with dedicated resources. Looks for opportunities across company to benefit the alliance. Fosters social development for alliance growth. Provides opportunities to strengthen and evolve the alliance. Spans many boundaries and layers.
Advocate	Sells the value of the relationship to alliance participants. Sells the value of the specific alliance in question. Develops support for the alliance. Constantly pushes the vision forward. Rallies the right people at the right time. Makes things happen deep in the company. Creates mechanisms for support and understanding within the alliance. Maintains a vigilant focus on the ongoing business of the alliance. Broadcasts its successes and achievements. Is internal to the alliance, hands-on and tactical. Actively owns the day-to-day alliance. Allows the alliance to have a large share of mind. Makes a significant emotional investment.
Networker	Relies on frequent contacts to expedite alliance business. Knows who to ask for help and when to ask. Put the right people together. Accesses resources quickly and efficiently through others. Creates connections between internal networks of partner companies.

Table 8.1 *(Continued)*

Primary Management Roles	Role Responsibilities
	Puts in face-to-face time to cultivate trust in key relationships.
	Engages in and encourages informal activities.
	Sees interpersonal activities as key.
	Bridges communication gaps.
Facilitator	Encourages open, honest, and straightforward communication among all parties.
	Facilities effective reviews of "state of the alliance."
	Conducts interactions with diplomacy, tact, and objectivity.
	Creates bridges between diverse parties with different interests.
	Resolves conflicts effectively.
	Exhibits sensitivity to the needs of all parties.
Manager	Shoulders responsibility for sustaining the alliance.
	Ensures that the alliance follows its prescribed path.
	Maintains relationships critical to alliance success.
	Maintains alliance momentum.
	Is daily and constant.
	Is more tactical than visionary.

Too often, however, companies select alliance managers for all the wrong skills, making the alliance worse not better. Many companies, especially U.S. companies, see an alliance assignment as an opportunity to give management talent an internationally broadening job posting for several years. The emphasis is on the individual's development less than it is on the alliance's needs. Other companies have put their strongest line of technical managers into alliances, simply because of their proven track record in that traditional line role.

Alliance Management Is Complicated and Complex

Being an alliance manager is far more complicated than simply replicating what has been done in another part of the business. Chapters 3 and 6 stress that relationships are important: the alliance manager is a critical linchpin in building those relationships and in balancing between business and partnership and the challenges, pitfalls, and possibilities of alliance evolution demand changing alliance management role and focus. Table 8.1 reviews the alliance management roles and typical actions required of those individuals throughout the alliance development.

Wanted: Multifaceted Individuals for Changing Management Roles

Though not explicitly stated, performing these roles well demands a managerial skill set broad enough to encompass many different talents, yet focused and deep enough to call on unique behaviors at the appropriate stage. Alliance management by definition creates an awkward set of relationships that require time and talent. Thus, alliance management needs multifaceted individuals with the ability to be flexible and adaptive to the stage of the alliance and to the role necessary, and with characteristics that enhance the alliance's mission. A good alliance manager is a unique individual, not necessarily a transplanted line or even general manager.

This is not to say, however, that with a good alliance manager all will be fine. The skills and competencies of that individual, however, make a huge difference in how the alliance functions and provide the best chance for getting out of thorny situations. A poor alliance manager is sometimes the reason, as Chapter 5 suggests, for making a reasonable situation worse. Such was the case for Hearne's predecessor, DeVries.[2] DeVries was all business and therein lies the problem. Although he was an expert marketer and had strong functional skills in petroleum retailing, he lacked the interpersonal savvy and competence that the alliance required and that the Italians had received from Radisson, the alliance manager before DeVries. What started off as a difficult situation quickly became worse, in part because DeVries had only one strong expertise (business), needed two (business and relationship), and (this is a most important "and") lacked the "extras" that Samuel Hearne brought to the joint venture.

Who was Samuel Hearne? He was an Englishman with impeccable credentials, born in South Africa and raised in India. His corporate background and experiences were anchored in the financial side of his company. His most recent assignment was as a country manager in Thailand for an ailing joint venture immersed in political instability and market volatility. He had a love of different cultures and learning, traveled extensively, and was fluent in several languages, though Italian was not one of them.

Underneath Hearne's resume credentials are characteristics that epitomize successful alliance management. These capabilities have as their foundation defined skills in business and relationship, but they go far beyond what he does into how he thinks and sees the world. Hearne's alliance strengths reside as much in his in his cognitive capacities and perspectives as in his behaviors. These qualities of strong alliance managers are not limited to alliances. These are management skills for the future. Learning about and from good alliance managers is also learning about management in and of the future.

Alliance Managers Are Boundaryless

Alliance managers have an extremely difficult task because they must attend to a broad range of strategic and operational issues while operating simultaneously on three levels: across two or more separate parent companies, within the parent companies, and within the alliance. Across companies, the alliance manager represents and manages the needs, resources, and desires of the partner companies. Within any one particular firm, the alliance manager represents and manages the needs, resources, and desires of his or her own company. If a joint venture is involved, the alliance manager maintains close contact with it and with the venture's general manager. On an interpersonal level, the alliance manager creates and maintains relationships with superiors, peers, and subordinates in the alliance and their partner organizations.

Working across different levels, who have different people who have different perspectives and agendas requires the capacity to be simultaneously in several places at the same time. Individuals must be able to take a broad, strategic, helicopter perspective, while knowing the details. Individuals must have design abilities and construction abilities, being as comfortable sketching what is to be as in building that structure. It requires individuals to be familiar with all stakeholders, their history, and the current state of the interactions among stakeholder groups. Such fluidity takes unique characteristics, which are easily understood when described, yet are sometimes difficult to spot and even harder to develop.

Competencies Are Identifiable

Strong alliance managers possess identifiable competencies. Some of these competencies are teachable; others are unteachable. Teachable competencies are imparted through an educational experience. They are the skill sets and abilities that individuals acquire through formal schooling, executive education, on-the-job training, or everyday work activities. They are generally easily defined and observable competencies, mainly because many can be viewed directly in behaviors and actions. Most of them are strongly associated with effective line management or general management skills. Unteachable competencies, on the other hand, tend to describe how an individual thinks and sees the world. While they may not be teachable in a traditional programmed way, they are learnable. The best and most effective alliance managers have already acquired these skills over time. In fact, managers like Samuel Hearne acquire unteachable competencies throughout their careers. How this happens is a welcome addition to the alliance management landscape.

Teachable Competencies

As discussed in this section, there are three clusters of teachable competencies: functional, earned, and interpersonal:

1. Functional competencies—
   Line skills/staff skills.
   Education.
   Functional expertise/experience.
   General business knowledge.
2. Earned competencies—
   Credibility and respect.
   Extensive networks:
      Organization.
      Industry/profession.
      Alliance.
3. Interpersonal competencies—
   Social skills.
   Communication skills.
   Tact/sensitivity.
   Cross-cultural awareness.
   Process skills.

Functional Competencies

Strong alliance managers have breadth and depth. Functional competencies relate to the actual business experiences and expertise required for general management strength. Strong alliance managers know the business, their markets, their products, the technologies, and general system management. They have a firm grounding, generally through direct experience, in both line and staff aspects of the business. More than likely, jobs and assignments over their career have taken them into different areas of the business from which they have acquired a general management perspective. They have both depth and breadth of work experiences.

Most likely, formal educational experiences have provided more targeted learning. If, for example, the business is highly technical, such as Corning's many ventures, the alliance manager is usually trained and educated in that technology. The person might be a scientist or engineer turned manager, such as many of Corning's senior managers with advanced degrees in disciplines core to Corning's glass and ceramic technology, or professional managers with general management experience. In nontechnical businesses, the functional competence may be in manufacturing, marketing, service, or quality, whatever is core to the firm.

Strong alliance managers have the background and knowledge aligned to the business core. Their experiences, both formal and informal, have deepened their expertise in the core while expanding into the surrounding areas.[3]

Earned Competencies

Strong alliance managers build robust and complicated networks. The competencies of the second cluster are less acquired and more "earned." The word earned connotes that these skills more often are the result of a job well done than of the expertise gained in performing the task. Past successes increase the credibility and respect acquired after years of building rapport within and through one's professional performance and interactions. Good alliance managers have paid attention to building networks throughout their career, taking advantage of opportunities to reach out to others, such as getting to know other company members, being active in professional societies on the outside, and never burning bridges during transitions or problem situations. The more career experiences a potential alliance manager has had, the greater are the chances that he or she has created a broad-based network of contacts. With a strong network in place, an alliance manager who is relatively new to a position is able to call just about anyone for information or assistance. Proficient alliance managers also know how to use their network-building skills to quickly tap into networks of their alliance partner. A "hired gun" may know the alliance well, but will not have the network know-how to get things done fast and right.

No individual contact is ever too small or inconsequential to be part of a manager's network because one never knows just if, when, or how a particular contact can help. A manager we know secured a great position in part because of a network connection made 17 years earlier and maintained all those years.

Networking within one's company is cited as the most important benefit of single-company executive programs on alliances (or any other topic for that matter). Actual content in such workshop scores second to the opportunity to mingle with others in similar situations. Strong alliance managers do not wait for a workshop. Networking—building connections with others—is part of their modus operandi throughout their entire career. Good alliance managers work diligently and persistently to earn and maintain credibility and respect.

Interpersonal Competencies

Interpersonal savvy is a must. Because alliances are so heavily dependent on relationships between people, an alliance manager's interpersonal skill can show little room for error. Thus, the third set of teachable competencies, as listed earlier, is a cluster of interpersonal abilities. These competencies have to do with the ability of alliance managers to interact appropriately in diverse social settings. Knowing how meals are taken in different cultures, how to make light social banter, how to engage in discussions of more serious topics, how to interact with business people in nonbusiness as well as business settings are necessary foundations to alliance management. If relationships are a cornerstone of strategic alliances, one's ability to form relationships often begins with simple social encounters.

Social stamina is internationally valued. Understanding the finesse needed in "meeting and greeting" is not inconsequential or frivolous in an alliance context. An Asian manager in one of our alliance workshops stated that the social skill most important to his company was a kind of "social stamina." Much business in his company is conducted over meals and over drinks, activities that can stretch long into the evening and early morning hours. For these managers, therefore, length of time spent socializing garners credibility and respect within the company.

Communication demeanor makes a difference. Interpersonal competencies also include communication skills. These communication skills encompass all the fundamental skills of speaking and listening well to others in a one-on-one situation, as well as the ability to make another, especially a manager of another culture, comfortable and at ease. This later skill is a skill termed mirroring. Strong alliance managers mirror their counterparts as they communicate. Mirroring is simply a term for matching another's gestures, tone, mannerisms, and emotional intensity. It is not mimicry; it is behaving with others in ways that create connections not distance.

The ability to mirror is an underrecognized skill in alliances. With all the cross-cultural arenas in which alliances operate, being able to communicate with very different others requires more than knowing how to listen. It involves knowing how to reflect back what you are receiving, thus reducing the cultural distance between individuals. Our interview with the man has been the Siemens alliance manager for the Siecor alliance for over 20 years gave us a front-row seat into the communication skills of a strong alliance executive. His self-presentation changed depending on the alliance partner he spoke of. When he was talking about the Spanish or Italian or Latin cultures, he was emotional and animated. His eyes brightened, his face echoed his emotion. This was in stark contrast to the demeanor he took on when talking about the Japanese or Chinese with whom he engaged. He made less eye contact, was more demure in this speech, and appeared quite reserved. This demeanor was again different than when he spoke of his fellow German managers.

Another strong root of interpersonal competencies has to do with cross-cultural tact and sensitivity. Strong alliance managers understand the power and impact of national culture in a business contact. They understand how to relate to others with different values or perspectives without demeaning themselves or their partner. We know of another alliance manager doing business in Saudi Arabia. Her engineering credentials were exactly what were needed in the alliance at the particular time she got involved. However, given the role of women in the Saudi culture, she alters her work methods. When she travels to Saudi, she is accompanied by a blood relative or her husband, because she can never travel alone. She is vigilant about her attire and is careful to cover her ankles and wrists. She wears the traditional Saudi veil out of respect for her alliance partners. While she may not share the same values, her actions demonstrate respect for the Saudi culture, thereby honoring herself, her company, and the others.

Same words, totally different meanings. Language and its use can be another demonstration ground for cultural tact and sensitivity. English and American are not always the same language, as the BA/USAir coordinating team discovered early in its preliminary negotiations in 1992. After vigorous and sometimes heated conversations, the coordinating team decided *to table* the contentious item. As a result, the British Airways representatives launched into their perspectives on the topic. The USAir representatives were confused and flustered. They had clearly heard agreement that the issue was to be tabled. Yes, said the British, that is what we are doing, tabling the item. Even though each spoke English, they spoke very different English. "To table" in Britain means to put on the table and discuss; "to table" in the United States means to take off the table and cease conversation. Each was in fact tabling the conversation, but neither understood the other.

The mind as internal translation machine. Imagine how difficult it is when business is being conducted in English and English is not the native language of either party. Nonnative speakers often think in their native language. A question in English prompts the following cycle. The question is translated mentally into his or her native language, reasoned out, and answered mentally in that language. That answer has a complexity and intricacy of design only possible in one's home tongue. Then, the formulated response is translated back into English, and finally the verbal English reply is given. The ability to completely express one's fullest thoughts is a function of access to vocabulary, sentence structure, and idioms. One executive told us such a process is similar to having an interpreter, a dictionary and a phrase book in one's head, all communicating with one another through a telephone modem. The process is slow, often interrupted, sometimes inexact and definitely tedious.

The last of the interpersonal competencies has to do with process skills. Good alliance managers understand group dynamics at a fundamental level. First of all, they understand the importance of the *how* as well as the *what*. When Samuel Hearne came into Shell Italia, his first actions involved changing key personnel that the Italians had been requesting for months. This was *what* he did. However, *how* he did this communicated volumes to the partner. After listening to the concerns and issues of the MontEdison and MonteShell executives, he realized that they needed to feel their voice could be heard. He understood that the process of demonstrating "I'm on your side" was more critical than any objective set of results or any words to the same.

On the one hand, all the competencies that have been noted here are competencies needed by effective managers in any global business. What distinguishes the best alliance managers are two aspects. First, the level of teachable competencies they possess is strong; and second, they have added that little extra of a Samuel Hearne, the unteachable competencies.

"Unteachable" Competencies

The Look and Feel of Unteachable Competencies

Consider the words of this alliance manager in response to the question: "What makes a good alliance manager?"

> It's more than what they know, what they've done or who they know. It's a state of mind that says: I know some things, I don't know others, but I'll learn. I have tools, but they may not be the right ones, so I'll improvise. Meeting new people, seeing new places is a challenge and a joy.

This description does not reflect the functional, earned, or interpersonal competencies just discussed. This description targets, however, the "unteachable" competencies that strong alliance managers possess. These unteachable competencies have to do with a way of thinking. Alliance managers *think differently and see the world differently.*

An exercise we often use begins to get at this competence. Consider these four quotes from four different alliance managers in response to the question, "Which one of these managers would you want responsible your alliance?"

> *Alliance Manager A:* I guess that I don't worry about being the new person in the alliance, or I haven't worried about that. I don't feel any obligation to bend over backwards or to go out of my way to yield or do something different than I would in the normal business transaction just because it is a strategic alliance. I think basically it is a business arrangement.

Alliance Manager B: My objective is very clear. Make as many connections as you can at the main distribution hubs. I am going to lose money on the routes I inherited from them in the short to medium term. I recognize that for the greater benefit of the alliance, we may need to do these things. However, if in three years time, life hasn't gotten any better on those routes . . .

Alliance Manager C: In 1978 there wasn't much business. It was still very developmental. Company A was putting in some field installations to see what worked and what didn't. Everyone was jockeying for position, so we kept on driving ahead, asking what business do we do next, what markets do we have to win, what challenges do we have to meet. There were lots of meetings and discussions; it was so helpful to sit down and talk for hours.

Alliance Mnager D: An alliance manager needs sufficient mental flexibility to adopt to the thinking and the situation of others. That is very important . . . if you have someone and this happens you may have narrow minded people who only look at their way of doing things, they will certainly fail in an alliance . . . you have to realize that there are other ways that can lead to success, if you can, you must look at these other ways and consider that they may be even better.

With little argument or dissension, alliance executives quickly dismiss Managers A and B. These managers, they argue, are not flexible; they are seen as too rigid, not expansive enough in their thinking, too cause-effect oriented for an atmosphere (alliances) that is much more dynamic and fluid. The strongest debate ends up around managers C and D. Manager C portrays a risk-taking sense of challenge, proactivity, and entrepreneurship that is relished. This manager also appears to understand the social noise inherent in an alliance. Manager D, however, is selected consistently. Alliance manager D is described as adaptive, flexible, and open-minded. This manager seems to understand what Manager A does not—a demonstrable concern for others' point of view. Both Managers C and D are effective in their alliances. They stand out, less because of the objective characteristics identified and more because they think differently, more expansively, in fact.

Managers C and D present elements of the unteachable competencies. Here are some of the attributes of thinking differently and seeing the world differently:

1. Simultaneously see multiple points of view.
2. Learn from the past, but not be constrained by it.
3. Think across time.
4. See patterns in data and chaos in routine.
5. Are clever, creative, constantly curious.
6. Possess true wisdom.
7. Engage diplomatically.
8. Orient toward learning.

Attribute 1. Seeing multiple points of view simultaneously. Strong alliance managers see in multiple dimensions because they are able to consider multiple points of view simultaneously. This is more than simply understanding the perspective of another and understanding that it is different. Good alliance managers actively use this information in explaining what is happening and in forming their solutions in real time. Take Samuel Hearne again as an example:

> The Shell family view of MonteShell was very negative and to a certain extent, rightly so, because it wasn't up to Shell standards. But, Shell may also have been a bit excessively negative and sort of hypercritical. There was no give-and-take, just both sides picking on principles. So I made a couple of quite significant concessions on things that had been festering for a while. I've got a long list of unresolved issues and, to break the ice—my object there was to try and break the ice and to show that if we traded off some of our issues, that at least some of the momentum could be won. They were and they weren't big things—but they were personal in a sense because the Italians, you know, the Italian culture very much is focused on honor. If they thought they had been wrongly cheated or undercut, they won't think things in terms of money, they'll think in terms of gestures and the messages that they send. I ended up moving out one guy that the other people thought was no good and that broke things open.

Hearne confirmed that he could see the view of the Italians, see Shell's view, understand the impasse, understand the reasons, imagine a different outcome, and offer that path in a way that allows both to come out ahead.

Attribute 2. Letting the past inform, but not direct. Another attribute of these unteachable competencies is the ability to learn from the past *and* not be constrained by it. Too often, managers want answers and solutions to their alliance problem. Managers want to know if others have coped with the problem being experienced. They want to know how the problem was addressed and exactly what steps were taken in what order. Their goal, often unarticulated, is to get a template, transport it into their alliance, apply it, and thereby solve the problem. This application technique does not work because alliances are living, breathing entities with unique developmental patterns, pitfalls, and possibilities, as seen in Chapter 6.

Principles may generalize, but the specific actions and the order of those actions may not. Each alliance is different, because of the interactions between the partners. Thus, solutions to issues are equally unique. What happened in the past (or in another company) is just that; something that happened in the past (or in another company). One alliance manager we talked with epitomizes this way of thinking: "I act forward by understanding backwards."

Attribute 3. Thinking across time. Good alliance managers know what is, imagine what is possible, and understand all the nuances in between. They think across time:

> I read an article about alliances. This article emphasized the fact that one gets all the facts, analyzes them, and puts the picture together and makes the decision based on that. The guys I see that are really doing best are very intuitive in their approach to things. They have done their homework [the past], they have a good data bank [the present] but they make decisions on the fly and they have to make them with incomplete information because in this day and time, by the time you get complete information, someone else has already done it [the future].[4]

Such thinking is reflected in a story told to us by a joint venture general manager. That manager remembers one of the biggest sales his fledgling alliance made in late 1984. His company received an order well above any volume the company currently produced or could produce. The purchasing manager wanted a guarantee that the quantity of material could be procured. Sales would not guarantee, and the situation landed in the office of the general manager.

I realized the situation wasn't about meeting an immediate order; it was connecting today to tomorrow. "I told everyone he'd have it. We managed it and we have 100% of their business ever since. You have to learn to live with those kinds of pressures and uncertainties."[5]

This general manager is demonstrating his ability to think across time and into the future without benefit of having that time.

Attribute 4. Seeing patterns in chaos and chaos in routine. Strong alliance managers have the unique and unusual ability to see patterns in data and disorder among order. A simple example brought this home. While waiting to meet with an alliance manager, we found ourselves staring at a painting in her office. One of us commented on the unusual and colorful abstract work. The other commented on the painting of the golfer swinging. During this exchange, the alliance manager entered. Her response was that both of us were right, which is why she loved the painting so much:

> Sometimes I see only colors and lines without a pattern. Others days I immediately see the golfer in the act of taking a stroke. To me it is much like my alliance work. I have to switch back and forth between figure and ground.

Attribute 5. Being clever, creative, and constantly curious. Good alliance managers are also clever, creative, ever curious, and questioning. These characteristics, like courage, are difficult characteristics to train for. But they are important ones, because managing an alliance requires a certain type of improvisation.

Many global managers, both U.S. and non-U.S., remember an American television show, McGuyver. McGuyver was forever finding himself in difficult situations and yet was always able to put together just the right ingredients or use just the right mix of items in his surroundings to fashion the perfect bomb, weapon, escape device, or aid to ameliorate the situation. So it is with strong alliance managers. They are McGuyver-like in the sense that they are able to fashion innovative solutions in the present because they see something more than what is. They see what is possible. They are able to create order out of whatever materials, or insights, or tools they have at hand. It has been said that if all one has is a hammer, then every problem becomes a nail. Instead of seeing a hammer, good alliance managers see a hammer, *and* they envision a prod, a wedge, a lever, and any number of other uses or characteristics for that hammer or its components. Furthermore, they retain this creativity under pressure, as McGuyver certainly did. The ambiguity and uncertainty of "not knowing" is not a fire retardant; it is live fuel for the creative flame. Some of the most recent discussions of leadership in the future highlight these characteristics.[6]

Attribute 6. Possessing true wisdom. Good alliance managers are wise. True wisdom is being wise enough not to know particular facts but to know without excessive confidence or excessive cautiousness.[7] Wise people know they don't fully understand what is happening right now. Less wise people assume they know. In alliances, there is a fair amount that is just not known completely and fully, making true wisdom a desirable, if not required, characteristic.

Attribute 7. Engaging diplomatically. Strong alliance managers engage diplomatically. Engaging diplomatically builds upon the interpersonal competencies of cross-cultural sensitivity, self-insight, and interpersonal and cross-cultural tact. Strong and effective alliance managers are never locked into a prescribed methodology, but have personal flexibility that allows them to adapt responses and approaches. Their skills emphasize creatively exploring differences and proactively raising issues and problems. They also include patience, giving relationships the time they need to develop and giving the time to relationships that they deserve.

Attribute 8. Orienting toward learning. Taken all together, strong alliance managers require a different kind of individual mindset, not to mention the corporate mindset described in Chapter 4. The term *mindset* refers to the distinctive viewpoints, needs, and agendas that determine how an individual views and engages at work.[8] Mindsets help executives make sense of and understand the business world and their daily interactions. As we have spoken to, worked with, and gotten to know many alliance managers, mindset appears to explain in the most solid form the unteachable competencies we've articulated.

An *alliance mindset* has at its foundation the ability to learn and exercise that learning using a broad repertoire. Diplomatic is a word often associated with strong alliance managers. Managers with a strong alliance mindset have strongly developed learning orientations,[9] are able to bring order to chaos, thrive on ambiguity and uncertainty, and engage artfully with others. Those conditions become a catalyst for learning, not a threat to the status quo. Recall the quotes from the four managers at the beginning of this section. Managers C and D had it; managers A and B didn't.

Of course, already possessing an alliance mindset is one thing; attaining one is another.

Good Alliance Managers Are Developed, Not Found Suddenly

Good alliance managers are hard to find. Few companies have the bench depth to carefully pick and chose among potential alliance managers. And, most companies do not design management development programs and experiences with an eye toward alliance bench depth.

Developing Alliance Talent Is Difficult and Time Consuming

One of the reasons the development of alliance managers is difficult is that there are so many traits that are difficult to identify, let alone "train" for. Alternatively, if companies merely throw an outstanding manager into an alliance, hoping for alliance development, that company is making a substantial expenditure of people and resources with uncertain results and high costs to the individual, the company, and potentially the alliance. Most companies should be leery. What firms need to be doing is thinking strategically about developing not just managers, not just global managers, but alliance managers, as they will run companies during the next century.

The Tension between High Potentials and Alliance Management Continuity

Another reason alliance managers are so hard to find is that the development of alliance managers takes time—in some cases, more time than companies are willing to invest or individuals are willing to endure. Short-term pressures for results are a disincentive for investing in alliance manager development. In American companies especially, managerial stars are identified early and promoted frequently. These are the individuals who work hard, desire challenge, and expect rapid movement upward. Companies who provide just that kind of atmosphere to young management talent are rewarded with their unending productivity and results.

Both the talent and their productivity are difficult to lose in today's business environment where speed, market savvy, and innovation all increase shareholder returns. Oftentimes, these same young managers are at the cutting edge of technology and changing competitive dynamics, making them even more willing and able to push out boldly with new ideas. Creating opportunities that meet these individuals' career needs, while broadening their perspectives in alliance skills, is a challenge. They want more sooner than alliance development may be able to deliver.

Continuity Is Critical

At the same time, continuity of alliance management is critical, particularly when dealing with other cultures where managers stay in their roles for long periods. In Japan, for example, one is an alliance manager for life, whether or not the current job is related to the business of that alliance. This point can best be illustrated by a story about the alliance managers of a joint venture that Corning had with Asahi glass. The two alliance managers, Decker from Corning and Kurata from Asahi, had known each other for over 20 years, as businessmen and friends. The business highs and lows they shared matched to the personal times they spent with one another. When Decker died, Kurata was unable to get to the United States for several months. On his first visit stateside, his foremost request after being picked up at the airport in Elmira, New York, was to visit Decker's grave. He spent 20 minutes pacing around the grave, speaking to Decker in Japanese. The Corning executives with him soon learned that he was not merely speaking his condolences, he was literally telling Decker everything that had happened in his absence. Decker was dead but the relationship and the alliance were still very much alive.

This kind of continuity and resultant dedication to an alliance is far removed from the selection procedures at some companies where alliance managers churn through the partnership. No sooner has one arrived than he or she is summoned elsewhere. We've heard from many Japanese or Korean or Taiwanese managers just how upsetting it is to them to have a manager change on them every three years. In fact, the same thing happens between functional areas in a company. Marketing people change from one position to another, one level to another, and R&D

folks generally stay in R&D for a career. One always ends up reeducating or relearning about the new person in the job. And in an alliance context, such reeducation is quite costly.

Development Begins with Recognition

Recognition is crucial. Companies need to acknowledge and appreciate the impact an individual manager can have on alliance development and success. This may seem obvious, but recognizing the need and importance of who is placed into an alliance is a good part of helping an alliance be successful. Alliance manager development is not just a human resources issue; as Chapter 9 explores, it is a question of developing corporate talent that belongs to the entire company.

Look beyond Experiences

Companies need to look beyond experiences when identifying alliance talent. Asking the right questions, such as those in Table 8.2, is as important, if not more necessary than an objective competence test of global leadership capabilities. These questions seek to identify the depth of teachable competencies and the strength of the unteachable competencies in a way that might not be accessible through a resume.

Escalate Alliance Experiences through Apprenticeship

These same managers can also learn what it means to partner, for the company and for the alliance. They learn continuity and the importance of the alliance (see Chapter 4). Here is Tom MacAvoy's apprenticeship:

> I was in R&D when we got involved with acquiring an integrated circuit company in California called Signetics. It was a very small company; I was the manager of the electronics research group in Corning, I must have been 32, I was young enough to still be considered an apprentice, and yet on the plane out I would fly out with the corporate controller and learn from him what was important about the balance sheet or the operating statement of the subsidiary. It was not totally owned, but a majority owned subsidiary. In the meetings I got to watch the alliance manager and the other people in the alliance, plus the managers in the joint ventures. And through this process, I gradually got to learn how such things worked. And then I got promoted, I was allowed to start a small alliance of interest to that business . . . here I could take more responsibility directly for it; and in fact it failed . . . it

Table 8.2   Alliance Manager Competencies: Questions for Selection Conversations

Functional Competencies

Does this person have the necessary or relevant line management skills for this alliance?
To what extent does this person understand the company, its products, and business?
How might this person's educational background enhance or detract in the position?
Does this person have a strong understanding of our business and of the alliance's business?

Earned Competencies

Has this person developed an extensive network within our company?
Does this person have an extensive business network in the industry of the alliance?
Has this person developed solid relationships within the partner company?
Does this individual have credibility in our company?
Does this individual have credibility and respect outside our company, especially with our partners and in the alliance?

Interpersonal Competencies

To what degree is this person comfortable in social business situations?
How does this person demonstrate sensitivity to differences between cultures?
Is this person considered an effective communicator in diverse settings?
To what degree does this person easily alter his or her behavior to fit with a new environment or setting?
Is the person attuned to nonverbal communication?
Can this person easily sense the mood of a group or individual?

Alliance Mindset

Does this person have an affinity for complexity?
Can this person think in terms of patterns, connections, and relationships?
Does this person thrive on challenges?
Does this person never stop learning from their experiences?
Is this person described by others as "thinking about and seeing the world differently?"
Can this person simultaneously consider multiple points of view?

was not a big alliance, but it was one that I could learn from and move on to the next one. I had a number of key mentors: Mal Hunt, who was responsible for the Signetics alliance, John Sheldon, a very wise and experienced technically oriented marketing person who was also a chemist as I am and who was older than me and could coach me constantly, almost unconsciously, and Bob Foster who was the controller of the company and who was very generous with his time in helping me understand how the business worked.

Thus, through escalating experiences, exposure to mentors, and role models, new management talent can learn from what the others are doing. The more diverse the models, the more broad the learning can be. And, emphasis is on the "can learn." The context is there; what Tom and what others have done is recognize and take advantage of the transformational opportunity they have been provided.

Summary

Alliance managers are an integral part of alliance development and alliance success. However, their development in part depends on their company seeing and valuing alliance activities and the related skills and competencies. Desiring strong alliance managers, but failing to reward allying behaviors or fostering an alliance spirit conducive to cooperation can undermine a company's efforts. Good alliance managers grow up in a culture that supports alliances and allying behavior; they reach their full potential in a company where the infrastructure and managerial processes reward and encourage cooperation and collaboration, with systems that reward the initiative and risk taking, inquisitiveness, and innovation that alliances demand. Without a supportive environment, good alliance management is incomplete. As Chapter 9 addresses, alliance competence includes not only doing alliances well, but having a context that encourages alliance and allying interactions. Senior executives running companies must be strong alliance managers as well.

9

Building an Alliance Competence

In Chapter 1, we introduced the idea that a firm's alliance capabilities are a potential source of competitive advantage. These advantages enable a firm and its alliance partners to outmaneuver and maintain an edge over competitors who are less nimble, less proactive, and less able to navigate through an increasingly uncertain world. Driven by significant globalization, rapidly evolving technology, and intense competition, successful companies will have to be more vigilant and responsive. Strategic flexibility[1] provides the ability to anticipate change and to respond quickly to competitive threats and changing conditions thereby allowing the firm to better develop its core competencies.

The goal of this chapter is to develop fully the concept of alliance competencies by discussing what they are and the role they play in building a stronger alliance. In addition, the chapter explains how a firm might become more alliance receptive and alliance capable. As stated in Chapter 1, both access to resources *and* an alliance competence result in a sustainable competitive advantage for a firm and its partners as it competes with other sets of firms. The interplay between these two building blocks of competitive advantage is illustrated in Figure 9.1.

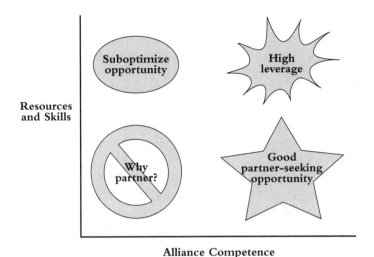

Figure 9.1 Resources plus competence = success.

What Is Meant by Core Competence?

Core competencies are the skills and capabilities that enable a firm to create a unique and sustainable set of benefits (value-creating activities) for its customers. The effect of competencies on competitive behavior is very different from that of a more traditional approach to competitive analysis. A traditional discussion of competitive advantage typically would focus on interproduct competition by making a side-by-side comparison between, say, jet engines produced by GE and Pratt & Whitney (PW). This comparison is competitor centered and examines on a firm-by-firm basis, their resource commitment and capabilities, relative cost structures, market share, and relative profitability. Attempts would be made to understand only the basis for competition between GE and PW.

This approach does not fully capture the true drivers of competitive advantage. If one focuses on core competencies, the analysis encompasses the more subtle skill-building activities and the capabilities held by these rival firms. The level of analysis for this comparison would shift to the firm as part of an extended enterprise. Now, one would compare GE and its constellation of alliance partners that together provide engines, financing, after-sale parts/service to PW's alliance partners that provide similar products, services, and technological capabilities to the commercial market consisting of both domestic and international air carriers. The extended analysis would compare the R&D effort, innovations, and complete array of value-adding capabilities that both engine manufacturers and their partners bring to the marketplace. These combined capabilities comprise the full set of competencies held by these formidable competitors.

An understanding of a firm's core competencies comes from the accumulated intellectual capital of the firm and is the sum of its technologies, experience, skills, and management processes. Competencies are not equally distributed, and some firms are better at developing capabilities and/or are more adept at gaining access to and internalizing skills held by others.[2] Competencies are dynamic and must be honed and redefined depending on the changes in both external factors and the firm's knowledge base. Merck, for instance, has a superior understanding of and ability to manage the R&D process such that its financial risk is lower and "hit rate" is higher than many others in the pharmaceutical industry. Other firms make superior alliance partners in that they better leverage the skills of their partners. It is difficult to have a discussion of core competencies and not also include learning. An ability to successfully leverage partners' skills is closely related to a firm's ability to learn. Learning occurs both for the teacher and the student; and the alliance is better for the transfer of skills to both.

A firm might have many kinds of competencies. A distinguishing characteristic, however, is that core competencies are often linked to making a critical contribution to an end product or service. Honda, for example, is recognized for its expertise[3] in small-size engines and can provide its customers one of the best price/performance trade-offs across many product categories (e.g., cars, lawn mowers, portable generators, motorcycles). Honda also has a set of alliance competencies that distinguish it from other automobile manufacturers such that it gains both a cost and a technological advantage in the marketplace. Honda's alliance competencies are but one illustration of the issues addressed in this chapter.

Types of Alliance Competence

An alliance competence makes a contribution to customer benefits, it should not be easily imitated, and it should be applicable across a range of relationships. The advantages that accrue to the firm that has developed an alliance competence are based on an ability to leverage both the firm's and its partners' resources more effectively. Alliance competencies fall into five categories:[4]

1. *Know-how.* This entails the deep understanding of a subject area. Corning's knowledge of all aspects of glass production and its related chemistry is a clear example. The know-how extends to all aspects of alliance management from understanding strategic intent and the role of alliances in one's business strategy, to partner selection, to managing the alliance over time and effectively handling alliance dissolution.

2. *Supportive Processes and Structure.* These processes result in the seamless delivery of superior products and services to the customer. They are mechanisms that enable and facilitate the sharing of alliance knowledge among partners as well as within the firm. Related to these processes are the systems and structures that allow partners to learn form each other. These processes and structures extend beyond the internal functions of the firm, and its business units, to include the firm's extended enterprise. With truly supportive alliance-related processes, the entire value chain should be poised to move in an integrated fashion to deliver unique value in the marketplace. For the extended enterprise champion, advantage results from an ability to orchestrate workflows and information sharing as though these independent firms were one.

3. *Mindset.* An alliance mindset encompasses a perspective that enhances the firm's ability to partner and effectively leverage the skills and capabilities of others. These activities might be ones associated with trust building and the skills associated with fostering commitment, and other key aspects of relationship development. These competencies capture those characteristics that engender positive feelings from potential partners and make it easier for them to lower their guard and feel less threatened engaging in alliance-like behavior. For example, one's reputation as a good partner has been shown to positively affect other's alliance-like behavior.

4. *"Bench-Depth."* Having bench-depth means having sufficient managerial talent with alliance-relevant skills ready to be placed in alliance positions. More importantly, it represents a purposeful commitment on the part of management to find, develop, and maintain a pool of alliance-competent managers.

5. *Learning.* Alliance learning addresses the institutional mechanisms by which alliance skills are recognized, taught, and then institutionalized. As a firm acquires alliance-related skills, it is not enough that they are resident in the minds of a few. The truly alliance-competent firm appreciates

its obligation to make alliance-related knowledge pervasive. Note that the term knowledge is used here. In Figure 9.2, knowledge[5] is distinguished from information and data; it is treated as a corporate asset that allows the firm to move on to the next innovation or idea. It is the creation of and access to alliance-related knowledge that distinguishes the successful alliance-competent firm from its less adept competitor.

Hewlett Packard has maintained over the years a relational database that inventories the range of its alliances. From this information storehouse, new alliance managers can benefit from the insights and experiences of others. Other companies rely on informal networks that develop through the natural rotation of personnel throughout the company. Shell Oil has rotated its managers from London to the field, to The Hague, and back to the field. Here, a side benefit is that managers learn a great deal about "who knows what," and can call on those experts when alliance-related advice is needed.

We have helped a company to catalog its entire set of alliances so that it can better understand the number, type, and names of the partners for each of its relationships. This exercise also showed that many of the firm's associations and relationships did not pass the alliance litmus test. To refer to a relationship as an alliance sets expectations in the partners' minds, and the disconnect between what the firm said and what it did was causing problems. This analysis revealed that when there is a high correlation between the firm's goals and the goals of the alliance:

- Management buy-in is stronger.
- Win-win solutions are sought.
- Thinking is more long-term, equitable, and honest.
- Managers emphasize relations *and* business.
- All sources of static are reduced.
- The firm better utilizes its assets, captures more of the value chain, and better leverages its partners' skills.

With further analysis, insights into alignment revealed that positive results that accrue when the partners are compatible. Armed with this information, senior managers can understand better why some of their JVs succeed and others fail, and can identify the enablers and the typical roadblocks.

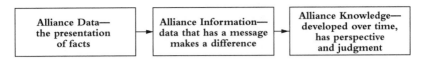

Figure 9.2   Knowledge as an outgrowth of data and information.

One premise of this chapter is that competencies should reside throughout the organization.[6] In a traditional hierarchy, the knowledge and competencies required to manage the business reside at the top and it is assumed that the leaders know how to create a competitive firm. Despite the scarce resources, some firms are more effective than others in leveraging and exploiting alliance knowledge. In part, these differences can be attributed to a company culture that fosters a climate of trust and encourages partners to share information. Without trust, the accuracy of information is diminished and partners are more guarded about sharing sensitive information. A sustainable competitive advantage can be achieved only through a commitment to learning. John Browne, CEO of British Petroleum, has said that any firm that thinks it does everything the best and need not learn from others is incredibly arrogant and foolish. Culture, knowledge creation, and other factors converge to develop an alliance competence, as depicted in Figure 9.3.

Alliance Know-How

A firm's alliance know-how is important throughout the entire alliance management process. The formative stages of alliance formation typically include strategy formation, partner selection, negotiation, and implementation. Although alliances fail during implementation, it is also true that if the formative stages are executed badly, there is little chance that the implementation will go well. Because alliances are relatively fragile entities, strong skills at one stage of the alliance's life cycle cannot fully compensate for weaknesses at other stages. Likewise if early stages of alliance formation are executed well, later stages are more likely to run more smoothly. If a partner understands better the role alliances play in its business strategy, is able to engage in a strategic conversation around the needs for and benefits derived from an alliance, and has a

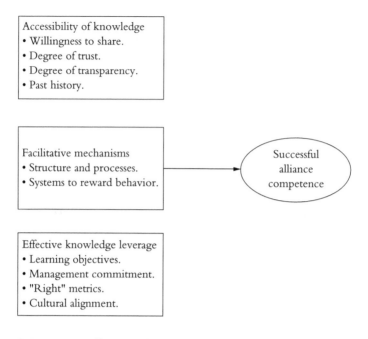

Figure 9.3 Factors affecting alliance competence. (*Source:* Modified from Andrew Inkpen, "Learning and Knowledge Acquisition through International Strategic Alliances," *The Academy of Management Executive 12,* 4 [1998]: 69.)

sophisticated approach to partner selection, there should be fewer conflicts down the road.

At the same time, if the negotiation process gets bogged down because of self-serving approaches to structuring the agreement, the advantages gained early are potentially lost, and the outcome is likely to be less gratifying to both partners. A favorable outcome gained from the prealliance work is rendered less effective due to heavy-handed, one-sided negotiation methods.

Respondents (alliance managers) from a sample of supply chain partners suggest that if the prealliance preparation work is thoughtful:

- Conflict incidents tend to be lower.
- Negotiations emphasize more of a win–win orientation.
- Partners better understand their roles.
- Satisfaction with performance tends to be higher.

Preparation work covers a range of prealliance activities associated with both strategy formulation and partner selection but deals with these activities on a fairly high level. Preparation addresses a partner's ability to understand strategic fit and partner leverage points, as well as determine opportunities for value creation. If managers understood better the purpose of the alliance and proactively sought partners who contributed value, the alliances had a more pronounced alliance spirit, partners treated each other with more respect, and behaviors were more supportive of a positive alliance experience.

Figures 9.4 and 9.5 show two charts that examine differences between higher and lower prealliance preparation.[7] If partners are chosen to fit a specific set of skills that are tied to the alliance's purpose and its value proposition, the outcome is quite encouraging and is likely to result in better alliance performance. Trusting behavior is stronger, information sharing is encouraged, partners are mutually dependent, and learning is both encouraged and transferred. It would appear that if partners trust one another, one partner is often willing to cede control to the partner whose expertise is greater.

Compare this finding with the observation that often alliances are formed defensively, in the heat of the moment, and with any remaining

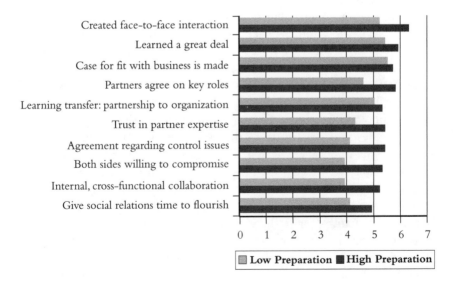

Figure 9.4 Level of partnership preparation by behavior.

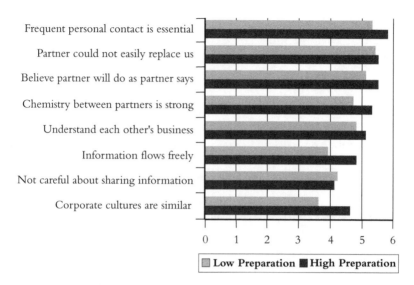

Figure 9.5 Level of partnership preparation by aspects of alliance behavior.

partner. When partners rush to form an alliance, have not fully thought about value creation and how each contributes to it, and have not engaged in comprehensive due diligence, the seeds of disaster are likely to have taken root. For example, data from a medical center shows that its alliance readiness is fairly low and its general approach to prealliance analysis seems to be driven by self-serving motives. The data also reveals a rather cynical approach to the overall alliance process. The senior medical staff understands the importance of alliances to their future strategy; however, they seem less willing to do the hard work required to make the investment in time and resources. Figure 9.6 summarizes the medical center's scores on questions that relate to the alliance spirit. Note the relatively low scores (the midpoint is 4). The findings also suggest that senior managers are unsure how alliances fit, do not appreciate the notion of leverage, and tend to believe that partners will act in their own interests. The contrasts among the organizations' perspectives are stark, despite the importance of alliances for both. It is apparent that competencies are not equally developed across companies.

During the negotiation stage, a win-win approach is best although many firms do not practice what they preach. This disconnect often occurs when the managers responsible for the alliance are not the ones who

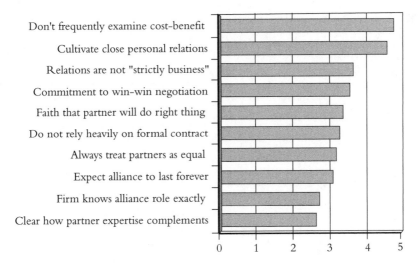

Don't frequently examine cost-benefit
Cultivate close personal relations
Relations are not "strictly business"
Commitment to win-win negotiation
Faith that partner will do right thing
Do not rely heavily on formal contract
Always treat partners as equal
Expect alliance to last forever
Firm knows alliance role exactly
Clear how partner expertise complements

Figure 9.6 Alliance spirit.

negotiate the agreement. Different agenda often emerge depending on who in the company takes the lead during negotiation. Agreements crafted by attorneys (who may lack full appreciation for the business case or do not understand the alliance rationale) often protect the firm to the detriment of the alliance. Typically, risk and reward are not shared equitably. Since legal counsel is typically charged with guarding the assets of the firm, they approach the alliance negotiations with a cautious, often self-serving perspective.

Remember, one manages a business and develops and nurtures a working relation but does not manage a contract. It would be better to base the agreement on an understanding of the alliance and its purpose. Armed with this information, the alliance agreement could enable the alliance-building process and not be seen as a roadblock. Lawyers are important to the process but probably should not lead the negotiations, and definitely should not conduct the negotiations without the managers who will run the alliance.

So, what are the lessons learned? Table 9.1 summarizes competencies that should become part of the alliance readiness inventory. The list is a guide to help determine whether your firm and its managers engage in these important behaviors. However, the alliance management process contains many steps and has a number of checkpoints to pass on the

Table 9.1   Alliance Management Know-How: Competencies Needed during Early Alliance Formation

Stage of Alliance Development	Key Competency Areas
Strategy formulation	Understands benefits/costs of the alliance versus going alone. Pinpoints major strategic issues, challenges, and risks. Understands the purpose of the alliance—what is the goal. Understands fit with your strategic direction and competitive landscape. Has vision and visioning skill. Can articulate the vision of what the future will be, given the alliance. Can engage in a meaningful strategic conversation. Can gain the buy-in of relevant managers and key stakeholders to help tell the story. Has humility and recognizes that go-it-alone won't work.
Partner selection	Understands leverage and can translate into partner complementarity. Looks for skill gaps and ways to fill. Understands the interplay between the business criteria and relationship criteria—zone of balance. Looks for signs of alliance capability and resource strengths. Understands the full meaning of partner quality. Assesses compatibility well and knows key touch points.
Negotiations	Is able to take the partner's perspective. Seeks to understand partners' strategic stake in the alliance. Fosters a win-win atmosphere that guides the process. Engenders trust and is viewed as an "honest broker." Focuses on the goal of the alliance and can build consensus. Keeps sights on long-term goals and understands importance of not reacting in the moment.

alliance journey. The sampling of competencies in Table 9.1 describes only the first steps in the journey.

Other competencies emerge during the later stages of the life cycle. On the individual level, they are based on a fundamental shift in how people interact both in and across the firm; the nature of decision-making authority and responsibility for alliance related issues; and, the manner in which work is executed. On a macro level, then, these factors shape alliance competencies:

- A recognition that information must be shared and should flow easily to those making the decision. Implicit here is a delayering of the organization and an empowerment of people to do the right thing on behalf of the alliance.
- A shift from command and control in which hierarchy rules and power resides at the top to a flexible (adaptive and boundaryless) form of structure in which hierarchy is less relevant, joint decision making rules, and trust and shared values set behavioral patterns. Governance changes and decision making are dispersed and shared both within the firm and across its boundaries.
- A change in the role of management from being in control (and, as such, making decisions for others) to the role of coach.

To think of managers as coaches has implications for alliance-like behavior within the firm. A coach has the following characteristics:

- Takes the long-term view.
- Helps others improve their own skills and competencies.
- Does little dictating and more orchestration.
- Is a facilitator and a guide.
- Shares the game plan willingly and shows how each plays a supporting role.
- Helps others grow as alliance managers.
- Does not look for mistakes as a means to punish; provides escalating experiences to learn; provides room to learn and lets go.
- Is a good example, lives the story and is credible.
- Builds a sense of team and encourages others to work on behalf of the alliance.

Consistent with the requirements of an alliance-capable firm, a coach emphasizes the long term, works hard to develop people, tends to view the system/enterprise as a whole and looks for integration and coordination to maximize the benefit to the partners. In the interest of learning, a coach will tolerate mistakes, try to make them learning experiences, and will share that learning over all alliances.

Many of the competencies required over the life of the alliance emanate from the different roles played by the alliance manager. Many of those competencies have been addressed in Chapter 8. The following list summarizes the competencies needed as the alliance progresses:

- Thinks big picture, is comfortable with nonlinear thinking.
- Is adaptive, anticipates change, and knows it will occur.
- Is comfortable with the contingent nature of alliance management—change is constant.
- Feels comfortable knowing his/her fate is interdependent and entwined with partner.
- Has a broad view and recognizes cost and benefit in the larger context.
- Knows that alliances ebb and flow and is comfortable with shifting advantage and contribution.
- Recognizes and devotes the time and energy to the alliance process.
- Feels comfortable with the role conflicts that naturally arise (boundary role problems).
- Welcomes diversity, values and seeks differences.
- Is not wary of information sharing but can draw line between what should be shared and what is out of bounds.
- Does not "keep score" for its own sake.
- Knows that goals are important but is comfortable with hard and soft measures.
- Does not get defensive, is willing to discuss position and listen with an open mind.
- Recognizes that the process and the results are both important.
- Makes commitments, fulfills obligations, and expects others to do the same.
- Is both a willing teacher and a student—alliances are about learning.
- Will help partners learn to be better alliance members.
- Failures are not used to blame others. Failures provide opportunities to learn and grow.

These range from developing a long-term perspective and an ability to look beyond the moment to the mutual benefits derived over time from the alliance, to being patient with the shifts in relative contribution that are likely over time.

Alliance-Supportive Processes and Structure

Alliance processes enable alliance-like behavior and enhance the ability of the partners to achieve their mutually compatible goals. Structures are the formal mechanisms that affect the coordination and integration among organizational units, functions, and external firms and networks that work together to bring value to the marketplace. Since alliance managers change, get promoted, and retire, it is the organization, its structure and processes that ensure continuity and enable the expertise of one manager to benefit others in the firm. Alliance-related knowledge that cannot be stored and transferred to others is wasted.

To understand the impact of structure and process on organizational performance, theorists talk about bureaucratic versus organic forms of organizations as a starting point for understanding how effectively a company adapts to uncertainty and change. Alliance-ready firms are more flexible and more responsive to change. More importantly, these firms facilitate alliance-like behavior and lay the foundation for the alliances to grow and prosper. An alliance-ready organization:

- Is not functionally bound. There is very little silo thinking and parts of the company cooperate and work together to bring value to the marketplace.
- Shares information. In a functional, or silo, oriented firm, information is power—why would one share it. It is in the best interest of the enterprise (or extended enterprise) to ensure that people have enough information to make a smart decision.
- Is decentralized. Decision making is dispersed and shared among those who can have an impact on the final outcome. Managers support and encourage others to take responsibility for their actions and proactively engage the business.
- Sets performance measures that encourage joint action and the pooling of resources. This is an important point since many companies that rely on an Economic Value Added (EVA) model of performance as a key tool for assessing performance. An EVA

model has no provision for the pooling of resources or bundling of services for the better of the firm. If the performance metrics emphasize "each tub on its own bottom," it is unlikely that managers will feel compelled to work jointly to solve customer needs, or to address opportunities in the marketplace. This is particularly true if it entails revenue, costs, and profit sharing.

- Encourages teamwork and rewards people for working on teams. These are two related issues. Relying on informal groups to work together to solve a problem and expecting them to work across formal boundaries requires both reward and reporting systems to facilitate these activities. Systems need to reward managers for their contribution to the firm and to the alliance if the alliance responsibilities are not a full-time job.

Tension exists between consistency and change. Bureaucratic organizations are more efficient for managing large process-driven businesses where variance in behavior and processes is likely to have a negative impact on the production process. Yet, these bureaucratic firms are less effective under conditions of higher uncertainty where alliance-relevant behavior becomes critical. These attributes are portrayed as process and structural competencies that the alliance-ready firm should adopt. These competencies are presented in Table 9.2.

An Alliance Mindset

Earlier in this chapter, the terms foolish and arrogant were used to describe firms that fail to appreciate the value of alliances. The firms that would boast about their level of vertical integration and the strength of their internal capability that allowed such integration might fill a lengthy list. Many of these firms have changed their tune. To a large extent, the prevailing attitude was that it wasn't worth building if you didn't do it yourself. Over time, these companies have seen the error of their logic and have become more willing to form alliances to achieve their goals. However, old attitudes die slowly, and these firms have been less than good partners since they have not checked their arrogance at the door. They manifest arrogance in ways that signal to partners that they are considered inferior; are lucky to be working with the alliance; and will

Table 9.2   Process and Structural Competencies That Enable Alliance-Like Behavior

Structure and Processes Factors	Types of Competency Engendered
Is not functional/silo bound	Lateral flows replace vertical ones. Informal networks complement formal reporting. An enterprisewide view emerges. *Not invented here* is not a problem. Has architecture that is already alliance friendly. Elements of coordination and integration processes are built in. Understands and is comfortable with interdependence.
Shares information	Information is a public good. Has processes to encourage transfer of information. Structure does not present roadblocks. Has permeable boundaries. Trusts information will be used as intended. Has a capacity to address shared intellectual property. Has built a broad bandwidth to enable sufficient alliance communications.
Endorses decentralization	Decision making flows to point of contact. Recognizes the importance of communication. Empowers and shares responsibility willingly. Decentralization does not mean out of control; has mechanisms to ensure objectives remain mutually compatible and achievable. Works hard to foster superordinate goals. Governance ensures coordination and cooperation. Mechanisms exist to check opportunism.
Has reward systems (performance and teams)	Thinks longer term, alliance productivity is on a longer cycle. Can reward for team and individual performance. Teamwork is valued. Has process to address performance outcomes and behavioral outcomes. Recognizes that alliance personnel get rewarded for alliance performance. Sets milestones and interim measures to monitor and self-correct; does not shoot the messenger.

be asked for any input that is needed (please do not volunteer). Sounds extreme? There are more subtle forms of arrogance. Insisting on a golden share in a joint venture, allocating personnel to key alliance positions, limiting the flow and direction of information, inequitable sharing of risk and reward, and so on all send the same signal. These actions speak to how much both the partner and the partnership is valued and to what degree decision making will be shared. Such attitudes and behaviors do not bode well for fostering a healthy alliance.

Firms with solid alliance reputations readily convey the importance of alliances to their future strategy and can easily articulate the importance placed on the value the partner brings to the alliance. First and foremost, these firms communicate that alliances are serious business and are essential to their future. Second, with this confession comes a humility that acknowledges its corporate ego will not be a barrier to forging an alliance. To effectively work with and educate a potential partner is in both companies' best interests.

These two factors convey a strong sense of commitment. There is a commitment to the alliance concept and its importance as a strategic tool and there is a demonstration that senior management also takes alliances and alliance-like thinking seriously. There is also an implied commitment

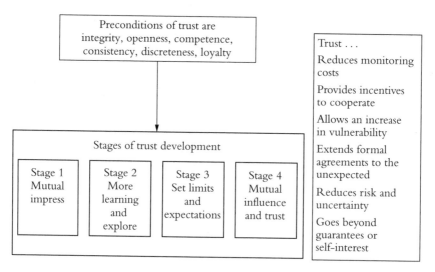

Figure 9.7   Trust develops over time and can be a virtuous cycle.

to one's partner. Such signals convey a high degree of trust. The process by which trust thrives in a relationship is captured in Figure 9.7. Integrity, loyalty, competence (good at what you do), and openness are viewed as important qualities. These qualities make it easier for the skeptical partner to at least be receptive to a discussion about why an alliance might make sense. They are open to a strategic discussion. All things being equal, one would choose to partner with a firm that possessed these traits than ally with a firm whose commitment was low and who seemed to be less trustworthy.

Our data examined the level of importance managers placed on alliance activity, and there are interesting contrasts between those who report high importance and those who do not. The findings show that a recognition of importance will affect partner behavior during the alliance. Figures 9.8 and 9.9 reveal that our sample of hotel alliance partners who perceive alliances as more important to their future business also report positive alliance-related behaviors as well as report faith in their partners' motivations and actions, and express clarity in role assignment and responsibility. Managers report both a positive feeling about alliances/alliance management and have instituted mechanisms to further their alliance capabilities. Extrapolating from the data, one

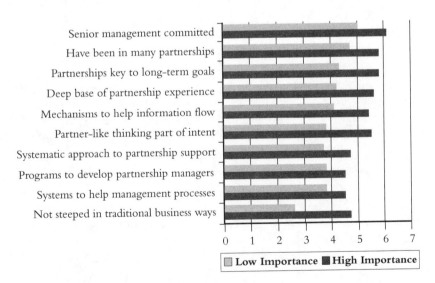

Figure 9.8   Alliance importance affects skill building.

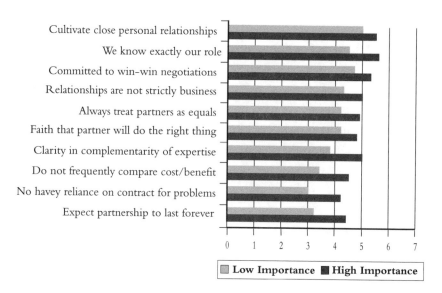

Figure 9.9   Recognizing that alliance skills make a difference.

would, in general, expect a successful alliance experience. This hotel chain is a market leader, has earned "bragging rights" but appears to be humble in its approach to alliances and willing to work with and develop its alliance partners. Similar findings were reported for the JVs found in the foreign energy company.

While it might appear symbolic, another observation is that virtually all of Corning's joint venture names carry the Corning name second. This is not accidental; nor is it an attempt to improve the pronunciation of the JV's name or to enhance name recognition. Corning purposively sends the signal that it is the reason for the alliance, the contribution of the partners' to the value adding activities of the alliance, and not the marquee value that is paramount. Humility is not a word often used to describe market leaders and many firms become ego-involved in these relatively small symbolic gestures. If a seemingly minor issue becomes a problem, what is likely to happen should more serious problems arise? To what extent, for example, would questions of control come to the fore if there is concern about which partner has his name first?

The importance of commitment is that it tends to be related strongly to alliance survival. If commitment or strategic intent/interest shift, it is likely that the alliance will suffer. Both shifts affect the attention, resources, and/or interest devoted to the alliance. Partners often, albeit subtly, communicate their faith in the durability of the alliance by their collaborative actions and relationship-building behaviors. These core relationship variables create an environment of mutual interest, promote a long-term vision, and demonstrate a willingness to invest on behalf of the relationship. Table 9.3 highlights attributes[8] related to positive alliance experiences. Each contributes to relationship value and makes it easy for one firm to partner with another. Not only do these qualities reduce the fears associated with opportunistic behavior, they embody a feeling that partners are, in fact, joined in a mutually beneficial quest, and they are willing to work hard to achieve their objectives.

Developing an Alliance Bench-Depth

Alliance-competent companies promote alliance-like behavior in the belief that it is essential to managerial development. High-potential managers

Table 9.3   Firm Attributes That Engender a More Positive Alliance Experience

Attribute	Description
Commitment	Implies the importance of the relationship.
Trust	Collaborative behavior is predictable and expected.
Cooperation	Complementary action in support of a mutual goal.
Mutual goals	Partners share goals that are accomplished through joint action.
Interdependence	Both recognize that they are jointly bound to the same goal.
Performance satisfaction	Past success leads to future interaction.
Structural bonds	Investments or commitments that make it hard for partners to separate.
Adaptation	One partner alters its processes, etc. to meet the changing needs of another.
Asset specific investments	Nonretrievable investments made in a relationship.
Social bonds	Personal ties and social relationships that make it hard to sever the relationship.

are identified early and are given increasingly more demanding alliance responsibility. The firm acknowledges that its alliance appetite is limited by the number of capable alliance managers. Moreover, the core values of the company support a culture that espouses the fundamental tests of alliance-like behavior. Strategic human resource development becomes an important factor in these activities.

Beyond its attempts to improve its bench-depth, management uses these opportunities to further inculcate an alliance mindset into the values of each manager. Developing its alliance strength through internal growth, rather than relying on external hires, is probably wise. In addition to developing an alliance mindset, effective alliance managers must be credible. Credibility is earned, and only through past interaction can one trust and have faith in the intentions of a colleague. Chapter 8 developed in greater detail the profile of a successful alliance manager. The challenge facing senior managers is the availability of resources to properly identify, nurture, and mentor the anticipated pool of further alliance managers to ensure sufficient bench strength.

Alliance Learning

Learning is the acquisition of new insight/knowledge that improves the firm's outcome. It is also defined as an ability to adapt to address problems or deal with uncertainty. Learning happens at several levels: at the alliance level, partners learn from each other; learning is captured and transferred within each of the partner organizations, and learning occurs at the individual level. Organizational learning is more than the accumulation of the knowledge of all the alliance managers, it encompasses also the learning systems and other processes developed by the company to influence the behaviors of others, to establish norms that support a learning environment, and to ensure that the knowledge acquired is passed from member to member.

In an alliance, knowledge transfer does not occur simply because partners select to work together. Exposure to new information is not enough for learning to occur. First, partners must have some common basis of past experience from which to absorb the knowledge. If the new knowledge is totally foreign to one partner, their ability to learn is greatly reduced. Second, there must exist a basis of trust between partners. The natural tendency is to be protective of one's expertise. Without trust, information sharing is low and partners are less willing to take risks associated with sharing valuable information

Third, some knowledge is more easily transferred than others. The more tacit the knowledge, the harder it is to acquire. The more open and visible the knowledge, the easier it is to learn, and the less valuable it is. It is through interaction, not observation, that a partner gets close enough to learn some tacit knowledge. Related to the question of tacit versus explicit knowledge is the concern for core versus noncore knowledge. While all core knowledge should be held dear, the most sensitive is tacit, core knowledge. In alliances, U.S. managers tend to focus on explicit knowledge—*what* is known rather than on the *how* or *why* it is known.[9]

One partner could attempt to hire away employees from the alliance (or the alliance partner) to gain access to this tacit knowledge. Such action often casts a dark shadow on the alliance and on the more aggressive partner; it is not uncommon for the injured partner to resort to legal remedies beginning with the enforcement of noncompete clauses. Bose, for example, has a specific statement in its agreement with its JITII™ partners that establishes the conditions under which employees can move from one firm to the other.

A fourth factor that affects the process would be the type of alliance used to acquire knowledge. Certain alliance structures and forms of governance can either enhance or inhibit the flows of knowledge. Licensing alliances limit the transfer of knowledge to the scope of the information licensed. When equity is shared and people comingle, the opportunity for greater knowledge transfer exists. These alliances enhance the opportunity to learn tacit knowledge. If joint activities are performed in sequence, rather than being pooled, the level of transfer can be controlled and limited to essential knowledge only.

A fifth factor relates to organizational processes and structures that enable the acquisition of knowledge. Organizational issues determine the way partners interact, affect decision-making styles and information processing, control the degree of formal versus informal exchanges and interaction, and influence the ease with which joint knowledge is created and disseminated. Flexible, adaptive, and open organizations are more conducive to high levels of interaction exchange, and knowledge transfer. Figure 9.10 illustrates how organizational issues affect learning in the foreign national oil company. As the alliance moves closer to the

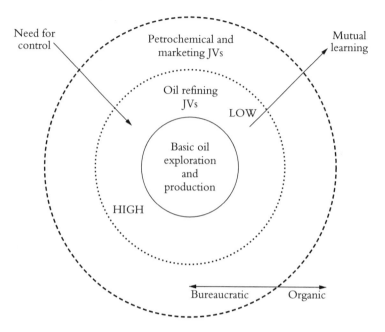

Figure 9.10   Organizational factors and knowledge transfer between partners.

core of the business and to oil itself, tighter control is exercised and there is less opportunity for learning. Geology and seismic information is not shared beyond making the report available to the "partner" who purchases the option to drill. As alliance activities move beyond activities such as distributing and refining the crude oil, to the production of chemicals and other petroleum derivative products and other downstream marketing ventures, alliance-like behavior becomes stronger, boundaries of the firm become more permeable, and greater learning occurs. Little learning is likely at the core since such tight control is exercised over access to the oil and the other natural resources. This is not unique to this company, as many firms try to protect their core. The irony is that by not allowing information out, no information enters.

A sixth factor affecting the partners' ability to absorb knowledge is the firm's culture. A culture supportive of trusting behavior, openness, inquiry, and experimentation is likely to reap more benefit from these alliances than a culture that avoids learning alliances because of the potential risks associated with knowledge transfer. Supportive cultures are open to continuous learning, encourage questioning behavior, and reward working hard to improve the quality and transparency of the information acquired through alliances and created internally.

As described in an earlier chapter, learnings that firefighters acquire at the site of a fire are transferred at the firehouse and shared widely. This is part of the learning culture. Similarly, the Israeli air force regularly reviews videotapes of missions to improve the quality of their pilots. All planes are equipped with cameras and all battle flights are taped. This quest for excellence is a key part of the culture and these rigorous after-action reviews are a standard part of training.

The factors that affect alliance partners' ability to learn from each other are summarized in Table 9.4. Two points should be mentioned. First, a learning alliance is a response to uncertainty that drives the motivation for partners to cooperate and increases the value of information to both partners. The ability to convert this acquired knowledge to a capability will result in competitive advantage. Second, the same uncertainty that drives firms to ally and share knowledge also creates the circumstances for partners' to behave opportunistically. As with alliances in general, there are tensions—factors that bring companies together also can serve to drive them apart. Table 9.4 also lists questions that should help managers identify the factors that could add to tensions in an alliance.

Challenges Affecting Learning Alliances

Learning alliances possess a darker side that challenges managers' abilities to develop alliance competencies devoted to learning. One challenge is the natural tensions that all alliances face; there is the dilemma of cooperation versus competition. Senior management must discover a process for enhancing the ability of the partners to learn from each other while, simultaneously, protecting their core technologies from an unintended leak or, in the worst case, outright expropriation. The second challenge is to ensure that learning happens at all three levels (i.e., firm, alliance, and the individual levels) so that maximum value can be achieved. All three levels are important and all contribute to knowledge creation and transfer.

A third, and more subtle, challenge is that learning is enhanced by a flexible structure. Permeable boundaries permit information to flow into the firm; yet, these boundaries also allow the unintended flow of sensitive

Table 9.4   Factors That Enable Alliance Learning

Factors That Enable Effective Learning Alliances	Questions for Assessing the Presence of These Factors
Common base of knowledge	If partners skills are complementary, to what extent is there overlap? How new is the knowledge being acquired? Do partners share a common base of understanding about this technology, innovation, etc.?
Trust	Are partners willing to share information? At what depth? Are partners worried about asymmetry in learning? How is it handled? Are questions raised about how knowledge will be used by the partners? Does one partner question the validity, content, worth of the information being shared? Are contracts and/or formal agreements used as a precondition to information sharing? Does one partner question the motives of the other? Is there constant evaluation of costs versus benefits?
Type of knowledge	How protective are partners of their knowledge? Is information departmentalized with some of it "open" and some treated as "private"? How accessible is the knowledge available through the alliance Are the "Chinese walls" real or perceived? Do partners continually get bogged down in trying to determine relative value of capabilities and skills? Do partners hold their cards close to their vest?
Type of alliance	How formal are agreements for technology sharing? Joint development of ideas, etc? Are partners encouraged to work closely on an informal basis? What is the governance structure for the alliance? How is performance defined? Do equity allocations dictate the degree of voice accorded partners? How embedded are the two partners?
Organizational structure and process	Do partners find that structural barriers inhibit the flow of information laterally? Do managers get rewarded for sharing information? What facilitating processes are used? Do partners have silo-like structures within their companies? Is information/knowledge held in the hands of many or few?

Table 9.4 *(Continued)*

Factors That Enable Effective Learning Alliances	Questions for Assessing the Presence of These Factors
	Does the compensation/reward system encourage/inhibit information sharing and joint discovery?
	How easily do the partners adapt to changes in their environment?
	How strong is the informal organization?
	Is the chain of command the preferred way to communicate in the partners' firms? Is it the default option?
Culture	How would you describe the partners' culture? Does the alliance have a same/different culture? How?
	Do managers show commitment to learning and espouse the importance of learning alliances?
	Is the culture open to new ideas and ways of solving problems?
	What are partners' tolerances for mistakes and errors?
	How aligned are the partners' cultures, values, objectives?
	Do managers dwell in the past and have a hard time unlearning bad past behavior?

knowledge out. The tension resides in achieving a healthy balance so that the information flows can maintain an equilibrium. Given that resources and absorptive capacity are not distributed equally among alliance partners, the equilibrium point is difficult to achieve. In the world of e-commerce and the Internet, many firms partner to share technology but also expend great effort to protect their proprietary part of the "puzzle." Partly, they achieve balance through industry norms that consider outright piracy to be a violation of accepted rules of engagement and such violators are treated as outcasts.

Partners must address other potential asymmetries that might occur. The degree to which a partner gains more nonalliance knowledge relative to alliance knowledge sets a tone that could affect the future of the alliance. The unintended acquisition of this expertise could affect one partner's future competitive position relative to its current partner. One outcome from such a situation is that the alliance might be structured to minimize the outflow of nonalliance knowledge while maximizing the flow of alliance-related knowledge. For example, rather than codevelop a new generation of software, the fearful partner licenses the rights to only the current version of the product. Such actions might protect one partner's interests but the alliance does not gain from the other partner's input. The question remains whether such balance is achievable and whether attempts to do so ultimately affect the intended spirit of the alliance.

Another imbalance is that partners do not learn at the same rate. Benefits from the alliance may accrue at different rates and one partner might feel disadvantaged. If one partner then pulls back or withholds information, the alliance and the partners suffer. If an aspect of learning is to acquire a new way to think about the future, all parties are less well off when the ability to acquire new knowledge is truncated.

Successful alliance partners seek more alliances and learn from their past mistakes. As alliance partners experience greater success in their ability to learn in their alliances and transfer that learning internally, they emphasize the qualities and characteristics that further enhance learning and knowledge sharing.[10] These firms become more trusting and more willing to share knowledge, and they invest in their people to build alliance competencies throughout the firm. Training and experimentation become valued and alliance capabilities become institutionalized. These alliance-ready companies know that if there is high turbulence and uncertainty, shared knowledge and a process for ensuring its widespread availability will separate the leaders from the followers.

Alliance Competence and Input to a Balanced Scorecard

As a firm develops an alliance competence, it will be more successful than competing firms that do not. The discussion regarding the impact of alliance competence on sustainable competitive advantage would lead to that conclusion. The data presented here show, over many different alliance contexts, that managers with greater alliance competence report higher levels of satisfaction with their alliance's performance than managers with less honed skills and competencies. In recent years, a balanced scorecard approach to performance has received attention as an approach to understand better one's corporate goals and objectives, financial results, and the drivers of these results.[11]

The scorecard is built around operating assumptions that are consistent with our view of factors that facilitate alliance-like behavior. These assumptions are delineated in Table 9.5. This table reflects many of the

Table 9.5   Factors Affecting the New Competition and the Need for a Balanced Scorecard (BSC)

Factors Influencing the New Competition	Tie to Alliance Competencies
Cross-functional thinking	Firms look for complementary skills and realize that specializing only on core skills is important.
Links to other part of the value chain	Follows from the above and recognizes that only through such linkages will companies be able to compete. Complementarity is the key.
Customer segmentation	While the emphasis is on mass customization, the underlying premise is value creation and the importance of alliances to provide unique valuable solutions to the marketplace.
Global scale	Alliances are a response to those who must compete on a global scale.
Innovation	Another reason for alliances; not only are the costs of innovation high but the life cycle of products and services continues to shrink.
Knowledge workers	People are key to the alliance process; a firm's ability to grow and disseminate alliance-related information throughout the firm is a key to alliance success.

external events mentioned earlier in the book and also captures issues that lie at the heart of the new competition.[12]

Beyond its ability to help managers clarify and translate vision and strategy, a BSC approach makes explicit the importance of measuring both the long-term outcomes and the short-term milestones in pursuit of those goals. The scorecard is built around four primary perspectives:

1. *Financial perspective.* Summarizes the economic consequences of actions taken.
2. *Customer perspective.* Addresses the value proposition one hopes to accomplish.
3. *Internal business process perspective.* Examines the internal processes that impact achieving one's goals as they relate to customers and financial targets.
4. *Learning/growth perspective.* Learning is key to long-term growth of the firm and must be attended to.

Alliances impact short- and long-term perspectives, try to achieve balance between objective and less quantitative measures, and affects firm, partner, and alliance outcomes. All these different perspectives must be balanced.

By understanding better how alliance thinking and alliance-like behaviors impact a firm's scorecard, managers will begin to ask additional questions about how their alliance strategy affects their overall business performance. Figure 9.11 illustrates the relationship between alliance thinking and the elements that compose the BSC. The effects of a firm's alliances impact each of the elements of the scorecard. The questions that are raised focus on implementation, as is the intent of the BSC, tie alliance thinking to the objectives of the four perspectives, and shed light on the initiatives senior management might develop to support the firm's overall vision and strategy. Alignment should exist among each of the alliance activities and the BSC elements. All this effort is directed to deliver value to the firm's chosen set of customers.

For the key themes associated with each perspective, there are alliance-related considerations that can affect performance outcomes. Table 9.6 presents questions that should help managers address alliance-related considerations in pursuit of their own balanced scorecards. Through these

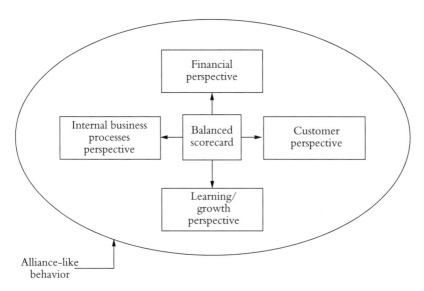

Figure 9.11   Alliance thinking and the balanced scorecard.

Table 9.6 Alliance-Related Activity and Its Efffect on Each of the BSC Perspectives

BSC Perspective	Key Themes for Each Perspective	Alliance Implications
Financial perspective	Revenue growth and mix. Cost reduction and/or productivity improvement. Asset utilization and investment strategy.	Does the alliance leverage partners' market, product, and/or technology advantage? To what extent are these leverage points complements or substitutes? If they are financial gains for one partner, are there gains for the other partner(s)? Do partners have access to their partners' other relationships? Do partners cooperate upstream and compete downstream? Has waste been reduced throughout the system or has the burden merely shifted from one partner to another? Using the alliance is greater value captured and delivered to the target customer? To what degree is this new alliance advantage sustainable? Are costs cuts shared equitably across partners? How is the risk/reward burden distributed? Have both partners realized benefits from better asset utilization? Do partners gain equitably across the different measures of financial performance?
Customer perspective	Market share. Customer satisfaction. Customer acquisition. Customer retention.	Do partners argue over who owns the customer? Have roles in the customer relationship development process been clearly understood? Is product/service delivery seamless from the customers' perspective? If one partner fails to execute, what is the impact on the alliance and on the other partner(s)? Do measures reflect the extent to which all partners contribute to and affect customer satisfaction? Are they compatible? Are partners selected because their concern for customer care, customer service, etc. are aligned? Can partners articulate how each contributes to customer retention/satisfaction? Can partners articulate the increment market share gains they hope to achieve from this alliance?

(Continued)

Table 9.6 *(Continued)*

BSC Perspective	Key Themes for Each Perspective	Alliance Implications
		Do partners acknowledge the long-term versus short-term tensions surrounding getting customers and keeping them? Is customer-sensitive information closely held or widely shared among partners?
Internal business process perspective	Innovation process. Operations process. Postsale service.	Have roles in the value creation process been clearly understood by the partners? Have provisions been made for sharing patents, inventions, etc.? Who owns what? How concerned are partners about sharing/leaking sensitive information? Are risks and rewards shared equitably? Is the venture equally important to both partners? Do partners share similar expectations regarding speed to market, time to break even, etc.? What are the partners' risk profiles regarding highly uncertain projects? Is NIH a big problem for partners? Is service delivery a seamless process through all levels of the value chain? If not, where is the bottleneck and why? Do partners have a silo mentality or is cross-functional cooperation encouraged and fostered?
Learning and growth perspective	Employee capability. Information systems capability. Motivation, empowerment, and alignment.	Do both partners value and invest in human capital? Do both partners share similar structures and processes to encourage the creation and dissemination of knowledge? Do partners treat information as a public or private good? Do partners share a similar view regarding the value of employee satisfaction and retention? What do partners spend yearly on technology and its infrastructure? Can partners link their systems easily and meaningfully? Do both partners make it easy for information to flow where it is needed, internally or externally? Do partners both value empowerment or do employees tend to delegate up?

Table 9.6   *(Continued)*

BSC Perspective	Key Themes for Each Perspective	Alliance Implications
		Do processes and systems within the partners' companies enable personal growth and commitment to the business?
		Are partner cultures aligned with core learning principles?
		Is risk-taking behavior encouraged or is failure seen as a black mark on one's career?
		Do partners support teams and other cross functional activities? Are they rewarded?
		How permeable are the partners' boundaries?
		Do partners worry about the asymmetries in learnings gained and the type of knowledge gained?

questions, one realizes that a firm's overall business performance is directly affected by its alliance-like behavior. Based on the reasons for forming alliances, one would expect that alliance-competent companies would have improved customer satisfaction and retention, would achieve these gains at lower costs and with higher profitability, would have more effective internal processes, and would be better organizational learners. However, alliances are not a panacea for poor performance. Our questions serve as a caution to those who might say: "alliances are the answer and I want some!"

The balanced scorecard discussion shows how alliance competency links to business performance. Other more subtle advantages are gained from such thinking. Since the BSC approach is based on input from managers throughout the organization, a hierarchical focus on top-down planning will not work. Although senior managers might set a vision for the future business and the role played by alliances, both the alliance process and the business-planning process cannot emphasize strategy formulation to the detriment of implementation. Implementation does not happen at the top of the organization; those who execute reside in the center of the firm. These lower-level managers must have access to information. To be effective learners, information must flow to the points where decisions are made. Teams and cross-functional activities become critical to the process as silo thinking just does not work. Alliance thinking and a balanced scorecard approach seem to support one another because both are based on a similar set of premises and values.

Summary

This chapter has focused on the building of alliance competencies and has attempted to build the argument that such competencies are part of the core competencies of a firm. It began with a discussion of alliance competencies, what they are and the types that exist, and how they enhance and improve alliance-like behavior. These competencies are a catalyst, a set of capabilities, and organizational factors that allow skilled firms to better leverage the potential gains that an alliance partner would bring to the alliance. Incorporating data from a number of studies to further enrich the presentation, we emphasized that building an alliance competence will positively affect alliance-like behavior, reduce the potentially debilitating effects of static, reduce conflict, and improve alliance (and corporate) performance.

A balanced scorecard approach was used to further stress the impact of alliance activity on business performance. The BSC became a vehicle to surface a set of questions that are relevant to each of the four components of the scorecard. Although alliance activity should improve overall business performance, there are no guarantees. Caution is advised as the list of questions implies. Alliances offer advantages and there are major benefits to be realized, but the process is complicated and all aspects of alliance management require attention and time. There are many obstacles to the development of alliance-competent firms. Old habits die slowly; power, information, and decision-making authority still reside at the top in many organizations. Many companies have begun the journey and are still at the stage where alliance skills are in the hands of a few. Alliance-relevant knowledge must be disseminated throughout the organization. Massive change is in order as the firm's culture, structure, systems, and processes must embrace this change to enable such learning. To acknowledge that alliances are important to one's future is one thing, to begin the journey and to develop alliance competencies throughout the organization is quite another.

10

Special Topics in Alliances

This chapter highlights three separate but related topics that have emerged as important alliance-related issues for managers. Although each topic presents unique challenges, the basic alliance concepts remain similar. The dual purpose here is to provide a contextual perspective and to show that the alliance concepts and principles put forth in earlier chapters are as meaningful across all of the following three topics:

1. Innovation and alliances.
2. Interimistic alliances.
3. Supply chain alliances.

Each issue is certainly important enough to receive a great deal more individual attention. However, we have limited our discussion to an overview since the topics are, to a large degree, special cases of more general topics covered earlier. The three topics can be viewed as expanded examples of current alliance activity. Innovation and supplier management present unique challenges for managers who rely on alliances to gain both access to technology and lower total cost of ownership. Interimistic alliances present different challenges because of the time-compressed relationship and the need to quickly reach value creation.

As a starting point, the *New York Times,* on Sunday March 7, 1999, ran several alliance-related stories. One story described the nature of coopetition[1] between Sony and Microsoft. One Sony executive describes the relationship as "sometimes we dance and sometimes we stand at opposite ends of the dance floor. The following key points are taken from that story:

- Both firms are in the midst of a convergence between consumer electronics and the PC. Microsoft and Sony are at the same time partners and competitors as the innovations brought to life by the Japanese require the software capabilities of Microsoft. Both are cooperating to produce a smart phone (in an alliance with Qualcomm) that can download from the Web and perform other functions that mimic a PC. Yet, despite the cooperation between these two giants, they compete as each covets the part of the market the other has traditionally ruled.

- There is a standards battle ensuing between Microsoft and its partners Mitsubishi and Honeywell, and Sony, Philips and six other consumer electronics makers to support home applications software. Each side has laid claim to its solution to have the PC monitor a full range of home appliances. The battle lines have been drawn with Sun Microsystems joining forces with Sony to create a system that is independent of a Windows© driven computer.

The article goes on to describe the complex interplay between the two giants. The relationship between Sony and Microsoft is one of partner, supplier-buyer, competitor, and complementor.[2] Relationships between companies do not get more complicated than the interaction between Sony and Microsoft.

To further illustrate the complexities in many corporate relationships, earlier the same week IBM and Dell announced a massive $16 billion alliance agreement. Not only will IBM furnish computer components to Dell, both will share technology development and will engage in broad patent cross licensing. In part, this alliance was driven by falling PC prices and thinning margins that plague both companies. They hope that this alliance offers them many opportunities: Dell gains access to new technology and IBM receives revenue from its components, patents, and technology. On the surface this appears to be the quid pro quo. However, the structure of the alliance takes different forms, and in one instance IBM and Dell have a supplier-buyer alliance; on another level, the two are engaged in a series of technology alliances. They foresee market opportunities in which their complex alliance allows each partner the opportunity to leverage the skills/capabilities of the other. For Dell, there is an opportunity to enter new markets and gain access to innovation and new technological developments sooner. For IBM there is the incremental revenue derived from its products, components, and technology, plus they have the chance to deploy their service organization more effectively.

A discussion of innovation and alliance activity follows. Next, we describe interimistic alliances, and then supply chain alliances are presented. There are linkages among the three types of alliances as the previous examples suggest. It is likely that companies will engage in all three types of alliances and also that the same partner might play three different roles. One purpose of this chapter is to help managers understand the complexities of each alliance context.

Innovation and Strategic Alliances

Background

Innovation is the lifeblood of corporate renewal. Although firms compete on different bases, sustainable advantage is achieved through products and processes that provide new opportunities for the firm. Historically, firms tended to rely on internal resources for their R&D and new product development efforts. To go "outside the firm" for innovation was seen as either an admission of poor management or a sign of failure. As stated earlier, one driver of increased alliance activity is that the cost of and time associated with all aspects of the innovation process (from ideation to commercialization) has increased substantially over the years. Very few companies have the luxury of enough resources or time; only through some form of partnership can they afford to engage in product or process innovation. Even if sufficient resources are available to the firm, the innovation process is serendipitous enough that only the strong are willing to risk odds that are not clearly in their favor. Beginning with ideation, for every 100 new ideas generated, there is less than a 5 percent chance of attaining a commercial success. Alliances provide a hedge against these risks (time, resources, and failure) and more and more the management of technology and innovation includes as a core capability the management of alliances. One finding that supports this assertion is that there is a positive correlation between the R&D intensity of an industry and the number of alliances found in that industry.[3]

The need for innovation has become a major source of strategic confusion among firms across a broad cross-section of industries. The problem is that the process itself is fraught with uncertainty and risk as depicted in Figure 10.1. Over time, uncertainty is reduced through learning but that learning comes at a cost; as with any alliance, there is a loss of control and autonomy. Through alliances, firms reduce technological risk because one partner relies on the capabilities of the other who has presumably journeyed down that path before or possesses knowledge that should lower the probability of failure. For example, Rover claims that some of its manufacturing costs were reduced by 30 percent as a result of its alliance with Honda. In addition to the impressive cost savings, Rover[4] asserts that it improved its supplier relationships, raised its quality, improved its cycle time for development, and developed sharper alliance management skills.

Generally speaking, however, technology alliances are formed to acquire technology that can fill an existing gap or preclude a technology from being acquired by one's competitor. These alliances can benefit the acquiring firm in different ways. Some firms[5] defined three kinds of alliances: learning, supply, and positioning. In both supply and positioning alliances, motivations are aimed at decreasing costs and gaining immediate leverage based on the partners' market access or product

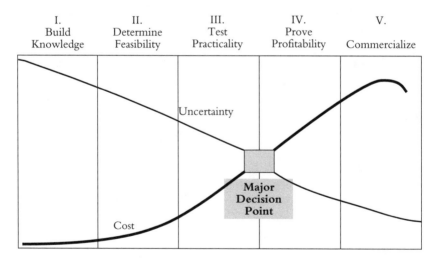

Figure 10.1   Risk and return through the stages of innovation.

portfolio. Oracle and CheckFree have signed an agreement whereby Oracle's software will be integrated into CheckFree's product. The objective is to increase the industry's acceptance of Oracle's solution. There is little intent to learn, the goal is to leverage CheckFree's market presence. To gain greater market exposure, Amazon.com and Hoover's Online have agreed to promote the other in their Web sites. Again, the objective is to leverage an already existing advantage.

Innovation Is Really about Learning

Learning alliances are, as the name suggests, intended to internalize knowledge and to decrease the partners' capabilities gap. Rover demonstrated that it learned a great deal from Honda over the decade they collaborated. Nortel partnered with Matsushita to access Panasonic's third-generation mobile phones that will include capability to send and receive motion pictures and voice. Beyond access to the Panasonic brand, both companies intend to experiment and test the feasibility of the technology and to assess the potential demand for the new service. This alliance is tied to both companies' core skills, allows them to expand their knowledge, and links technology and innovation to both firms' strategic intent. When an alliance is tied to defined corporate objectives and intent, there is a higher probability of success.

Since technology changes and innovation often take circuitous paths, it is also important that the partners can adapt and, in real time, reassess the alliance's direction. Because some alliances pursue basic research problems (as opposed to applied problems), they need to monitor performance and establish milestones as partners search for answers to questions that might not have been asked before. Beyond the checkpoints (gates) through which the innovation process proceeds, the importance of developing trust cannot be emphasized enough. When the rationale for the alliance is vague both within the partner companies and among the partners, instability will affect the partnership.

Although this section is about innovation, it is really about knowledge creation since innovation is a true form of experimentation in which we learn from our successes and our failures. Alliances are the catalyst for stimulating and leveraging such experimentation. In periods of rapid technological growth, one firm is unlikely to possess all the capabilities needed to be successful and must rely on different forms of alliances to reduce the inherent uncertainties associated with novel products or new markets. Figure 10.2 illustrates the many ways in which a firm might explore a new opportunity. The range of possibilities provides different options for assessing risk and return as well as the degree to which the firm must commit resources.

Innovation through Different Alliance Types

Figure 10.2 shows a range of approaches for transferring knowledge from one partner to another. Regarding explicit knowledge, one can observe and learn but the knowledge gained and the ability to successfully innovate from such observation is limited to how transparent the process is. First, the insight gained is marginal at best since the information is available to all and offers no sustainability. If one company can observe, why can't another? Yet, in recent years, companies have limited the extent to which visitors are permitted to tour their facilities. While the value gained here can be minor, little if any resource commitment has been made. The knowledgeable observer, however, can learn a great deal. Steve Jobs learned about new technology from his visit to Xerox's PARC. The MacIntosh is said to be based on Xerox-inspired technology. Similarly, a Corning scientist learned the specifications for the practical application of optical fiber from a visit to the British Post Office. Partly this is a mindset problem in that different

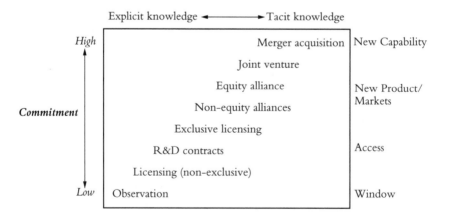

Figure 10.2 Innovation through alliances: The options. (*Source:* Adapted from D. Leonard-Barton, *Wellsprings of Knowledge* [Cambridge: Harvard Business School Press, 1998].)

people see the world differently. By seeing differently, one see opportunities that others don't.

At the opposite end of the continuum, firms either merge, or are acquired, in hopes of gaining access to the core competence on which the innovation or technological gains have been made. On paper, this approach has merit—one firm now *controls* the source of the innovation and the intellectual storehouse that birthed it.

Merger. Two immediate problems surface when one considers the merger/acquisition approach to innovation. One problem is that innovation is partly social phenomenon and the culture of the dominant firm might impede or inhibit the same level of innovation that existed prior to the merger or takeover. This unintended outcome is found in countless examples of smaller firms that were acquired by larger ones whose processes and structures have killed the innovation spirit that the larger firm so admired.

The problems associated with postmerger integration are nontrivial. Often the focus is on the need to cut costs first but the importance of maintaining the innovative momentum of the partner is essential. The second problem is that a firm can buy the company but it does not own the people. The talent can and often does walk out the door leaving the acquirer with an empty shell. When IBM bought Lotus, the fear was that the talent that developed Lotus Notes would become unhappy and would leave taking the "crown jewels" with them. Lotus and IBM have very different corporate personalities and IBM had been down this same path before with other acquisitions (e.g., Rolm).

The lesson to be learned is that values and cultural norms are hard to change and merely acquiring the assets does not ensure that innovation will continue. A third, but less immediately recognized problem, is that if technology is changing quickly, or there are periods of discontinuous technological change, a merger/acquisition limits the firm's ability to react quickly if its chosen technological option is not viable. The exit costs associated with the purchase or merger are often high and the firm might find itself unable to quickly adapt to the significant changes in technology.

Joint ventures. A joint venture offers some degree of flexibility when compared with the merger but there are also limitations here as well.

Often partners contribute hard assets to the joint venture and the exit costs for them are also very real. It is probably best to start small and to limit the amount of investment at the outset. For example, in 1998 Nexstar Pharmaceuticals formed a joint venture with SKW Trostberg of Germany to produce products to diagnose and treat certain genetic illnesses. Nexstar and SKW combined units from each company to form this venture. Should the products fail to live up to expectations, because both companies committed significant resources, it would seem difficult for them to just walk away from the venture. Many times, the sunk cost argument is not convincing and firms do not respond as they might with less significant commitments. On the flip side, because partners have higher levels of commitment, they often work more diligently to solve problems and will try to weather the storms. Joint ventures allow greater opportunity to absorb technology and enable greater acquisition of tacit knowledge; yet, they also present greater risk if technology is changing rapidly. In addition, these complex relationships sow the seeds for greater potential conflict, partly as a result of the unintended flow of proprietary information from one partner to the other.

Other alliances. Nonequity alliances provide greater degrees of freedom under conditions of significant technological change. In yet another alliance aimed at the convergence of home electronics and the PC, Sony is working with General Instrument to develop digital set-top boxes for cable operators. This alliance is part of Sony's home network software solution. If the competing standard is accepted, there is more room for Sony to maneuver than had they invested significant resources to buy a company to accomplish the same objective. If there are competing standards and the alternative option prevails, as a general rule the less flexibility associated with the partnership, the more difficulty the partners will have adapting to the change required to remain competitive.

Where partners desire more flexibility there are either licensing agreements, dedicated sourcing, or other even less restrictive alliances through which partners can achieve their joint objectives. AOL and Sun have both developmental and marketing alliances in which both have focused on offering end-to-end e-commerce solutions. Again, the e-commerce arena is overflowing with alliances in which partners and competitors posture for their slice of what is estimated to be an enormous opportunity. Whatever the estimates are for the consumer market, the business-to-business market is estimated to be ten times the size. As discussed later in the chapter, many of the emerging e-commerce alliances would qualify as interimistic in nature since they are short-lived and exist to accomplish a specific task in a time-compressed manner.

Licensing provides access to a technology or a process that enriches the licensee's current capabilities. Merck has a licensing pact with In-Clone Systems for a cancer treatment that fills a void in Merck's own pipeline of new products. Similarly, Eli Lilly and Sepracor have formed a licensing agreement for Sepracor's R-fluoxetine, a modified form of an active ingredient in Prozac©. Lilly will exclusively develop and commercialize the product as well as retaining the rights for all indications and uses. Prozac is the single largest revenue producer for Lilly and its ability to extend the efficacy of the drug through this license is an important strategic decision. In both instances, licensing is used to provide pipeline protection for the companies by relying on others to provide key innovations. Also, the knowledge transfer is explicit and can be easily circumscribed to a defined set of compounds and/or drugs, or processes. For the smaller firm, the license provides much needed cash (in the Lilly example the payments total approximately $100 million) and, more importantly, protect their intellectual core from the expropriation of tacit knowledge and proprietary technology.

Consortia. Another alliance form that enables the innovation process is the consortium. Consortia are often loosely aligned networks of firms that combine resources and talent to jointly explore a new technology or process. Consortia also form to pursue standards setting and other approaches to gain commonly accepted view of an industry problem. Consortia have been formed to investigate HDTV, electric cars, and new generation computer chips. Companies join forces with both other companies and with universities. A university consortium often is used to conduct basic research that can then be taken into the firm for more applied problems. Here, companies might cooperate in the early stages of development and then compete later as each takes the output of the consortium and uses it inside their respective companies.

Innovation and the Ability to Absorb Knowledge

A fundamental issue here is the firm's relative absorptive capacity, which was introduced in Chapter 2. It relates to a firm's ability to recognize the value of external knowledge, assimilate it, and apply it to commercial ends. As discussed in Chapter 7, there exists a natural tension between the desire to acquire knowledge and the need to protect core capabilities. Nonetheless, to benefit from the availability of external knowledge, there are certain behaviors that enhance one's capacity to learn:[6]

- *Create porous boundaries.* Managers must be open to new ideas and not limit themselves to what they know. Many firms shun innovation and new ideas either because they have too much invested in the status quo or are listening too closely to their existing customers.

- *Scan broadly.* Do not limit your sights to what is known or what is comfortable. Innovation comes from varied sources and many times flows from outside the dominant paradigm. Encouraging scanning behavior that takes people from their comfort zone is probably wise and increases the probability of exposure to novel ideas. Remember that one's perspective limits one's imagination. The dominant paradigm presents strengths and weaknesses.

- *Provide for continuous interaction.* Knowledge is not gained at one point in time and is not limited to idea generation. Constant monitoring, experimentation, and probing throughout the innovation process takes time and resources but improves the quality of information gathered and results in better solutions.

- *Nurture technological gatekeepers and boundary spanners.* To the extent possible, look for well-connected managers who have both an extensive internal and external network. These managers might also play the role of alliance manager orchestrating the flow of information among alliance partners. This will facilitate the creation and dissemination of knowledge.

- *Fight not-invented-here.* To reject knowledge simply because it comes from the outside makes no sense but is part of the emotion and culture that drives many organizations. To think one has the answers and that others do not know is the height of arrogance and does not fit within an alliance mindset.

Summary

R&D alliances play a central role in many companies' technology strategies and are one approach to improving their innovation capability.

Firms have many reasons for collaborating to gain access to technology. The three major categories of motives for these alliances are summarized in Table 10.1. Although there are many reasons for such alliances, the success rate is relatively low. Partly, failure is a function of the fragility of alliances in general. Failure is also attributable to the nature

Table 10.1 Motives for Innovation Alliances★

Technology reasons	Much technology knowledge is tacit and is difficult to transfer. An alliance provides mechanisms to facilitate the flow of knowledge.
	Emerging technology represents the confluence of different areas of knowledge (e.g., bioengineering). Alliances expand the scope of knowledge available to the partners and ease access to these skills.
	Due to the costs and risks associated with new technology, uncertainty is high. Alliances reduce the costs of such attempts at innovation.
	Since information technology is pervasive both within and between firms, alliance-like behavior and information sharing are enabled.
Competitive reasons	Alliances often raise barriers to entry and can preclude competitors from gaining scale, resources, or a capable partner.
	Alliances improve the firm's global reach by providing access to both technology and markets.
	Through closer customer/supplier linkages, alliances provide an ability to be more nimble and more responsive.
	Alliances have demonstrated that partners improve time to market and decrease the development times.
	In markets where standards have not been established, alliances provide a vehicle by which partners can jointly create and promote their "design."
Firm reasons	Alliances are sometimes used as a precursor to mergers. Technology alliances allow firms to experiment and "get to know each other."
	Given that many mergers and acquisitions fail to achieve their stated objectives, alliances are a less costly alternative.
	Where technology is just emerging, a critical mass of effort might be needed to achieve gains in strategic technologies seen as important to the national interest.

★ This discussion is based on M. Dodgson, "The Strategic Management of R&D Collaboration," *Technology Analysis and Strategic Management 4,* 3 (1992): 227–44.

of innovation alliances in particular. Many of these alliances are experiments—they are probes into untested technology. Given the inherent uncertainty and unpredictable change often associated with emerging technology, it is difficult for partners to maintain focus and strategic direction. Such alliances are often fraught with tension because of the unpredictability of the innovative process. Researchers might start a project looking to learn about X and find that they discover Y.

Interimistic Alliances: A New Breed of Alliances

Interimistic alliances represent fast-developing, often short-lived alliances in which partners combine their skills and/or resources to address a transient, albeit important, business opportunity. While some of these alliances might enhance the innovation process through the access to technology, the opportunity includes other advantages such as access to customers or key segments. Interimistic alliances are typically found in swiftly evolving industries/markets, marked by rapid technological change and/or uncertainty. These alliances appear in nascent industries, such as biotechnology which has been spawned by new technological developments, such as recombinant DNA or the Internet. They are found also when companies must join forces to develop an industry standard or complete a similar short-term project.

These alliances appear to challenge conventional academic wisdom with respect to how partners develop relationship attributes necessary for the creation of alliance value, at what levels these attributes must exist, and the definition of alliance success. Most alliance thinking has typically taken a long-term view of alliance creation and suggests that certain key relationship characteristics that enable value creation are developed over a considerable length of time.[7] Our own research suggests that it can take alliances close to three years to work through start-up problems. When we share this information with managers from high-tech industries, they recoil at the thought and state that they don't have two months, let alone two to three years.

Because of the need for immediate strategic impact, interimistic alliance partners must "hit the ground running." Partnership characteristics necessary for the effective operation of the alliance have to be either in place or developed in a compressed period of time. Because interimistic alliances are truncated, relationship attributes, such as commitment and norms, exist but in modified form. For example, commitment appears to be more task-bound than broadly based, and norms tend to be tied to expectations derived from the industry instead of being established through the relationship. At its core, what drives these alliances is time pressure.

Finally, interimistic and more long-term (or sustainable) alliances are often evaluated on different measures of success. Interimistic alliances are focused on achieving success that is narrow in scope and less final results oriented than that pursued by sustainable alliances. These alliances help firms achieve milestone targets on the path to an ultimate objective. These alliances accomplish goals that, if not reached, make it difficult to attain the final objectives.

Interimistic alliances are often designed to achieve narrowly defined objectives, such as acquiring specific know-how, producing a new product, or influencing industry standards. Cybercash, a small high-tech company that focuses on problems associated with e-commerce security, has alliances that cover the full range of topics mentioned earlier. Figure 10.3 illustrates the extensive web of Cybercash's alliances. As technology

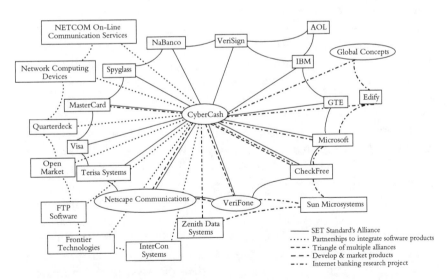

Figure 10.3 CyberCash, Inc.: Shaping the future of cash—spider's web of some of CyberCash's alliance involvements.

advances and/or as partners align, becoming advocates for their proprietary protocol, it is apparent that no one company possesses all the pieces to the puzzle. There are many more skills and capabilities needed than can be held by one company. Complicating matters further is that the "puzzle" is a moving target. Not only are alliances formed to solve a section of the puzzle, the technology is constantly changing and the puzzle must adapt to these changes. Once a section is solved, partners then disband and continue down their different paths. At a later point in the development of another part of the puzzle, partners might ally again and so it goes.

A Comparison of Life Cycles

As discussed in Chapter 6, alliances have no set pattern to their productive life and using length of time as a measure of alliance success might lead to false conclusions about the efficacy of an alliance. In Silicon Valley, alliances to exploit new technology partly account for the high growth among gazelles[8] (i.e., small firms that have revenue growth over 20% during each of the past four years). A predominant theme among these alliances is that time is critical and partners help each other minimize time to market and lower the costs associated with innovation. These firms come together, part ways, work with other partners, and seemingly re-create themselves according to the Schumpeterian notion of creative destruction. Alliance duration is partly explained by the industry and the pace of change, and partly by the scope of the alliance and the activities performed. Thus, different kinds of alliances might reach a productive life in shorter period of time and others might sustain the level of productivity longer.

Despite the differences in the length of alliance life cycles, all alliances must pass through common stages. Reverting to another biological analogy, different species mature over different periods of time. Yet, the pattern of growth (i.e., the stages) is similar. A life cycle comprises a series of stages, or changes in form or function, through which an organism passes. Scientists, for example, use fruit flies in their research because fruit flies' genetic structure is similar to that of humans. Generations of fruit flies can be studied in a relatively short period of time since their entire life cycle is less than 45 days. In the laboratory, researchers are able to study, over a decade, genetic changes in hundreds of generations of fruit flies. Generally speaking, a fruit fly and a human share the same number and similar types of life cycle stages. Each of their life cycles progresses through birth ➔ growth ➔ maturity ➔ decline; however, fruit flies develop in a highly compressed period.

Comparing the Development of Relationship Attributes

Attributes associated with the relationship partly predict alliance performance and are necessary for an alliance to reach a value creation stage. The manner in which these attributes evolve, and the level at which they exist in interimistic alliances is often different from that found in the traditional model of alliance development. An understanding of these attributes and how they evolve is critical to alliance managers since part of the problem facing partners is how to manage expectations about the interactions associated with an alliance. These attributes include trust, mutual goals, norms, interdependence, social bonds, commitment, and performance satisfaction.

Trust

One way in which trust develops is that the partners make adaptations over time, such that each partner earns the trust of the other. In interimistic alliances, the pressure to partner quickly makes "trial and testing" difficult. Trust often must be a preexisting condition, developed through previous dealings and/or reputation. As a consequence, prospective partners are trusted within the narrow bounds of the newly defined alliance's goals and scope.

Three important points surface:

1. Trust is expected to exist at a threshold level *before* the alliance partners consummate an interimistic alliance since there is little time to let trust emerge. The alliance decision becomes a binary: there is sufficient trust; there is not sufficient trust. Past behavior becomes the predictor of future expectations about partnerlike behavior and one's trustworthiness.

2. Trust is context-specific and is limited to the scope of the alliance. There are different expectations surrounding the domains in which trust will extend. (Recall that many interimistic alliances are nonexclusive.)

3. Partners ally to combat a mutual threat or to capitalize on a joint opportunity. Thus, trust places partners in positions of mutual dependencies.

Time is an obstacle to the more deliberate, and cautious, trust-building process. These alliances must be nimble and develop quickly as discontinuous change is more the norm. Because interimistic alliances often compete for resources, skills, and/or marketplace access against other alliances, or networks of alliances; partners have a significant incentive to work together in a nonopportunistic fashion for the duration of the alliance. One can think of trust in these instances as related to the notion of "enlightened self-interest." For example, in alliances where the goal is standards setting, it is in the interest of *all* alliance partners that standard X be accepted over standard Y (e.g., standards for operating systems and Internet security). Once standards have been set, it is expected that the partners will resume their competitive actions. Cooperation was stimulated by rival alliances that advocated their own dominant design. Once standard X is accepted, each firm can then participate in a market from which they might otherwise have been precluded.

Mutual Goals

Mutual goals reflect the degree to which partners share goals that can only be accomplished through joint action. The broader the alliance's mandate, the longer the time period required to reach consensus among partners. Mutual goal development in interimistic alliances is mainly a result of a mutually acknowledged transient business opportunity. Potential partners are presented with a moment of crisis, or a brief window of opportunity, that gives them clear reasons for working together. For example, the confluence of communication, computer, information, and entertainment technologies makes it inherently clear that firms need to work with partners from these complementary industries to emerge as a player in the new convergence industry. Because of the rapidly changing technological opportunity, much of the broad thinking about why partners should collaborate is truncated.

The reason to cooperate is obvious; failure to align now could preclude a viable competitive response later. Interimistic alliances are driven by an opportunity, and mutual goals become part of the "contract." In this sense, goal compatibility is conditional on the turn of environmental events that can drastically change industry demands. Both partners recognize that influences beyond their control can make initial motivations for the alliance irrelevant and, hence, eliminate goal congruence. At that moment partners may decide to disengage; or, they might agree to refocus their energy and jointly pursue the new opportunity. Nimbleness is a virtue.

Norms

Norms are expectations about behavior that a group of decision makers share and use as rules for establishing joint values. They are based on the expectation of mutuality of interest and are designed to enhance the well-being of the relationship. In an interimistic alliance, it is accepted that parties have expectations about potential individualistic or competitive actions and are less obligated to the continuity of the relationship. There is a mutually expressed, or sometimes tacit, understanding that the firms will work together as long as the alliance makes good business sense. For example, Visa and MasterCard International cooperate in such areas as standards setting, encryption, and basic smart card technology and then knowingly and vigorously compete once agreement has been reached. They know that without agreement on fundamental strategic points facing the whole of the bank credit card industry, both will face limited opportunities.

External pressures often dictate that partners *rapidly* develop working norms that are likely to be tied to the alliance task. Personal commitment is less likely to emerge given the time horizon of the alliance. Instead there might exist a general set of accepted norms that are set by the culture of the industry and the expectations that have built over time among firms. In Silicon Valley, where nonproprietary and nonexclusive alliances appear to be widely accepted, companies have developed over the years sets of norm-governed behaviors. For example, when e-mails are not promptly returned, it is likely that the alliance has ended.[9] A clanlike culture exists among these firms, whose managers migrate from company to company bringing their past experiences, expectations, and contacts with them.

Some firms have developed an alliance competence through their participation in many such alliances, which allows them to shortcut the norm development process. Successful interimistic alliance partners have a high capacity to learn and possess a level of adaptability; both are important precursors to norm development.

Interdependence

In interimistic alliances, mutual dependence, and hence a desire to collaborate, is less motivated by investments and outcomes over time as it is by risk and transient opportunity. Partners view dependence as limited to the task or opportunity at hand. Once the mission of the alliance has been accomplished, partners often look to untangle, or redefine, the alliance. To ensure that decoupling can occur, partners rely less on psychological ties, and they often intentionally limit the boundary permeability between firms through such activities as "black-boxing" technology or know-how. A concerted effort is made to limit alliance "touch points" to those required to accomplish the task at hand and to minimize the potentially detrimental effects of future competition between partners.

Social Bonds

Social bonds develop through personal interactions, and there is an expectation that future interaction is affected by past alliance behavior. The limited shelf life of interimistic alliances does not provide, nor require, the time necessary to develop *substantial* social bonds. Although some threshold level must exist, interimistic alliances tend to have a lower level of social bonding than sustainable alliances. In many instances, interimistic alliance managers have a far-reaching social network, often as a result of previous dealings. Key players are known and social bonding is more a function of corporate/industry contacts. Past experience and existing relationships coupled with reputational effects seem to facilitate the development of social bonds.

Commitment

The cornerstone of a successful alliance is a high level of commitment by the partners from the beginning of the relationship development process. Without high levels of commitment, the alliance might languish since each party is less willing to devote the resources necessary for success. Or, commitment might be uneven because partners value the alliance differently.

In interimistic alliances, commitment to the alliance's objectives tends to be greater than commitment to partner. Shared enlightened self-interest exists, and partners are committed to their own future success. Yet, their success is partially dependent on the outcome of the present effort. A firm might commit its best R&D people with the intention of learning from the alliance. The higher order commitment is to advancing the state-of-the-art technology, so that both partners gain relative to other competing alliances. It is likely that each partner will later use that technology to complete in an expanded marketplace. Expanding the pie is better than retaining a large share of a small piece.

Performance Satisfaction

Performance satisfaction is the degree to which the business transaction meets the performance expectations of the partners. In interimistic alliances, project-oriented measures of success are utilized to the exclusion of social outcomes. These measures include developing a strategic portfolio of technology options for the future, acquiring know-how, signaling to partners/competitors/customers, or simply taking the only avenue open to the firm if it wants to be a player in an emerging market. Success is really a staging point or intermediate position on the way to a future competitive gain. Parties might successfully partner now so that each can successfully compete later in what is expected to be a much larger market. If this first alliance fails, neither partner will have acquired the requisite skills/knowledge or influence over the market to compete later. These early, interimistic alliances are necessary but not sufficient conditions for a larger, future opportunity. Think of a series of interimistic alliances as building blocks in the accomplishment of a larger set of alliance objectives.

Implications

Due to the ever-increasing rate of technological change, interimistic alliances are likely to grow in importance. If this is true, several implications emerge. These alliances are a different alliance form and present challenges to the most seasoned alliance managers. Time is a critical consideration and there is little tolerance for mistakes—change happens too quickly.

Importance of reputation. Because partners have different temporal expectations about interimistic alliances, partners play by a slightly different set of rules. Since interimistic alliances tend to exhibit a higher degree of enlightened self-interest and bounded commitment, partners must adopt a stance of duality tinged with opportunism. The question here is how can the partners manage the existence of such seemingly diametrically opposed postures without jeopardizing the collaborative spirit that must exist between the partners for them to quickly create value. Partly, expectations must be shaped to tolerate a certain level of self-interest. A more significant factor is the ability of the partners to balance self and alliance interests, and quickly bring the alliance up to speed. Here, *reputation* plays a critical role. The partners' reputation as a *fair-dealing and competent* alliance partner is critical to shortcutting the relationship development process. Reputation becomes the platform from which the partners take the leap of faith necessary for quickly achieving close collaboration. Just because an opportunity exists, one cannot act opportunistically! The alliance-competent partner is an enabler, a facilitator, who achieves heightened alliance results by minimizing the nonproductive energy associated with alliance formation and value creation.

Firms that have enough market power to incent others to partner, without a desirable reputation as an alliance partner, are potentially sabotaging the gains they might achieve from interimistic alliances. For example, if one has a reputation for being a potentially opportunistic partner, it might take longer for these alliances to reach a value-creation stage. Partners simply behave more cautiously and structure more complex alliance to protect their own interests.

Different definitions of success. Interimistic alliances are built on the belief that competitive success ultimately hinges on discrete but related events. To achieve success, one might have to rely on a different set of partners all of whom contribute unique skills/competencies but none of whom singularly possesses the range of needed capabilities. In light of the high levels of uncertainty, these skill sets might not be known with precision but are revealed over time as partners learn more about the emerging market/technology. The firm's success is predicated on a series of intervening alliances that culminate in achieving the final measure of firm success. Each interimistic alliance is a partial solution contributing to the larger corporate plan and objectives.

Rapid environmental/technological change necessitates navigating the future nimbly and with few long-term encumbrances. A series of intense, interimistic alliances allows flexibility and an opportunity to develop performance metrics that are suited to the narrowly defined task at hand. As the pace of technological innovation begins to significantly affect almost every industry, firms will need to develop strategies for dealing with such change. Interimistic alliances allow firms to stay current with evolving trends, hedge bets, influence the development of industries, and/or learn. These alliances provide firms with the ability to renew and maintain advantages that are constantly eroded by technological change. In this respect, success becomes a series of intermediate, achievable milestones that, when taken together, result in future profits and/or market share.

Summary

Interimistic alliances are a step to understanding better the notion of network alliances since many of these relationships involve more than two parties. Often the arrangement that evolves is a constellation of firms working together in what are sometimes referred to as spider web alliances. The addition of a third party to the alliance creates messy problems and often adds geometrically to the complexities of these alliances. Now the wishes of three partners must be balanced against three different cultures, sets of expectations, and management styles. All the considerations that make alliances fragile and hard to manage, make networks even more complicated. Adding to these problems is the reality that firms often participate in competing networks as a strategy to hedge their bets.

If windows of opportunity are brief and/or a threat is imminent, it is necessary that the magnitude of the alliance reflect the realities of the marketplace. A long-term alliance with a broader mandate than the opportunity at hand might be preferred, but high uncertainty might necessitate an interimistic alliance with its limited expectations. Preexisting trust, possibilities for future competition against one partner, nonexclusivity, and the like are bound to make the most seasoned manager nervous and hesitant to act. Here, hesitation can spell doom. Failure in the first alliance might mean an inability to participate in the second alliance. Interimistic alliances allow firms to proceed in a measured fashion, attempting to piece parts of the puzzle together knowing that the complexities are such that one partner is unlikely to have all the parts.

Toward More Effective Sourcing and Supplier Management

Today's competitive pressures compel business leaders to continually seek new sources of sustainable advantage to survive, let alone flourish. Often competitive advantage resides with the relationships and linkages that the firm can forge with its supply chain partners.[10] With the new dynamics of these supply chain alliances, we can no longer talk about suppliers and customers as though they are independent entities managed in isolation. Many CEOs have identified supply chain management as a key initiative for their companies. Look at the numbers: they tell a compelling story. Purchased goods and services typically represent from 50 to 70 percent of a company's value potential: 70 percent of revenues, as well as 70 percent of a typical company, is defined by the components, materials, and services it acquires from outside sources.

Vertical integration has become less and less credible, serving only to burden many organizations with noncore activities. Recent data on the use of outside suppliers show that GM buys 58 percent of its parts from outside suppliers versus 72 percent for Ford, and 77 percent for Chrysler. This equates to approximately $800 in additional costs per automobile for GM for the same basic materials. Ford and Chrysler rely on their supply chain to achieve efficiencies that GM has failed to realize internally.

For many companies, there is an emerging realization that solidifying effective relationships at every link in the supply chain is a prerequisite of success. Sources of competitive advantage include the ability to leverage purchasing knowledge and expertise across the extended enterprise built on the benefits of supply chain information management systems. In addition, these supply chains focus on reducing the total cost of ownership, improving quality, and, ultimately, increasing shareholder value for all members of the supply chain. The potential of effective sourcing and supplier management represents the shift from denominator management (i.e., cost reductions) to becoming a major contributor to the numerator (corporate revenue).

At the core of this new sourcing paradigm is a systemwide effort to harmonize individual self-interests; align values; adopt compatible technologies; address the problems of distorted information; and pursue complementary core competencies across the entire supply chain. These sourcing principles, combined with the quality of partnerships across each supply chain, form the basis of effective supplier management. In fact, some propose that achieving excellence in supply chain management will ultimately result in a significant increase in a firm's stock prices.[11] Among the critical factors that affect effective sourcing and supply management are:

- Integrating suppliers into the supply chain.
- Information sharing and trust.

We highlight these two factors and discuss their impact in gaining the advantages espoused by effective supply chain management. Despite the efforts made thus far, it is possible to work closely with one's supply base and never integrate them into your planning or other essential processes. Partly, this reluctance is a function of trust (a lack thereof) and a resistance to share information. Both concerns emanate from the traditional adversarial role between buyers and sellers. The goal of this section is to equip managers to think differently about what it means to partner within the context of a supply chain.

Integrate Suppliers into the Supply Chain

Despite the claims espousing some form of "partnership" among a wide range of suppliers and customers, our own research has shown that attempts at partnering have met with mixed success. Many companies (and their procurement managers) openly fear becoming too reliant on suppliers and worry that these so-called partners might take advantage based on that dependency. Our data[12] show that while buyers advocate closer ties with fewer suppliers, they tend to focus mainly on price when making sourcing decisions. Achieving supply chain integration involves an understanding of the organizational drivers that relax these price-driven tensions by sharing information and developing trust. Practically, it means integrating suppliers by pursuing leading edge practices and incorporating key sourcing dimensions in strategy, systems or processes, and operations concurrently with the supply base as shown in Figure 10.4.

Companies that have learned to leverage procurement have mastered the alignment suggested in Figure 10.4. They actively develop close supplier relationships because such ties will reduce cycle times, improve quality, achieve greater end user value, and enhance two-way learning across the supply chain. These firms implement programs to bring productivity improvements to all levels of the supply chain. True exemplars, such as Honda, have the best of their suppliers participate in product design and prototype development as well as share in other technology innovations throughout the product/service life cycle. According to Dave Nelson (former senior vice president of purchasing and corporate affairs

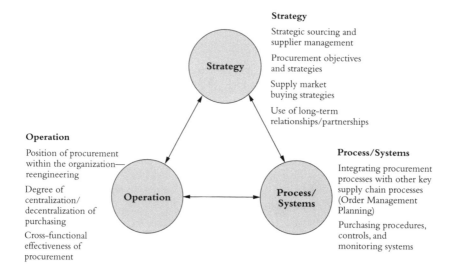

Figure 10.4   Key sourcing dimensions required for alignment.

for Honda of America, who now holds a similar position at John Deere), suppliers helped design the 1998 Accord and, as a result, saved over 20 percent of the cost associated with producing the car. Such integration can occur only when one has reduced one's supply base.

The supplier rationalization process begins by simplifying the procurement process by taking waste and redundancy out of the supply chain. To begin, one examines the underlying fundamentals of supply chain relationships and estimates how each linkage contributes to the value perceived by end-use customers. At the core of this process is understanding the linkages that comprise the total value chain and determining who is best suited to perform which sets of activities. Critical success factors are leverage and synergy: the opportunity capitalizes on mutually beneficial alliance-like interactions between buyers and suppliers. Strong relationships with a limited number of high-quality suppliers position the supply chain to respond quickly to market shifts and demands.

Leveraging the supply base necessitates finding innovative ways to unleash supplier creativity through such strategies as vendor-managed inventory and outsourcing. The ability to gain reduced inventory-carrying costs and improved service levels that benefit the whole supply chain

Table 10.2   Integrating Suppliers into the Supply Chain

To what extent do the following apply within your supply chain?	Low Performers (N = 85)	High Performers (N = 75)	Total Sample (N = 160)
Suppliers initiate planning, shipment, and production.	3.26+	4.11★	3.66
There are tight linkages between customer and supplier.	4.76	5.78★★★	5.32
There is IT integration with all customers/suppliers.	2.44	3.62	3.08
Sub-tier suppliers are an indispensable part of our overall supply.	2.89	2.62	2.76
We have strong relations with this supplier's suppliers.	2.89	2.62	2.76

★ $p \leq .05$, ★★ $p \leq .01$, ★★★ $p \leq .001$.

+ Responses range from 1 to 7, where 1 connotes "not at all" and 7 equals "to a very great extent."

results in better monitoring of systemwide material usage, demand, and availability through information sharing.

The data presented here examined the impact of better integrating suppliers in the supply chain.★ Each of the five items shown in Table 10.2 suggests that high-performing supply chains are more likely to have tight linkages with their suppliers, rely on their suppliers to initiate aspects of the inventory replenishment process, and are more likely to integrate these suppliers into their business processes. Higher performers report also that there is more likely to be information technology integration among their suppliers and customers. High-performing supply chains attempt to make the ties between suppliers and buyers seamless. Yet, these close relationships must be based on a willingness to share information and trust.

Information Sharing and Trust

Substituting information for inventory is a powerful source of new competitive advantage, and this more intense information exchange creates both entry and exit barriers. Sharing information is not a simple request

---

★ For the interested reader, the Appendix describes in detail the study, the methodology, and the measures reported in the Tables 10.2 to 10.5.

and, at its core, the key issue is based on trust. These close relationships beg the question: to what extent should a company be prepared to trust its trading partners with this depth of information? This concern is very real if a supplier is, or could become, a competitor. Consider, for example, that GE is United Technologies' third largest supplier and is Pratt & Whitney's most significant competitor. Both companies are careful about the amount of information shared and the content that flows between the two companies. Yet, both acknowledge that sharing information between Carrier and GE's small motor division is critical to Carrier's ability to compete against other air conditioning companies. Herein lies the tension.

Companies must grapple with what information to share and at what level partners are asked to participate in decision making. The central premise of supply chain integration is based on the open and honest sharing of information among trading partners.[13] The results shown in Table 10.3 show that high-performance supply chains are

Table 10.3   Information Sharing

To what extent do the following apply within your supply chain?	Low Performers (N = 85)	High Performers (N = 75)	Total Sample (N = 160)
We share supply chain performance measures.	3.55+	4.56★★★	4.05
We share supplier/customer (S/C) satisfaction measures.	4.31	5.12★★	4.71
Suppliers are an operational part of demand planning.	3.64	5.55★★★	5.35
We exchange technical information with this supplier.	5.12	5.55★	5.35
We exchange design information prior to the final design.	3.78	4.20	3.99
We transfer effective tools/techniques to this S/C.	3.62	4.42★★	4.02
We willingly share technical information with this supplier.	4.57	5.42★★	4.99

★ $p \le .05$, ★★ $p \le .01$, ★★★ $p \le .001$.

+ Responses range from 1 to 7, where 1 connotes "not at all" and 7 equals "to a very great extent."

active information exchangers. They are more likely to share technical, design, and performance measures with other supply chain members, and also tend to incorporate suppliers as part of their demand planning process. One can infer that high performers are more likely to share best practices with their supply chain partners. Implied here is the notion that effective supply chains are "learning" networks in which it is incumbent upon supply chain champions to transfer knowledge to their partners. The goal of systemwide learning is to raise the competence level of *all* supply chain members. This position can be contrasted with supply chains in which information asymmetry is practiced to gain a position of power over one's suppliers/customers.

The idea of information asymmetry violates the basic tenets of trust. The data in Table 10.4 strongly support the notion that high-performing supply chains exhibit higher levels of trust. Managers in high-performing supply chains perceive that their suppliers are more trustworthy, feel that these suppliers are more committed, and believe that they are treated fairly and equitably. In addition, these high performers evidence greater confidence in their suppliers' motives. Fair dealing and a sense of equitable treatment, commitment, confidence, and longevity of relationships

Table 10.4 Trust in the Supply Chain

To what extent do the following apply within your supply chain?	Low Performers (N = 85)	High Performers (N = 75)	Total Sample (N = 160)
We believe that this supplier is trustworthy.	5.6+	6.46★★	6.0
We believe this supplier is committed to us.	5.04	5.95★★★	5.46
We have complete confidence in this supplier's motives.	5.2	5.85★★	5.5
Maintaining this relationship is vital.	5.2	5.38	5.87
We share with this supplier a similar sense of fair play.	5.55	6.23★★★	5.87
Rewards are shared equitably between us and this supplier.	3.94	4.47★	4.19

★ $p \leq .05$, ★★ $p \leq .01$, ★★★ $p \leq .001$.
+ Responses range from 1 to 7, where 1 connotes "not at all" and 7 equals "to a very great extent."

have been discussed previously as antecedents to the building of trust among partners.

The data support the centrality of trust to effective sourcing and supply chain management. Recall that buyers and suppliers have historically had adversarial relationships; here, trust builds slowly as both parties enter the relationship with long-established patterns of behavior. Change tends to be more difficult for the buyer who can always ask for price concession by withholding the order, or by threatening to do so. To focus on the total cost of ownership, and not the purchase price, is more than a change in perspective, it takes a strategic dialogue with senior management to fully align procurement thinking with the strategic intent of the firm. If a procurement manager is rewarded on variance to stated price, there is no wonder that a key decision factor is price!

The Use of Technology as an Enabler

If information sharing is a key enabler of effective supply chain management, technology is the vehicle through which this information exchange becomes possible. Competitive advantage accrues to those who effectively adapt information technology to better disseminate information within their supply chains. In many industries, the ability to link electronically has become a right of entry and a prerequisite for consideration as a potential supply chain partner. Often viewed as a productivity tool, information technology now links supply chain partners through the design phase of new product development as well as into full production via just-in-time (JIT), electronic data interchange (EDI), and enterprisewide resource planning systems (e.g., SAP or Oracle). As firms compete on a worldwide basis, information technology is the means through which end-use customers are satisfied and value is created. The data summarized in Table 10.5 support the notion that high-performing supply chains use information technology to a greater extent than do lower performers. However, the technology has not been applied beyond the traditional information exchange associated with logistics and other components of workflow (e.g., raw material cost, delivery and quality tracking; shipment tracking, WIP). Absent from the findings is an exchange of information based on EDI or other more sensitive kinds of information. It appears that firms in our sample talk a better information-sharing game than they deliver. Information related to workflow is willingly shared but information

Table 10.5   The Use of Technology

To what extent do the following apply within your supply chain?	Low Performers (N = 85)	High Performers (N = 75)	Total Sample (N = 160)
EDI supplier links.	2.66+	2.75	2.71
Raw material cost, quality, and delivery tracking.	4.72	5.37★	5.05
Shipment tracking.	4.09	4.94★★	4.51
WIP tracking.	3.9	4.72★★	4.32
Total configuration at the point of sale.	2.82	3.68★★	3.27
Integrated manufacturing, planning, and control systems.	3.64	4.09	3.87

★ $p \leq .05$, ★★ $p \leq .01$, ★★★ $p \leq .001$.

+ Responses range from 1 to 7, where 1 connotes "not at all" and 7 equals "to a very great extent."

that lies closer to the core knowledge of the firm appears to be held dear. Such a guarded posture is not uncommon, but it must change!

The process of developing the technological capability for intensive information exchange through JIT systems, EDI, POS systems, or even the Internet is not the major hurdle confronting supply chain partners. The basic problem, again, hinges on trust. Absent trust, the likelihood exists that self-serving behavior will emerge and partners will be unable to leverage each other's skills and capabilities. At a minimum, transaction costs are increased since partners must now more closely monitor their dealings.

Trust develops through personal relationships and builds through a process of mutual adaptation that occurs only by repeated interaction. Some businesses have begun to formalize this process by creating opportunities for key managers to meet on a regular basis, often informally, to build these interpersonal ties. Supplier councils are a variation on this theme that has met with significant success. Other companies have developed senior management (top-to-top) programs in which interaction and relationship building extend beyond the buyer-supplier relationships. In these alliances, trust builds over time; yet, once trust has been violated, it is difficult to rebuild.

Not All Supply Chains Are Integrated, Nor Should They Be

Although the companies that use integrated supplier chain management increase almost daily, a number of laggards still fear such close ties and, to their own detriment, continue to engage in adversarial, often opportunistic, behavior. It remains far easier to extract price concessions than to develop, nurture, and leverage the skills of a capable set of trusted suppliers. For many buyers, such a change in perspective is a significant paradigm shift.

Through their sourcing strategies, high-performing companies manage their supply base as a valued resource. Beyond engaging in behaviors that run counter to the traditional wisdom of "three bids and a cloud of dust," a key challenge is the proper selection of partners. True supply chain partners have abandoned their unilateral, win-lose perspectives and advocate an approach that favors mutual gain, shared value, and total system costs. Both formally and informally, these partners share information on strategic plans, customer needs, capacity utilization, and supply chain costs. The *Financial Times* (December 1, 1998) reported that effective supply chain management provides competitive advantage that traditional sources no longer can. The ability to gain global superiority results from synchronizing supply chain activities to both reduce costs and improve end customer satisfaction.

The importance of supplier integration cannot be applied indiscriminately across one's entire supply base. Simply, not all suppliers are created equally, nor should they be. Some supplier relationships are still best managed as an "open-market" exchange. Different contexts demand different approaches to sourcing; one size does not fit all! Those trading parties chosen for supplier partnerships should be selected with care; supply chain partnerships are far too time and resource intensive to treat lightly. Different levels of sourcing and supplier relationships are described in Table 10.6. These categories reflect a range of supply chain relations from more traditional notions of purchasing management to a more comprehensive view of supplier management. The key dimensions used to differentiate among the categories are length of planning horizon, level of corporate involvement, the criticality of the purchased product/service, and the level of shared norm development.

Table 10.6 Different Supplier Strategy Portfolios

Category	Description
Supplier management	Necessary for planning and controlling a select few absolutely critical items—high in volume, short in supply.
	Centralized management.
	High-level involvement.
	Time horizons up to 10 years.
	Collaboration *and* coordination of supply chain activities.
	Use of strategic alliances and sharing of long-term strategies.
Sourcing management	Necessary for planning and controlling a select few, absolutely critical items—high in volume, short in supply.
	High-level involvement.
	Time horizons up to 10 years.
	Cooperation *and* coordination of supply chain activities.
	Necessary for specific bottleneck operations—unique or specialized produces—that are critical to operations.
	Management emphasis on performance of individual components and assurance of supply and cost.
	Global sources, if necessary.
	Central coordination, local administration of purchasing.
	Planning horizons that vary according to market and technology factors.
	Reduction of supply base.
	Working with remaining suppliers over extended periods of time, if performances warrant it.
	Supplier required to invest in additional assets, specialized personnel, technology, or other commitments.
	Cooperative joint technology development (codesign and build).
	Use interorganizational teams to solve specific problems.
	Collaboration in the supply chain.
Materials management	Routine procurement of items with potential impact on profit.
	Concern with supply reliability and low cost through routine, localized procurement.
	Planning horizons between 12 and 14 months.
	General concern with materials, although there may be some specific component items as well.
	Routine purchasing for items with high profit impact; may require the full purchasing power of the organization and possible use of multiple vendors to encourage competition.

(Continued)

Table 10.6 *(Continued)*

Category	Description
	Respect and mutual trust related to repeated transactions. Operational alliances with some sharing of ideas and people. Build only—supplier receives specs and prints. Joint problem-solving on specific commercial issues. Coordination in the supply chain.
Purchasing management	Routine procurement necessary but noncritical low-value items, often using multiples sourcing. Commodity: catalog items supplied to specifications. Short planning horizons (normally less than 12 months). Primary emphasis on procurement efficiency, which takes place locally. Reliance on standard product specifications and order processes to minimize transaction costs but balanced against inventory efficiency. Judicious use of procurement cards warranted. Information shared as necessary to facilitate transaction.

Most companies should plan to engage in relatively few highly collaborative relationships: the kinds where the mutual risks and rewards are significant enough to define corporate success or failure. Beyond the heavy resource demands required, strategic partnerships are hard to execute; strategic objectives and operating criteria frequently conflict; and cooperation can be maintained only as long as mutual competitive advantage can be derived. Traditional, open-market interactions (e.g., with companies supplying commoditylike products) are still likely to represent the bulk of sourcing relationships.

Figure 10.5 arrays the categories of supplier relationships according to levels of commercial and technical complexity. These dimensions are best defined according to industry and supply chain characteristics and are developed from the buyer's perspective. Table 10.5 describes the general characteristics of each category using parameters that apply to effective supplier management and integration. High complexity on both dimensions connotes "mission critical" purchases that are best managed through a closely knit alliance between buyer and supplier. Longer-term planning horizons, high levels of information integration, and the commitment of senior managers appear to be the norm. Conversely, when

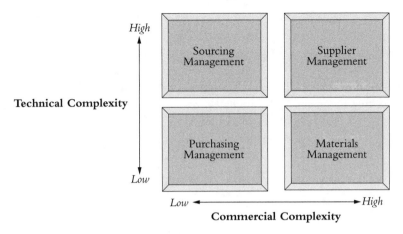

Figure 10.5   Classification of supplier relationship based on levels of complexity.

the levels of complexity are low on both dimensions, multiple sourcing in a more arm's length fashion is appropriate.

A systematic and disciplined approach to effective supply chain management reduces the cost of externally purchased products and services and maintains high levels of quality, service, and technology. Those efforts engage the enterprise to think beyond functional barriers and apply leverage to its supply chain partners. In developing a firm's intellectual capital, a key element is the ability to capture and easily transfer information across organizational boundaries. Part of the leverage and synergy to be gained is the transfer of knowledge and learning between supply chain partners. This is transformational thinking for which not all managers are presently equipped.

What Needs to Be Done

In the final analysis, effective supply chain management is predicated on developing and inculcating these principles into the basic fiber of the organization. In addition, there must exist a basic change in operating philosophy. World-class companies will become more selective and will ally and align with fewer supply chain partners. Companies with outstanding sourcing strategies appear to share two characteristics. They typically enjoy executive level commitment to building the organization's sourcing capabilities and view sourcing as a cross-functional capability that is linked to strategic and operational objectives while focusing on people and process. These organizations also relentlessly deploy these capabilities across the entire enterprise by creating and implementing an infrastructure of organization, measures, and technology that support the tenets put forth here. To meet the demands of the new competition firms must first identify core and noncore activities and then they must strategically select partners to fill the gaps.

APPENDIX

The Study

The purpose of the original empirical study was to focus on "best practices" from the perspective of managers, from different levels of the supply chain, who were responsible for procurement related activities. The intent was to understand better those principles that contribute to the differences between high- and low-performing supply chains.

The Sample

The original study is part of a larger project and represents the responses of 22 *extended* supply chains from North America, Latin America, and Europe across five broad industry groupings—Life Sciences, Oil & Gas, Consumer Products, Agricultural and Food Processing, Utilities and Manufacturing (High Tech Electronics and Automotive). Life sciences comprised 4.3 percent, oil and gas 9.4 percent, utilities 4.4 percent, consumer/retail 13.8 percent, agricultural/food processing 29.4 percent, and hi tech/manufacturing 28.8 percent of the sample. The remaining 9.9 percent was made up of a diverse set of businesses. This convenience sample was drawn from the client list of a major consulting company's supply chain practice. The range of businesses in the final sample is diverse enough that these results can be generalized. The sample contains companies located in Europe, Latin America, and North America; however, the majority of the sample (85 percent) represents supply chains located in both Latin and North America. The sample consists of 160 (75 percent response rate) surveys of 188 that were returned.

An *extended* supply chain reflects the response of different levels (e.g., upstream and downstream) within the supply chain relative to a focal company.[i] The sample comprises respondents from different functions in the firm (operations, procurement, materials management, and marketing) and from different levels of the supply chain (suppliers and customers). For example, marketers responded to questions about their internal suppliers (operations/procurement) and their external customers;

275

similarly, operations/procurement managers responded to questions about their external suppliers and their internal customers (marketing). These perspectives reflect an *extended* supply chain view of certain key dimensions of effective sourcing strategies.

Performance Measures and the Questionnaire

To determine high- and low-performing supply chains, respondents reported the degree to which their supply chain partners contribute to key performance measures. These measures ranged from traditional measures, such as decreased inventory levels and improved quality, to more robust metrics that focused on end-use customer satisfaction and marketplace concerns, such as competitive differentiation. The survey examined the extent to which these measures were used as part of the evaluation of supply chain performance. These are proxy measures of performance; actual performance was not measured. The emphasis on end-use customer performance measures[ii] is consistent with and highlights the importance of buyers' concern for resource enhancing factors and not just cost-based performance measures.

To focus on performance related to end-use customer considerations, we selected five items based on their face validity (contribution margin improvement, customer satisfaction, value added, customer value, and increased account penetration). These items were evaluated statistically for internal consistency and the scale yielded a Cronbach's alpha of .73. The sample was separated into high and low performers by dividing at the median value of this measure. There were no significant differences between high and low performers across type of industry, geographic location, or classification according to operations/marketing, supplier customer, up/downstream, or buyer/seller distinctions.

The final research instrument examined a range of procurement-related factors related to strategic sourcing and supplier management. For each section of the questionnaire we approached the research by examining the supply chain literature with a broader scope of inquiry and attempted to encompass elements of logistics, distribution, marketing, operations, and procurement in the survey design. Throughout the study, the primary goal was to understand, broadly, the factors, processes, motivations, and behaviors that support and encourage more effective sourcing and supply chain management practices.

11 | Concluding Remarks

An Alliance Competence Is Key to Success

Throughout the book, we have spoken about alliances and the development of alliance strategies as a journey and not an end state. The simple fact is for many companies the journey is both arduous and subject to failure. Alliances are fragile entities that require a sense of purpose and a realization that they are about the business of people and not just about business. We built a strong case for the importance of the people side of alliances. However, the central focus of the book has been on alliance competencies. As alliances become more central to firms' quest for competitive advantage, management's ability to develop, grow, and sustain alliance-like behaviors among its managers will partly differentiate success and failure. In addition to the development of managerial talent, firms will have to develop processes, systems, and structures that encourage and enable the preservation and institutionalization of an alliance-supportive culture. This means that the values and beliefs that contribute to an appreciation of a strong alliance spirit must woven into the fabric of the firm.

What does this mean? Should managers approach all potential partners with a willingness to ally or does one follow a process that forces discipline and attention to detail prior to narrowing the set of suitable partners? It is important to have a disciplined approach to alliance management. Even interimistic alliances must fit a firm's strategic intent. An opportunity does not mean one can act opportunistically. Does one assume a basis of trust if there has been no prior experience with a potential partner? While trust is a precondition for a successful alliance, trust is earned and is the result of repeated interaction. If trust is an essential ingredient, the effects of reputation cannot be ignored. Firms that are widely recognized as alliance competent are sought out as partners. Similarly, those who engage repeatedly in self-serving behavior are either shunned or are treated cautiously. In both instances, the potential benefits of the alliance are diminished because monitoring behavior adds to the costs associated with running the alliance and often inhibits the level of exchange and depth of interaction achieved in strong alliances.

Alliance-competent firms are highly desirable partners and are in great demand. At the same time, they are selective in their choice of partners since they have a disciplined and well-honed approach to the alliance process. Their willingness to form relationships is limited (i.e., selective) and, therefore, these potential partners should be considered a scarce resource.

Alliance competent firms will engage in elaborate due diligence and will avoid firms that do not share their vision of appropriate alliance-like behavior. As alliance-competent companies look for potential partners, or respond to others' request to partner, a key selection criterion becomes the degree to which one advocates and lives up to the norms and values of a positive alliance spirit. The companies that embrace the tenets of collaborative behavior admit that alliances enable value creation that they could not easily replicate without an alliance partner. The strength of the alliance is related to the quality of the partners.

Driven by an articulated alliance strategy, these firms focus on defining a set of partners with whom they share both a strategic vision and an understanding of what it means to partner. Alliance-competent companies are more likely to leverage the full potential of their partner for the benefit of the alliance and are less likely to suffer the debilitating effects of static and conflict that can ultimately derail even the most desirable alliance. In addition, these firms work hard to raise the overall effectiveness of the alliance by helping their partners gain insight into what it means to be a good partner. Improving the quality of the partnership will increase the value the alliance brings to the marketplace. In the end, the alliance will gain a competitive advantage over rival alliances that are less skilled in maximizing partners' full potential. A central premise here has been that a sustainable competitive advantage is a function of both partners' resources and skills *and* their alliance competence. Technological skills, marketing prowess, access to resources are all important to the partner selection process but, alone, are insufficient criteria. True leverage and maximum value in the marketplace accrue to the alliances that can best harness the skills of their members.

Competence Is Not Only an Individual Characteristic

In part, alliance competence is defined by the capabilities of managers charged with alliance responsibilities. The alliance manager (AM) has been featured as a linchpin in the alliance management process—the one who orchestrates the interaction among alliance partners. The AM is a central character in both creating demonstrable value from various alliance activities and smoothing the bumps that might occur as the alliance progresses over its productive life. To be sure, the role of the alliance manager is key to the success of the alliance and a strong alliance can suffer at the hands of a poor AM. As the alliance develops over time, different skills are required. Alignment is essential between the AM's skill set and the requirements of the particular life cycle stage.

One can be a proficient line manager and lack the ability to be a successful alliance manager. The specific details about teachable and unteachable alliance management skills were presented in Chapter 8. Some of these skills are difficult to develop. However, all the requisite skills can be identified. Beyond identification of these skills and talents, firms must proactively manage the talent pool of future alliance managers. Companies tend to underestimate resources and senior management time that are needed to create sufficient numbers of alliance managers. The true challenge, however, is to incorporate alliance management skill building as part of the firm's career development and succession planning. These skills are so critical to the firm that they cannot be left to chance or managed in an ad hoc manner.

Having a cadre of alliance managers is not sufficient to ensure a firm's long-term alliance competence. A small number of talented managers must be supplemented with a supportive culture as well as a set of systems and processes that are aligned with the objectives of the alliance and facilitate its growth and success. Many companies tout the virtues of alliance-like behavior but have rigid structures and systems, and support legacy processes that run counter to the spirit and intent of alliance-like behavior. If, for example, reward systems, decision-making processes, and communications flows support mainly short-term goals, encourage highly centralized decision-making authority, and tacitly reject risk-taking behavior; it is easy to see the disconnect. A small number of key people might be alliance savvy, but the firm is not supportive and widespread alliance-relevant skills will never be valued. Because alliances depend on cross-functional interaction and the flows of information across company and discipline boundaries, alliance thinking must be widespread and consistently supported.

An Individual Competence and a Supportive Infrastructure Are Critical

While alliances are about people and relationships, enabling mechanisms must exist on two distinct but related levels. On one level, there must be alignment as suggested. People, processes, systems and structures must be collectively supportive. Too often there is a gap between what we say and what we do. On the other level, firms must work hard to institutionalize the learnings gained from their alliances. Alliance skills that cannot be shared across the organization are wasted diminishing their full value. While individual expertise is important, it is far better to create opportunities for others to learn from these experts than to rely on them to be solo contributors to the alliance process. The goal is to create a storehouse of knowledge from which all can benefit and from which best practices can be cataloged and disseminated throughout the firm. It is here that the true advantage of an alliance competence is realized. By creating a repository of alliance knowledge, the firm ensures that these competencies are widely spread and that a broad base of expertise is developed. In addition, these skills are passed to future generations. Thus, an alliance competence becomes part of the firm's core values; it is part of its genetic code. The ability to accumulate this alliance experience is invaluable and will contribute to a sustainable competitive advantage.

Now the firm has begun the process of making alliance-like thinking and behavior a central component of its core beliefs and norms. As part of the process, the company is transformed—it becomes a knowledge-based company. Part of its knowledge base is alliance specific, which bodes well for competing in the twenty-first century. The message is clear—success will come to those firms that master working both cross-functions and cross-borders. As firms attempt to work in a seamless global context, the ones that become alliance competent will manage effectively the accompanying upheaval and uncertainty.

Balancing the Key Elements

Three elements must work in concert if the firm is to be alliance competent. *People* are clearly essential, but more importantly it is the development of one's people and a dedication to improve their abilities to work in alliance-related roles. Alliances are about relationships and relationships are about people. The challenge facing the firm is how to develop, keep, and sustain a full complement of capable alliance managers and instill the belief that these skills are important to the overall management of the company. Within an alliance context, empowerment, accountability, and access to information are core issues for the firm and it must support these tenets to be an alliance-ready organization.

A process for *knowledge management* is the second element that must be in place. Our focus here is limited to alliance-specific knowledge but the successful firm will store and distribute best practices, competitor and customer intelligence, and other critical information to all its personnel wherever they are located. If one subscribes to the notion that knowledge is power, the thought of sharing, collaborating and building a common base of corporate wide knowledge requires a major change in behavior and in thinking. To think of information as a corporatewide asset that is available to those who need it means that one willingly cedes a potential base of power. Alliance-specific information should be a shared asset from which the overall firm benefits; even one's alliance partners should be better off.

The third element relates to those *process, systems, and structural factors* that facilitate the alignment among each of the elements. These factors are the enablers that make it easy to combine skills across disparate parts of the business; improve cooperation and integration among business functions and units to bring value to the marketplace; and extend these integrative mechanisms to one's partners in support of the alliance's objectives and goals. Through these linkages, both internal and external firms support alliance-like behavior, develop alliance managers, and transfer relevant knowledge to the point where it is needed.

The challenges here are two. One is to gain alignment among the three elements as each must be present. They are mutually supportive and each alone is insufficient to allow the firm to be successful as an alliance-competent firm. Second is the ability to spread these elements among all members of a broader network of alliances. The first challenge is probably more easily accomplished since one does not have to grapple with the complexities inherent in working across company boundaries. Nonetheless, in both instances, managers must be prepared to transfer skills, share knowledge, and exchange best practices. In the first instance, the sharing is cross-functional or cross business unit. In the second, sharing is among alliance partners. Such behavior flies in the face of "information is power" and the tendency for a firm to act in its self-interest instead in the mutual interest of the alliance.

Alliance Competence Requires a New Paradigm and a Plan

There are paradoxes in the quest to develop the notion of an alliance competence. The first is the term *alliance management*. Management implies a chain of command, or having an ability to control. Yet, alliances are not about control, they require shared decision processes, open flows of information, and trust. Trust supplants the formal organizational structure and ensures that partners perform as they say they will. The second paradox is that alliances, despite all the cautions, are seen as an important component in many companies' strategic options. Alliances are acknowledged to be fragile, often awkward, and require an extraordinary amount of management time and attention. Some might protest and argue that given the commitment of time needed, a go-it-alone strategy might be the preferred option. Thus, managers rely on alliances and alliances are for some not highly reliable.

Third, firms have a natural tendency to protect their core and act in their own best interest while recognizing that such behavior runs counter to the alliance spirit. Here, the tension is quite visible. Managers want to learn from their partners but would prefer that the door swing one-way. To open oneself to the possible expropriation of sensitive information is not a positive outcome. We have discussed ways in which one can share technology but not give away the crown jewels. Above all, expectations need to be shaped early and trust needs to be preserved.

Even within these paradoxes, the alliance revolution is here—no industry is immune and few firms have the luxury to remain alliance free and attempt to succeed in a global marketplace. Although alliances might not be the default option for all the firm's relationships, where alliances do make sense managers should proactively seek them and nurture them. Competence does not develop overnight nor does it come without significant change to all aspects of the firm. Recall that alignment is needed among systems, processes, people, strategy, and structure if the company is to become alliance competent. Where does one begin? As with large-scale change,[1] there must be a road map—change should not be left to chance. Developing an alliance competence is for many companies a significant change from business as usual. Resistance is expected since the norms of an alliance-competent firm are not consistent with those found in more traditional hierarchies where barons rule the silos, decision making rests at the top, and empowerment is a term. The following steps will be helpful.

Step 1. Create a Sense of Urgency

Significant change can only occur if there is a perceived need for change. The sense of urgency, however, is not enough if there is not a plan for action. Senior management must not only create the "burning platform" but must convincingly argue why the future looks as it does and why alliances will become more central to the firm as it defines its future direction. The need for change must also show the path to a favorable outcome. For the firm in crisis or facing hard times, the sense of urgency might be real and the words ring very true. However, if the crisis is too severe, there might not be enough time to forge the alliances needed. Even if alliances can be formed, there is often insufficient time to engage in the long-term behaviors that support a positive alliance spirit. Alliances are not a panacea and are certainty less useful for the firm in trouble. Alliances require too much attention and effort. The reality is that sick companies are often distracted and lack the discipline to develop the needed skills. Here, alliances might help in the immediate term but there are longer term issues to resolve.

For the healthy and even successful firm, why fix what isn't broken? Success often breeds hubris and with it comes an arrogance that has the firm embrace the concept of alliances but not develop the requisite skills and competencies to manage them effectively over time. Senior management understands the need for alliance-like behavior, but old habits die slowly. Here, the process of alignment becomes critical as all systems, processes, and structures must reenforce the new alliance strategies.

Failure will result in suboptimal performance. The result is that management often views the alliance strategy as flawed instead of looking to the implementation process for the problem. There are likely to be many naysayers. Alliance-like behavior threatens those who have a silo mentality, are kingdom builders, and see information as power. Nonetheless, it is the healthy firm that will benefit more in the long term from adopting an alliance mindset and competence.

A sense of urgency is not the battle cry: "My competitors have alliances, I want some!" Urgency is captured in a realization that change is the only way to long-term survival. The risks to the business are too great and the firm cannot sustain its competitive position by relying on its internal strengths. There needs to be a wake-up call, a realization that the past cannot predict the future and that tried-and-true strategies fit the old world; they are inappropriate for the new challenges facing the firm. Employees have to understand and appreciate that change is on the wind and alliance-like activities make sense as a strategic option.

Step 2. Create an Alliance Vision and an Alliance Strategy

There are several key points here. First, companies should not develop strategic alliances, they should develop alliance strategies. First and foremost, to espouse the virtues of alliance competence, one must articulate a vision and clearly demonstrate how alliances fit into the future of the firm. Vision paints a picture of the future and explains why it is important for the firm to head in that direction. At the same time, it is necessary to explain what will happen once the firm arrives at that future state. Vision without an appreciation of the likely outcome—the objectives and performance expectations of the future state—may leave people cold and uncommitted to change. Setting aggressive but reachable targets is advisable. Stretch goals rally interest and create an additional sense of urgency. At the same time, one must create a future that people can imagine and see as feasible. From this vantage point, a firm can better develop its alliance strategies *if* there is a realistic frame of reference.

Beyond creating an urgency for change, it is essential that there be a sense of the final destination. The end point need not be precisely described since senior management should reserve flexibility in which to maneuver. The future is fraught with uncertainty, and plans do not always unfold as intended. At the same time, it is necessary to be able to articulate the desired future state. Vision without an ability to communicate its virtues leads to both resistance and confusion. The plan should be tied closely to the firm's key stakeholders and constituent groups. One should never have to ask: Why does this alliance strategy make sense? How are we and our customers better off? Recall the elevator test; there should be no question why alliances make sense. This knowledge and commitment must be resident throughout the firm.

Step 3. Begin to Build a Team of Committed People

Plans without a committed group of people to design and implement the requisite changes will not succeed. Agents of change lie throughout the firm and are not limited to senior management ranks. Senior management commitment is essential but middle management's involvement also is critical. Senior managers become advocates and champions; set the tone; and begin the process of changing the firm's culture. But middle managers must be involved in the process. It is on their shoulders that the alliance process is carried forward and success rests. At the senior levels, one can begin building trust, designing an organization that supports alliance-like behavior, and modeling the behaviors that will drive the change process. If there is little alignment among the management ranks, the likelihood of success falls dramatically. Consistency throughout the organization is important since in alliance-competent organizations senior management willingly cedes control and decision-making authority, and middle managers are equipped to assume control. Finger-pointing will kill the alliance-building process. Consistency throughout the organization is a must.

Step 4. Build a Supportive Infrastructure

Understanding the need for change and accepting the future vision of the firm's alliance strategies is not sufficient. Enabling structure, processes, and systems must support the change as the firm begins to develop its alliance competencies. A central theme has been the need for alignment, and the importance of a supportive infrastructure cannot be underscored enough. Changing culture and adapting the organization to facilitate these changes is not a small task and yet it must be done if the firm is to institutionalize alliance-like behaviors and encourage alliance relevant thinking. It is important that the business model and the organization show high degrees of compatibility in form and substance. Effort entails more than empowering employees and giving local control for alliance management. It is the ability and the process to translate vision into desired behaviors that are sustainable as the firm transforms itself to becoming more alliance ready and capable.

Step 5. Look for Quick Wins

Since the data on alliance success are not encouraging and it is likely that many in the firm would prefer the status quo, the alliance strategy needs to show strong promise early in its development. The accomplishments should be visible and important in that they demonstrate that the strategy does, in fact make sense and that the firm is on the correct course. This implies that large-scale, complex alliances might not be a good first alliance attempt—start small and build skills before trying to take on a large, complicated alliance. If a complex alliance is unavoidable by virtue of the opportunity afforded, try to establish milestones along the way that enable these small wins to attract attention and stand on their own. One outcome is that these incremental wins help to establish credibility and commitment. Over time, these incremental wins begin to shape expectations. Positive alliance experiences engender greater alliance activity. This process begins to build on itself and the changes in infrastructure that are required to facilitate or support such behavior gain momentum. Managers gain self-confidence and are willing to experiment with more and different kinds of alliances. While practice cannot make perfect in an alliance context, those with more experience show more favorable performance results.

Step 6. Constantly Communicate Change, Culture, and Congruence

Alliances, or the development of an alliance competence, have never failed because people communicated too often. The changes required for an alliance-competent firm strike at the core of the firm. The process requires adaptations that eliminate silo thinking, reduce the degree of central control and decision-making authority, and generally threaten the status quo. One can only begin to appreciate the challenges inherent in developing an alliance competence. To begin the process of linking these changes to the firm's new alliance-friendly culture is an attempt to ensure that alliance competence becomes part of the firm's core values and accepted as part of its norms. Without an anchor to the firm's core values and culture, either old habits will resurface or new habits will not be reinforced. Either way, the development of requisite skills might be short-lived. This transformation process will not occur naturally and must be orchestrated. The process can derail in many ways.

The leadership challenges are rigorous. The final destination is often uncertain and the vision of the future becomes less clear as the changing environment becomes more turbulent. It is difficult to orchestrate profound change as there are too many variables to consider. A balanced score card (see Chapter 9) approach can assist in navigating these uncharted waters. Staying true to the vision and communicating the story in a simple, albeit compelling, manner helps considerably. Leading by example is also key to the process. Patience is required although actions must be deliberate and send a clear message—the time for change is now, our future success depends on it!!

Let the Journey Begin

To become alliance competent takes hard work, dedication, and a mindset that embraces the willingness to change. We have charted a course that should help managers better develop alliance-competent companies. This book has also presented a realistic sense of the journey and has highlighted hazards and troublespots along the way. The journey is fraught with challenges; yet, the prepared firm can adapt and proactively negotiate these obstacles. We have blazed a path for travelers that is better marked and easier to travel. Yet, companies have attempted the journey and have failed. Many things can go wrong, even for those who are prepared. Although we urge caution, we remain optimistic.

Teaching at the University of Virginia makes it tempting to compare our alliance journey and explorations to that of Mr. Jefferson's famous explorers, Lewis and Clark, but our challenge fades in comparison. We admire those who search where others have not traveled. While we also have attempted to map unknown territory and present a narrative of the journey, our task has been far less daunting. Nonetheless, we have shared part of our journal; this book is the record that documents our alliance journey.

Notes

Chapter 1

[1] In 1997, there was less of an urge by small biotechs to seek alliances with large pharmaceutical firms to remain financially viable because the strong equity market had become a source of capital.

[2] See, for example, S.G. Bharadwaj, P.R. Varadarajan, and J. Fahey, "Sustainable Competitive Advantage in Service Industries: A Conceptual Model and Research Propositions," *Journal of Marketing 57*, 4 (1993): 83–100; M. Porter, *Competitive Strategy* (New York: Free Press, 1983); and George S. Day and Robin Wensley, "Assessing Advantage: A Framework for Diagnosing Competitive Superiority," *Journal of Marketing 52* (1988): 1–20.

[3] FedEx has tied part of its future to e-commerce and views itself as part of the total value-adding capabilities of doing business over the Internet. Wall Street is beginning to view FedEx as an "Internet stock."

[4] See Darden case UVA-G-0485 for a presentation of the competitive interplay between FedEx and UPS from 1982 to 1996.

[5] This discussion is based on Richard Reed and Robert J. DeFillippi, "Causal Ambiguity, Barriers to Imitation and Sustainable Competitive Advantage," *Academy of Management Review 15*, 1 (1990): 88–103.

[6] A discussion of transaction costs is based on work by Oliver E. Williamson and is best summarized in *Markets and Hierarchies* (New York: The Free Press, 1975).

[7] While there is not uniform agreement as to what constitutes failure, the figure cited has been reported in K. Harrigan, *Managing for Joint Venture Success* (Lexington, MA: Lexington Book, 1986).

[8] This topic is covered in greater detail in C. Jay Lambe, "Alliances and Sustainable Competitive Advantage: An Exploratory Examination," unpublished doctoral dissertation, University of Virginia, The Darden Graduate School of Business, May 1998.

[9] Seven E. Prokesch, "Unleashing the Power of Learning: An Interview with British Petroleum's John Browne," *Harvard Business Review 75*, 5 (1997): 146–62.

[10] An illustration of best practices can be found in John Harbison and Peter Pakar, Jr., "Institutionalizing Alliance Skills: Secrets and Repeatable Success," Booz Allen and Hamilton Series on Alliances (1997).

[11] Cooper & Lybrand, "Partnerships Pay Off for the Growth Companies," *Trendsetter Barometer* (Jan. 6, 1997).

[12]D. Ernst and M. Stern "Managing Alliances—Skills for the Modern Era," www.allianceanalyst.com/Mckinsey.htm (March 18, 1996).

[13]G. Urban and John Hausen, *Design and Marketing of New Products* (New York: Prentice Hall, 1980).

[14]C. Jay Lambe and Robert E. Spekman, "Alliance, External Technology Acquisition and Discontinuous Technological Change," *Journal of Product Innovation Management 14,* 2 (1997): 102–17.

Chapter 2

[1]See Oliver E. Williamson, "Comparative Economic Organization: The Analysis of Discrete Structural Alternatives," *Administrative Science Quarterly 36,* 2 (1991): 269–96; and Bryan Borys and David B. Jemison, "Hybrid Arrangements as Strategic Alliances: Theoretical Issues in Organizational Combinations," *Academy of Management Review 14,* 2 (1989): 234–49.

[2]T.K. Das and B.S. Teng, "Between Trust and Control: Developing Confidence in Partner Cooperation in Alliances," *Academy of Management Review 23,* 3 (1998): 491–513.

[3]Joel Bleeke and David Ernst, *Collaborating to Compete: Using Strategic Alliances and Acquisitions in the Global Marketplace* (New York: John Wiley & Sons, Inc., 1993).

[4]Sue Cartwright and Cary L. Cooper, *Managing Mergers Acquisitions and Strategic Alliances: Integrating People and Cultures* (Oxford: Butterworth Heinemann, 1992).

[5]See British Institute of Management (1986), *The Managers of Acquisitions and Mergers,* discussion paper #8.

[6]Arvind Parkhe, "Strategic Alliance Structuring: A Game Theoretic and Transaction Cost Examination of Interfirm Cooperation," *Academy of Management Journal 36,* 4 (1993): 794–831.

[7]See again Das and Teng, "Between Trust and Control."

[8]A.C. Inkpen and P.W. Beamish, "Knowledge, Bargaining Power, and the Instability of International Joint Ventures," *Academy of Management Review* 22, 1 (1997): 177–203; and Bruce Kogut, "Why Joint Ventures Die So Quickly," *Chief Executive (U.S.) 51* (1989): 70–4.

[9]David T. Wilson, "An Integrated Model of Buyer-Seller Relationships," *Journal of the Academy of Marketing Science 23,* 4 (1995): 335–46.

[10]See R.J. Lewicki, D.J. McAllister, and R.J. Bies, "Trust and Distrust: New Relationships and Realities," *Academy of Management Review 23,* 3 (1998): 438–59.

[11]See William G. Ouchi, "Markets, Bureaucracies and Clans," *Administrative Science Quarterly 25* (1980): 129–41.

[12]Michael Y. Yoshino and U. Srinivasa Rangan, *Strategic Alliances: An Entrepreneurial Approach to Globalization* (Boston: Harvard Business School Press, 1995).

[13]This discussion is based on work presented in Das and Teng, "Between Trust and Control."

[14]Embeddedness is a term taken from Provan 1993 and refers to the extent to which alliance partners are mutually dependent and are physically tied to one another. In an alliance where resources and personnel are comingled and the boundaries between firms are blurred, embeddedness is high. Conversely, where the interaction between partners

is sequential (one performs a task and then hands-off to the partner) or the ties linking the two are weak, the degree of embeddedness is low. See Keith G. Provan, "Embeddedness, Interdependence and Opportunism in Organizational Supplier-Buyer Networks," *Journal of Management* 19, 4 (1993): 841–57.

[15] See Andrea Larson, "Network Dyads in Entrepreneurial Settings: A Study of the Governance of Exchange Relationships," *Administrative Science Quarterly 37*, 1 (1992): 76.

[16] Cooper & Lybrand, "Partnerships Pay Off for the Growth Companies," *Trendsettter Barometer* (January 6, 1997).

[17] Ranjay Gulati, Tarun Khanna, and Nitin Nohria, "Unilateral Commitments and the Importance of Process in Alliances," *Sloan Management Review 35*, 3 (1994): 61–70.

[18] A discussion of transaction costs is based on work by Oliver E. Williamson and is best summarized in *Markets and Hierarchies* (New York: The Free Press, 1975).

[19] See D.H. McKnight, Larry L. Cummings, and Norman L. Chervany, "Initial Trust Formation in New Organizational Relationships," *Academy of Management Review 23*, 3 (1998): 473–91.

[20] The difference between data (a set of discrete, objective facts about an event), information (data that has meaning and relevance) and knowledge (information that is blended with experience that provides a framework for action) is taken from Thomas H. Davenport and Lawrence Prusak, *Working Knowledge* (Cambridge: Harvard Business School Press, 1998).

[21] Geert Hofstede, *Culture's Consequences* (San Francisco: Sage Publications, 1980). This work also focuses on differences in national cultures.

[22] As referenced in John R. Harbison and Peter Pekar, Jr., *Smart Alliances: A Practical Guide to Repeatable Success* (San Francisco: Jossey-Bass, 1998).

[23] David Lei, John W. Slocum, and R.A. Pitts, "Building Cooperative Advantage: Managing Strategic Alliances to Promote Organizational Learning," *Journal of World Business 32*, 3 (1997): 203–24.

Chapter 3

[1] All executive quotes are from interviews conducted with alliance managers as part of the research methodology for the book by Robert Spekman, Lynn Isabella, Thomas C. MacAvoy, and Ted Forbes, *Managing Alliances and Partnerships* (Lexington, MA: International Consortium of Executive Development Research, 1996).

[2] See G.P. Hamel and C.K. Prahalad, *Competing for the Future* (Boston, MA: Harvard Business Press, 1996).

[3] Ibid, p. 24.

[4] Model used in a presentation given by Peter Shaw at the Stuttgart Forum, International Consortium of Executive Development Research, Stuttgart, Germany, October 1994.

[5] This term has been used by Jeanne Liedtka and John Rosenblum, "Shaping Conversations: Making Strategy; Managing Change," *California Management Review, 39,* 1 (1996) 141–157.

[6] Ibid.

[7] See Jennifer James, *Thinking in the Future Tense: Leadership Skills for a New Age* (New York: Simon & Schuster, 1996).

[8] See Robert P. Lynch, *Business Alliances Guide* (New York: John Wiley & Sons, 1993).

[9] The technique of dialogue is described in Peter Senge, *The Fifth Discipline* (New York: Doubleday, 1990). For suggestions on the managerial use of dialogue, see Lynn Isabella and Ted Forbes, "A Note of the Dialogue Technique" UVA-OB-0595, University of Virginia Darden School Foundation, Charlottesville, VA, 1995.

[10] Called deferrence trust.

[11] Different kinds of trust are discussed by Roy Lewicki and Barbara Bunker, "Developing and Maintaining Trust in Work Relationships," pp. 114–139. In R.M. Kramer and T.R. Tyler, *Trust in Organizations* (Thousand Oaks, CA: Sage, 1996).

[12] See Morgan W. McCall, Jr., *High Flyers: Developing the Next Generation of Leaders* (Cambridge, MA: *Harvard Business Review*, 1998).

[13] See, for example, Ed Nevis, Joan Lancourt, and Helen Vassallo, *Intentional Revolutions* (San Francisco, CA: Jossey Bass, 1996); John Kotter, *Leading Change* (Cambridge, MA: Harvard Business School Press, 1996).

[14] See Lynn A. Isabella, "Evolving Interpretations as a Change Unfolds: How Managers Construe Key Organizational Events," *Academy of Management Journal, 33,* (1990) 7–41.

[15] See Daniel Goleman, *Working with Emotional Intelligence* (New York: Bantam Books, 1998).

[16] The work on learning mindsets is based on Lynn A. Isabella and Ted Forbes, "The Interpretational Side of Careers: How Key Events Impact Executive Thinking." Paper presented at the Academy of Management Annual Meetings, Dallas, Texas, 1994. See also "Learning Mindset: Who Has It? Who Doesn't?" *Harvard Business Review,* March/April, 1994, p. 10.

Chapter 4

[1] Excerpted from a copy of a speech presented by Carlos Borregales, "Strategic Alliances at Work with Orimulsion," Petroleos de Venezuela, S.A. Senior Management Seminar on Global Strategy and Strategic Alliances, Caracas, Venezuela, October 31, 1996.

[2] For a complete discussion of the psychological contract, see D.M. Rousseau, *Psychological Contracts in Organizations: Understanding Written and Unwritten Agreements* (Thousand Oaks, CA: Sage Publications, 1995).

[3] The four types of marriages are: fantasy, rescue, companionate, and traditional. Each type implies a basis for interaction between the partners in the marriage. For more information on these four types of marriages, see J.S. Wallerstein and S. Blakeslee, *The Good Marriage* (Boston, MA: Houghton Mifflin, 1995).

[4] Rousseau, p. 9.

[5] These concepts are based on the work of Ravi S. Achrol, "Changes in the Theory of Interorganizational Relations in Marketing: Toward a Network Paradigm," *Journal of the Academy of Marketing Science, 25,* 1 (1997) 56–71.

[6] Peter Senge speaks about a company's "undiscussables," those issues that impact the workings of the firm but are considered off limits for discussion. See Senge and Associates, *The Fifth Disciple Fieldbook* (New York: Doubleday, 1994) for additional explanations.

[7] Ibid.

[8]Ibid.

[9]See Daniel Goleman, *Emotional Intelligence* (New York: Bantam, 1998).

Chapter 5

[1]Quote taken from *Shell Italia,* Case number UVA-OB-0536, University of Virginia Darden School Foundation, Charlottesville, VA, 1995.

[2]See Robert Spekman, Lynn Isabella, Thomas C. MacAvoy, and Ted Forbes, *Managing Alliances and Partnerships* (Lexington, MA: International Consortium of Executive Development Research, 1996).

[3]Ibid.

[4]Ibid.

[5]For more specific discussions of scenario planning, see Kees van der Heijden, *Scenarios: The Art of Strategic Conversation* (New York: John Wiley & Sons, 1996). Also see Arie de Gues,*The Living Company* (Cambridge, MA: Harvard Business School Press, 1997) and T. Irene Sanders, *Strategic Thinking and the New Science* (New York: The Free Press, 1998).

[6]Sanders, p. 110.

Chapter 6

[1]In January 1999, Ford announced the $6.8B purchase of Volvo's worldwide car operations. Many of the arguments given for the purchase were similar to the reasons given in 1991 for the alliance between Volvo and Renault.

[2]Reported in *Fortune,* Dec. 7, 1998, David Kirkpatrick, "The E ware War,": 102–12.

[3]This discussion is based on M. Serapio and W. Cascio, "End Games in International Alliances," *Academy of Management Executive* (1996): 62–70.

Chapter 7

[1]Cyrus Freidheim, *The Trillion-Dollar Enterprise: How the Alliance Revolution Will Transform Global Business* (Reading: Perseus Books, 1998).

[2]John R. Harbison and Peter Pekar, Jr., *Smart Alliances: A Practical Guide to Repeatable Success* (San Francisco: Jossey-Bass, 1998).

[3]Empirical studies in the field of marketing have examined relationships between buyers and suppliers and channel partners. Typically, these studies have focused on the negative effect conflict has on performance. See, for example, work by James C. Anderson and James A. Narus, "A Model of Distributor Firm and Manufacturer Firm Working Partnerships," *Journal of Marketing 54,* 1 (1990): 42–59; and Louis P. Bucklin and Sanjit Sengupta, "Organizing Successful Co-Marketing Alliances," *Journal of Marketing 57,* 2 (1993): 32–47.

[4]Adapted from David Strutton and Lou E. Pelton, "Negotiation: Bringing More to the Table than Demands," *Marketing Health Services 17,* 1 (1997): 52–9.

[5]This discussion is based on an article by W. Ross and J. LaCroix, "Multiple Meanings of Trust in Negotiation Theory and Research," *International Journal of Conflict Resolution 7,* 4 (1996): 313–60.

[6]Robert E. Spekman, Lynn A. Isabella, Thomas C. MacAvoy, and Theodore M. Forbes, III, *Alliance and Partnership Strategies* (Lexington, MA.: International Consortium for Executive Development Research (ICEDR), 1997).

[7]Richard D. Lewis, *When Cultures Collide: Managing Successfully across Cultures* (London: Nicholas Brealey Publishing, 1996).

[8]Xiaohua Lin and Richard Germain, "Sustaining Satisfactory Joint Venture Relationships: The Role of Conflict Resolution Strategy," *Journal of International Business Studies 29,* 1 (1998): 179–97.

[9]This research is summarized in Robert J. Pearce, "Toward Understanding Joint-Venture Performance and Survival: A Bargaining and Influence Approach to Transaction Cost Theory," *Academy of Management Review* 22, 1 (1997): 203–25.

[10]See Jeanne M. Brett, Debra L. Shapiro, and Anne L. Lytle, "Breaking the Bond of Reciprocity in Negotiations," *Academy of Management Journal 41,* 4 (1998): 410–25.

Chapter 8

[1]Name has been disguised. Story is part of a case study, "*Shell Italia A and B,*" UVA-OB-0586 and UVA-OB-0587. These case studies are published by University of Virginia Darden School Foundation, Charlottesville, VA, 1995.

[2]Name disguised.

[3]This has recently been called "T" types by Dorothy Leonard, *Wellsprings of Knowledge* (Cambridge, MA: Harvard Business School Press, 1998).

[4]Bracketed material added for emphasis.

[5]From a personal interview.

[6]Several recent books and articles have hinted at these characteristics. See Shona Brown and Kathleen Eisenhardt, *Competing on the Edge* (Cambridge, MA: Harvard Business School Press, 1998); Morgan W. McCall, Jr., *High Flyers* (Cambridge, MA: Harvard Business School Press, 1998). See also Hal Gregersen, Allen Morrison, and J. Stewart Black, "Developing Leaders for the Global Frontier," *Sloan Management Review,* Fall 1998, 21–32.

[7]A number of the ideas on wisdom have been adapted from Karl Weick, "The Collapse of Sensemaking in organizations: The Mann Gulch Disaster," *Wildfire Magazine* September (1996): 1–16.

[8]See Samuel A. Culbert, *Mind-set Management: The Heart of Leadership* (New York: Oxford University Press, 1996).

[9]These ideas are drawn from some ongoing research based on learning orientations. Preliminary themes of this research have appeared in "Learning Mindset: Who Has It? Who Doesn't?" *Harvard Business Review,* March/April, 1994, p. 10.

Chapter 9

[1]See Michael Hitt, Barbara W. Keats, and Samuel M. DeMarie, "Navigating in the New Competitive Landscape: Building Strategic Flexibility and Competitive Advantage in the 21st Century," *The Academy of Management Executive 12,* 4 (1998): 22–4.

[2]Gary Hamel, "Competition for Competence and Inter-partner Learning within International Strategic Alliances," *Strategic Management Journal 12* (1991): 83–103.

[3]This expertise carries skills that run the gamut from design, to production, to after-sale service.

[4]Briance Mascarenhas, Alok Baveja, and Mamnoon Jamil, "Dynamics of Core Competencies in Leading Multinational Companies," *California Management Review 40*, 4 (1998): 117–33.

[5]This discussion is modified from Thomas H. Davenport and Lawrence Prusek, *Working Knowledge* (Cambridge: Harvard Business School Press, 1998).

[6]Ron Ashkens, Dave Ulrich, Todd Jick, and Steve Kerr, *The Boundaryless Corporation* (San Francisco: Jossey-Bass, 1995).

[7]Higher and lower were determined by mean splits based on a scale of 1 to 7; where 7 connotes *my company does an extremely good job* and 1 connotes *my company does not do a good job.*

[8]See David T. Wilson, "An Integrated Model of Buyer-Seller Relationships," *Journal of the Academy of Marketing Science 23*, 4 (1995): 335–46.

[9]Andrew Inkpen, "Learning, Knowledge Acquisition, and Strategic Alliances," *European Management Journal 16*, 2 (1998): 223–29.

[10]See P. Senge, *The Fifth Discipline* (New York: Doubleday, 1990).

[11]Portions of this discussion are based on materials in Robert Kaplan and David Norton, *The Balanced Scorecard* (Cambridge: Harvard Business School Press, 1996).

[12]See Michael Best, *The New Competition* (Cambridge: Harvard University Press, 1990).

Chapter 10

[1]The term *co-opetition* comes from a book by Adam M. Brandenburger and Barry J. Nalebuff, *Co-opetiton* (New York: Doubleday, 1996).

[2]A complementor enhances the value of your product when its product is offered in conjunction with yours.

[3]See Walter W. Powell, Kenneth W. Koput, Laurel Smith-Doerr, "Interorganizational Collaboration and the Locus of Innovation," *Administrative Science Quarterly 41*, 1 (1996): 116–45.

[4]See Ronald L. Schill, Roland G. Bertodo, and David N. McArthur, "Achieving Success in Technology Alliances: The Rover-Honda Strategic Collaboration," *R & D Management 24*, 3 (1994): 261–77.

[5]Benjamin Gomes-Casseres, *The Alliance Revolution* (Cambridge: Harvard University Press, 1996).

[6]Dorothy Leonard-Barton, *Wellsprings of Knowledge:Building and Sustaining the Sources of Innovation* (Cambridge: Harvard Business School Press 1995).

[7]See Robert F. Dwyer, Paul H. Schurr, and Sejo Oh, "Developing Buyer-Seller Relationships," *Journal of Marketing 51*, 2 (1987): 11–28; Peter S. Ring and Andrew H. Van deVen, "Developmental Processes of Cooperative Interorganizational Relationships," *Academy of Management Review 19*, 1 (1994): 90–119; Nils H. Hakansson, "Changes in the Financial Market: Welfare and Price Effects and the Basic Theorems of Value Conservation," *Journal of Finance 37*, 4 (1982): 977–1005; David T. Wilson, "An Integrated Model of Buyer-Seller Relationships," *Journal of the Academy of Marketing Science 23*, 4 (1995): 335–46.

[8]John Micklethwait, "The Valley of Money's Delight," *The Economist 342,* 8010 (1997): S5–S8.

[9]This comment was made recently in a conversation with an executive from a company in Silicon Valley.

[10]Much of this discussion is based on R.E. Spekman, J. Kamauff, and J. Spear, "Towards Effective Supplier Management," *European Journal of Procurement and Supply Management,* accepted for publication 1999. The Appendix contains information about the study and how the data were gathered.

[11]See Stephen C. Johnson, Gery Marsh, and Gene Tyndall, "The Path to Higher Shareholder Value," *Chief Executive (U.S.),* 136 (1998): 38–42.

[12]See Robert E. Spekman, John W. Kamauff, Jr., and Niklas Myhr, "An Empirical Investigation into Supply Chain Management: A Perspective on Partnering," *Supply Chain Management 3,* 2 (1998): 53–67.

[13]From the results, it can be seen that we refer to both customers and suppliers. This reference is based on the fact that we examined different levels of the supply chain such that suppliers refer to customers and buyers refer to suppliers when they answer their specific version of the survey.

[i]A focal company represents the "entry point" for the survey. Once a focal point was identified, we gathered information from certain key managers relative to suppliers and supply chain management. Then, we gathered data from both upstream and downstream supply chain partners. The term extended implies that responses were gathered from both upstream and downstream companies rather than from a single informant's attempts to respond on behalf of the supply chain.

[ii]Focusing on revenue-enhancing factors permits the most robust evaluation of performance since fewer supply chains attempt to gather such information and tend to emphasize instead more traditional purchasing performance metrics (e.g., price, delivery, quality). In addition, such a focus is consistent with our attempts to convey leading edge practice.

Chapter 11

[1]The steps described here have been influenced by John P. Kotter, *Leading Change* (Cambridge: Harvard Business School Press, 1996).

Index